BLINDED BY SCIENCE
The social implications of epigenetics and neuroscience

David Wastell and Sue White

D1612656

First published in Great Britain in 2017 by

Policy Press
University of Bristol
1-9 Old Park Hill
Bristol
BS2 8BB
UK
t: +44 (0)117 954 5940
pp-info@bristol.ac.uk
www.policypress.co.uk

North America office:
Policy Press
c/o The University of Chicago Press
1427 East 60th Street
Chicago, IL 60637, USA
t: +1 773 702 7700
f: +1 773-702-9756
sales@press.uchicago.edu
www.press.uchicago.edu

British Library Cataloguing in Publication Data
A catalogue record for this book is available from the British Library

Library of Congress Cataloging-in-Publication Data
A catalog record for this book has been requested

ISBN 978-1-4473-2234-4 paperback
ISBN 978-1-4473-2233-7 hardcover
ISBN 978-1-4473-2237-5 ePub
ISBN 978-1-4473-2238-2 Mobi
ISBN 978-1-4473-2236-8 ePdf

Cover design by Lyn Davies
Front cover image: www.alamy.com

For Geraldine, Imogen, Joe, Tom and the latest (epi)genetic incarnation, baby Jesse.

Contents

List of figures and tables

Figures

Tables

Acknowledgements

We would like to express our sincere gratitude to Mike Seltzer for a very detailed read of our manuscript and further insights into the historical continuities, and Paul Martin for advice on some of the technical aspects. Any errors in the published work are our own.

The book was informed by discussions with our colleagues in the research team on Leverhulme Trust Research Project Grant 'How does inequality get "under the skin"'? Epigenetics, health disparities and the making of social policy'. Particular appreciation goes to Maurizio Meloni who has pointed us in the direction of a great deal of useful material.

Our encounter with Basil Bunting was facilitated by Joe White. Thanks Joe.

Finally, we would like to thank the team at Policy Press for their support and encouragement from commissioning all the way through to publication.

Preface

[F]or decades we've all been told: you are what you eat. You are what you drink. You are how much, or how little, you exercise ... And yet a quiet scientific revolution is changing that thinking. For it seems you might also be what your mother ate. How much your father drank. And what your grandma smoked. Likewise your own children, too, may be shaped by whether you spend your evenings jogging, worrying about work, or sat on the sofa eating Wotsits. (Bell, 2013)

The pronouncements of leading biotechnoscientists are listened to with respect previously given only to the most eminent of nuclear physicists, today they advise government and industry, and give well-received lectures to the world leaders at Davos. (Rose and Rose, 2012: 277)

The biological sciences, particularly neuroscience and genetics, are currently in the cultural ascent. Aided by advances in informatics and digital imaging, these 'techno-sciences' increasingly promise to provide a theory of everything in the natural and social worlds. Social policy has not been slow to conscript biology into its legitimating stories. Beginning in the United States with the decade of the brain in the 1990s, neuroscience was first on the stage, but developments in genetics, known as epigenetics (referred to in the first epigraph), also have potentially profound implications for society and culture, and the responses of the State to intimate family life and personal choices. In the chapters that follow, we aim to provide a review of these nascent technological biologies and their claims. We examine the actual and potential applications of contemporary biology in social policy, and the implications which flow for moral debate and State intervention.

Our purpose, in part, is to explore how the new technological sciences 'think', how their scientific practice is conducted, the issues on which they focus, and the assumptions that have to be made in the interpretation and application of their findings. If we are to perceive, question and debate their social implications, science and scientists must be part of the story. It is not simply, as we and others have argued, that the original science can be lost in translation into policy, but sometimes the preoccupations of the laboratory itself lead in distinctive, controversial directions. Experiments on the maternal behaviour of rats, for example, make assumptions about what good mothering looks like; these experiments then inform debates on human maternal lifestyle, which in turn influence policy and so forth.

Technological biology has the capacity to shift profoundly the relationship of the State with its citizens. If brains can be damaged or boosted, should we not be boosting them or preventing the damage? If gene expression is adaptive, and can be changed for the better at the molecular level, should we not get swiftly to work? If the genome is re-conceptualised as a malleable entity, and vulnerable to lifestyle and patterns of nurture, will this create ever more moralised domains and responsibilities, judgements of what is good or bad? What implications are likely to ensue from a moral imperative that requires each generation to maintain the quality of the human genome (and epigenome) and pass it on *in no worse condition* than that received by the present generation? How does it change your relationship with your mother if you see yourself, not as the latest in a line of anxious people, part of a family of worriers, but instead as a neurologically and epigenetically compromised individual, damaged *in utero* or in early childhood by your 'neurotic' or distracted mother?

In seeking to examine critically the seemingly self-evident virtues of the aspiration for human improvement driven by scientific progress, we as authors inevitably put ourselves into a position of some moral delicacy. We are, of course, in favour of social improvement and understand the impulse to deliver the good life for the many, but we will show that contestable choices are being made about who to help, who needs to change and how money is spent on creating a better world. Our arguments are sometimes complex to deliver, and perhaps prone to be misunderstood. Before we venture forward, we will briefly summarise what we are intending to argue and, crucially, what we are not.

The aim of this book is first to provide a critical introduction to the biology itself, so that readers may appraise its promises, its threats and its implications for policy and professional practice, for example, in social work, education, law and medicine. Second, we seek to locate this within the historical movement of post-Enlightenment thought. Thus, we have drawn on concepts from social science to explore how ideas move from the laboratory to the policy world, and further afield into public discourse. Behind apparently uncontroversial programmes for social improvement, there are fundamental assumptions and myths; possible alternative actions can be obscured behind policies which seem benignly self-evident. For example, it has become unfashionable in the helping professions to accept that some people find it harder to parent and may need long-term practical help rather than, or perhaps as well as, a targeted programme, rigorously evaluated with clear 'outcome measures'.

The imperative for everyone, including increasingly the old, to participate in the labour market and be economically active may also strip communities of resilience and assets. Notions of vulnerability and damage are double edged; possibly more resources flow, but they are conditional on 'compliance', 'engagement' and surveillance. Targeting, and its associated drive for evidential outcomes, is (as we shall see) paradoxically expensive to deliver, soaking up resources which might be better deployed in direct support. Academic careers are made on the long and winding road to the *properly* evidence-based intervention, creating further perverse incentives within the scientific community itself. The war on poverty is no longer 'on trend', and because the majority of folk in adverse situations bring up their children perfectly well, on biological and psychological grounds giving ordinary resources to the poor could come to be seen as wasteful. In contrast, changing selected parents increasingly comes to be seen as the right response, crucial to securing the economic capacity of today's children. All this has commercial implications. Big Pharma companies gather around emerging findings from animal studies which appear to dangle the prospect of a chemical cure for biological traces of 'social disadvantage'. Elsewhere, other global interests seek to protect themselves from potential litigation arising from emerging work on the epigenetic impact of environmental and workplace toxins.

In proposing that some of the current settlement is misguided or limited, we are not suggesting that the amelioration of suffering and disadvantage are inappropriate policy aims. The goals of eliminating poverty, and providing universal education, were 18th- and 19th-century attempts genuinely to help people, but their impetus came also from a desire to 'cure' criminality and induce more socially apt aspirations and desires. There is no doubt that these policies improved the lives of populations, but we must remember that these same lives had already been disrupted by the consequences of rapid industrialisation and urbanisation. It was not these forces that interventions of philanthropists and the State sought to stem; there were many powerful interests, including those of many of the philanthropists themselves, ensuring this was not the case.

Behind the current dominant motifs stands a range of potent actors and interests. In the interests of informed conversation, these need to be made visible. The path of accumulated assumptions needs to be cleared in order for new conversations to begin. But in clearing the way, we are not aiming to produce a blueprint for a new fix. That is beyond our reach here, and needs the involvement of a wider, more inclusive public beyond the 'expert'. Rather, to paraphrase Raymond Tallis (2011: 348), we aim to clear the ground just a little in the hope that we can open the conditions for progress by acknowledging the limits of what we know, how little we are likely to know any time soon, and by asking whether we are really looking in the most appropriate places to resolve contemporary problems.

We have written the chapters that follow so that each is relatively self-contained. While there are some dependencies and cross references, it should be possible for the reader to be selective and nonlinear in the way they approach the book if they so wish. There is a clear narrative thread though which runs through the chapters. We are concerned about contradictions and unintended consequences of the understandable desire to cure the human race of a range of ills and disadvantages.

The intended readership is interdisciplinary and there is a variety of ways in which the arguments might be approached. Part I of the book, chapters one to three, reviews the technical vocabularies which are at play within the primary sciences. Beginning in chapter one with a broad sweep across our core argument, we review the origins of the project of human improvement, the yearning for a utopia, free from misery, disorder and disease. We trace the ascendency of developmental psychology and 'infant determinism', which has always been a key part of the project of human improvement. Chapter two provides an introduction to some key concepts from the philosophy and sociology of science and technology, which we will draw on to examine how the sciences 'think'. These are foundational for much of our analysis of the technological biologies and their ways of making knowledge. We review two exhibits in this chapter, 'neuroscientism', a form of thought whereby neuroscience is given a status as a privileged worldview, and the 'epigenetic' thought style.

Chapter three then examines the ways in which biology has been brought to bear in understanding forms of behaviour variously known through the ages as madness, mental illness or developmental disorder, culminating in the current preoccupations with finding the genetic markers and neurological traces for a variety of manifestations of human deviance. These opening chapters are written using some of the vocabulary of these areas of science themselves, as we want to show how scientists think about and make sense of the complicated things going on inside our bodies. The chapters are not handbook summaries, but instead are intended to illustrate for the reader the real perplexity and complexity of the movement of ideas in science and their path dependencies. Readers who are already familiar with these fields might find new, more sceptical ways of looking at them by reading these chapters. Readers who have no scientific knowledge might find the material quite challenging, but we have provided accessible examples as we go, and encourage such readers to take the plunge.

In Part II of the book, we switch register and examine the way biological thinking is coalescing with the project of human improvement. Chapters four and five review recent policy, tracing the ways in which neuroscience in particular has been invoked to relocate an older moral project of child welfare on the high hard ground of scientific rationality. In chapter six, we explore the thought style of 'prevention science', where scientific method is brought to bear to nip human dysfunctions in the bud. At the end of this chapter, we will encounter epigenetics starting to enter the fray. Chapter seven then focuses on this new biotechnology, introducing a cast of laboratory animals, examining how they are bred and handled experimentally to produce findings which seem to transfer so convincingly from the laboratory cage to the disadvantaged housing estate. Chapter eight then examines how epigenetic understandings are being applied to human beings, reviewing seminal work on the impact of natural disasters on the epigenome and revisiting the familiar terrain of gestation and early infancy, reconfigured as a process to be understood and perfected at the molecular level.

Our final chapter reviews our arguments and makes the case for a more inclusive approach to the project of social improvement, informed by social science. Here we reappraise the new biologies and debate their possibilities, utilities and potential dangers in the domain of social policy. Drawing on a range of commentators, we make a case for the biological worldview as but one strand of thought. Policy and professional practice can be enriched by understandings from the physical sciences, but there is much that these cannot explain. We examine where the biological project may take us and propose some alternative or complementary ways forward. We conclude that it is vital for the policy and practice communities, and the public at large, to be emboldened to ask awkward questions about vested interests, laboratory rats, human disadvantage, resilience and flourishing.

Part I
Getting to grips with the thought styles

ONE

Biology and the drive for human improvement

In this chapter, we begin with a brief introduction to the recent developments in the biological sciences. We go on to examine how these are joining with older projects to improve the human condition. We review the origins of these projects in the natural yearning for a utopia, free from misery, disorder and disease. We then trace the ascendency of developmental psychology and 'infant determinism' which has always been a key part of the project of human improvement.

The application of molecular biology and neuroscience to the treatment of diseases such as cancer or Parkinson's disease may be relatively morally uncontroversial, but we are seeing a shift in the range of matters to which biological understandings are being applied. This is why the exploration of their translation into policy and practice is so pressing. The 'neuro' prefix, for example, is now applied to disciplines as disparate as economics, the law, aesthetics, pedagogy, theology and organisational behaviour. The term 'neuromania' has been coined (Legrenzi and Umilta, 2011; Tallis, 2011) to refer to this proliferation.

Although some critics have lampooned this ebullience, speaking flippantly of parts of the brain 'lighting up' in overly simplistic laboratory experiments, there are many, very real implications in seeing the human condition in this way. Social policy is making increasingly significant use of neuroscientific evidence to warrant particular claims about both the potentialities and vulnerabilities of early childhood, and the proper responses of the State to these. Neuroscience is also making its mark in the area of criminal justice, where it often appears to offer 'liberalising' benefits: developmental neuroscience has been used, for example, to make the case for raising the age of criminal responsibility. However, alongside these apparently progressive trends, there lies the seductive (and somewhat sinister) idea that violent crime can be attributed to a small group of intrinsically aggressive individuals, and that neuroimaging (or genetics) can yield 'biomarkers' which may be used to identify risky people and to 'target' interventions at them. This potentially prefigures a future in which new biological technologies play an increasing role in pre-emptively isolating risky subgroups and identifying how to prevent their predicted deviance.

The last decades have thus seen a profound shift in our understanding of biological processes and life itself. At the heart of neurobiology's ascendancy is a paradox, described by Rose and Rose thus: '[Biological] discourses are at once essentialist and Promethean; they see human nature as fixed, while at the same time offering to transform human life through the real and imagined power of the biotechnosciences' (Rose and Rose, 2012: 24).

Whereas genetics has conventionally focused on examining the DNA sequence (the genotype), epigenetics examines additional mechanisms for modifying gene expression in manifest behaviours, traits, physical features, health status and so on (the phenotype). It provides a conduit mediating the interaction of the environment and an otherwise immutable DNA blueprint, and invites a natural interest in the impact of adverse conditions, such as deprivation or normatively deficient parenting. The implications for social policy of this new 'biology of social adversity' (Boyce et al, 2012) are far reaching. 'Hard' heredity, in which genes were seen as inherited and fixed for life (insulated from environmental influences, life chances and choices) drove the eugenics movement of the late 19th and early 20th centuries. In its extreme form, the 'barbarous utopia' of the Nazis (Meloni, 2016: 28) banished biology from the acceptable face of politics and social reform, but epigenetics shows every sign of rehabilitating biology, making it politically acceptable again. As Meloni notes, freeing us from the determinacy of our genetic inheritance might help make the case for more resources to 'fix' or prevent damage to the epigenome of disadvantaged groups, but it may also have less pretty effects:

> This all sounds desirable, but how likely is it in a society where class, race, and gender inequalities remain so vast? What is our society going to make of the notion that … the socially disadvantaged are also (epi)genetically damaged? … And what will oppressed groups do with this flurry of epigenetic studies concerning their own condition? (Meloni, 2016: 221)

Political positions are already emerging. The slavery reparations movement in the United States is using epigenetic arguments to support its case for compensation for the privations of enslavement in previous generations.[1] There are also claims that the offspring of Holocaust survivors show enduring epigenetic changes (Yehuda et al, 2015). Legal scholars and ethicists are further commenting on the implications for litigation in relation to the effects of a range of environmental and workplace toxins: 'Insurance policy claims and tort liability may have a 'long tail' if the toxic effects from agents acting via an epigenetic mechanism are not manifested until one or more generations into the future' (Rothstein et al, 2009: 11).

As we shall see, whether the current science supports some of the bolder claims is contestable. Even within medicine, where epigenetically based drug treatments have promise and are beginning to appear, and where the moral arguments for their use are less contentious, the science is as yet unsettled. In fixing one thing we may very easily finish up breaking another. Epigenetics, for example, is starting to challenge the wisdom of previous public health interventions. A case in point is the use of folic acid fortification in cereal to prevent neural tube defects such as spina bifida. This has been called into question by the apparent effect of these substances on unrelated parts of the epigenome: if folic acid switches off undesirable effects, might it also switch off some desirable ones, thus causing iatrogenic disease in the population?

Epigenetic arguments potentially engender newly racialised and stigmatised identities consequent on 'damage' to the epigenome, and the related moral imperative to 'optimise' the uterine environment in particular (Mansfield and Guthman, 2014). These may be resisted by those very disadvantaged groups who have come under the epigenetic gaze. The following online comment from a Glaswegian citizen, responding to the publication in the press of the results of a study about the inhabitants of his city, is an illustration of how the stories may be received:

> "I am just flabbergasted by this latest research – I am 81 years old and was born into what I would describe as extreme poverty … but with caring parents who were not into accepting 'charity' but gave me and my siblings the best they could in spite of a lot of unemployment. I have led a useful life, was pretty intelligent at school, and held responsible jobs, have married successfully, had children … and feel I was anything but deprived or damaged. Just grateful that these statistics weren't available in my past!" (Cited in Meloni, 2016: 221)

Epigenetics, like neuroscience, also promises to identify biomarkers of vulnerability and risk, thus creating the potential for State intervention to prevent 'suboptimal' human flourishing and to correct intergenerational social injustices. The new genre of explanations for health inequalities, associated in particular with the research programme on the developmental origins of health and disease (DOHaD), gives a flavour of the moral arguments at play:

> It might be possible to design environmental or pharmacological interventions for reverting the potential adult consequences of a particular mothering style at the molecular, cellular and physiological level. One implication ... is that there is a prima face duty of justice to intervene: the possibility of reverting programmed traits, when epigenetic information is a reliable biosensor, might efficiently prevent a process of life-time accumulation of disadvantage that ends up in disease. (Loi et al, 2013: 149)

Significantly absent from many of these sophisticated analyses is the proper response of the State to those who refuse to comply with actions deemed to be in their own best interests, or in the interests of their future offspring. Yet, these are thorny matters indeed, as Rothstein et al note:

> Epigenetics raises difficult questions about the obligations of society to preserve the soundness of the human genome and epigenome for the benefit of future generations. In developing a principle of intergenerational equity for the human genome and epigenome, optimum social policy lies between indifference to the health burdens of future generations and eugenic notions of manipulating heredity to improve the human condition. (Rothstein et al, 2009: 27)

The ascendancy of technobiology, in the form of neuroscience and epigenetics, seems to usher in new imperatives for the State to act. But such actions will inevitably have unintended as well as intended consequences, particularly in fields where knowledge is unsettled and claims to predictive power outstrip current understanding. There are serious implications for the State and its mandates to act in 'our best interests' (Kahn, 2010; Rothstein et al, 2009), but these nuances are unlikely to dampen the enthusiasm of politicians for robust and urgent action on a range of matters perceived to be within the State's ambit of concern.

These enthusiasms go back a long way and have a chequered history. Current developments in biotechnology are not historically unique; arguably they form part of an enduring project to 'fix' people which has, in its various guises, both liberal and conservative valences, but tends to drive policy and professional reasoning in particular directions. Prevention and targeting are prominent motifs in an increasingly residual and conditional welfare settlement, providing a natural slot for technologies which can claim to tease out individual susceptibilities. As we shall see, rather than challenging orthodoxies, both neuroscience and epigenetics are presently being co-opted to support old moral arguments, regardless of what the scientists might anticipate and debate among themselves.

The utopian legacy, policy and practice

Utopias are mythological, imaginary places, good or bad, which are expressions of desires, or fears (Carey, 1999). Perhaps, most usually, they are a little of both. Usually mistranslated from the Greek as a 'good' place (creating a need for its antonym, dystopia) utopia actually means 'no-place'. The origins of utopian aspirations in our emotions naturally invite public sympathies: we want the world to be a better place; we seek the elimination of suffering, unrewarding toil, inequality, crime and madness. Utopias, in all their fictional and political forms, are granted a special place in our imagination because they embody contradictions. The most important of these relates to the human race itself.

> The aim of utopias ... is to eliminate real people. Even if it is not a conscious aim, it is an inevitable result of their good intentions. ... to aim to eliminate real people might not be as bad as it sounds ... visitors to utopias are often informed that criminals of every description have been made obsolete. That has undeniable attractions, however keen we may be on preserving the rich and varied tapestry of human life. (Carey, 1999: xii)

The durability of the utopian project would seem to belie its status as a myth. By myth we do not refer to a false belief, but rather, after Barthes (1973), to the linguistic trick of presenting as wholly natural a particular cultural set of values or concepts. Myth is a system of 'signs', linguistic or visual, which have a meaning beyond their literal significance, conveying fundamental 'truths' about the nature of the world, its origins, composition, ordering. A pertinent example from *Mythologies* (Barthes, 1973) is the Myth of Einstein's Brain. Although we may allude metaphorically to his 'massive brain', it is not Einstein's brain which is prodigious, but his intellect. Mythically, the trope reduces the mystery of genius to the properties of a material object:

> Einstein's brain is a mythical object: paradoxically, the greatest intelligence of all provides an image of the most up-to-date machine … a photograph shows him lying down, his head bristling with electric wires: the waves of his brain are being recorded. … Thought itself is thus represented as an energetic material, the measureable product of a complex (quasi-electrical) apparatus which transforms cerebral substance into power. (Barthes, 1973: 68)

In fact, Einstein's brain was bequeathed for medical examination and no remarkable features have been found, but that is not the point: the myth 'says' that his mind, and therefore all minds, are but powerful cognitive machines. This provides our first encounter, of many to come, with what is known as the 'mereological fallacy'. In general, the fallacy consists of localising properties to a part or aspect of something, which makes sense only when applied to the whole. In the present context, it amounts to ascribing psychological phenomena to the brain, which only make sense as properties of living conscious human beings. The fallacy, as we shall see in due course, is particularly rife in neuroscience (Bennett and Hacker, 2003).

As with brains, utopia is not a myth in the literal sense that it does not exist, but in the normative sense that it prescribes how things ought to be, depicting this (crucially) as the natural condition of humanity, rather than a cultural product reflecting a particular moral orientation. The 'perfect family' is arguably a core motif of contemporary utopian mythology: this provides a superficial identity (all perfect families are the same): 'difference' is thus seen, not as injustice or simply otherness, but as defect. While there are socialist utopian[2] projects, where social structures and political economy are the focus of revolutionary effort, at present the dominant aspiration, in 'western' civilisation especially, is to fix individuals, with the State assuming the moral imperative to do so. Potent symbols gather around the utopian myth (of technological progress, images of 'damaged' brains, the prestige of laboratory science) holding in place a prospectus about what should be done to, and for, whom.

> The method of producing ideal citizens found in utopian thinking from Plato onwards is through attempts to control human reproduction and child rearing. How to

beget excellent offspring has always been a prime utopian concern, and it offers, supposing it could be made to work, an absolutely foolproof way of replacing real people with utopians. (Carey, 1999: xvii)

As we shall see, many of the policy and practice applications of the technosciences are focused on the early part of the life course and on the female reproductive years. They are resolutely and classically utopian both in their contradictions and in their moral certainties. For the first half of the 20th century, the ambition to ensure the excellence of the next generation was manifested in the science of eugenics. In 1896, the socialist Sidney Webb urged the Fabians to 'take property from idle rich and children from the unfit poor' (Perry, 2000: 7). Eugenics was popular and respectable up until the Second World War when, sullied by fascism under National Socialism in Germany, it hung its head for a while. It is arguably back in new clothes, fuelled on the one hand by environmental concerns with population control, and on the other by those seeking to eliminate social disadvantage and its associated suffering and unhappiness.

The social engineering of human reproduction, and the process of parenting and child rearing, enjoy support from both left and right of the political spectrum, as the entitlements of the very young are not tainted by any moral stain that their parents may carry. It has proved popular with the World Bank, for example, as an apolitical aspiration, apparently transcending ideology: 'The idea of giving people equal opportunity early in life, whatever their socioeconomic background, is embraced across the political spectrum – as a matter of fairness for the left and as a matter of personal effort for the right' (Paes de Barros et al, 2009: 18).

The focus on early childhood has a long history in developmental psychology. Ways of thinking about parents and children in this discipline will be familiar to many readers. It is worth summarising the evolution of this approach, not least because it informs the direction of much of the primary work in neuroscience and epigenetics, particularly that with policy aspirations. The precariously normal womb, foetus and infant remain the bedrock of the enduring project of social improvement. In its heyday, the vocabulary of psychology, like those of neuroscience and epigenetics, provided the allure of science and rationality.

Developmentalism and precarious normality

> Broadly conceived [mental hygiene] … consists first in
> providing for the birth of children endowed with good
> brains, denying as far as possible, the privilege of parenthood
> to the manifestly unfit who are almost certain to transmit
> bad nervous systems to their offspring … and second, in
> supplying all individuals, from the moment of fusion of the
> parental germ-cells onward, and whether ancestrally well
> begun or not, with the environment best suited for the
> welfare of their mentality. (Beers, 1921: 299)

The turn of the last century witnessed a number of progressive
movements, aimed at the promotion of public health via the control
of communicable diseases and the sanitation of the environment
(Bridges, 1928). The mental hygiene movement, originating in 1908,
forms a filament in these developments. The Beers extract, dating from
the early days of the movement, illustrates the aspirational shift from
concern with disease to concern with prevention of both personal
and social malaise. The responsibility of parents to provide an optimal
environment for the child is striking.

The early years of the child's life continue to have a pivotal
significance in welfare policy and practice, giving rise to the dominance
of developmental psychology in professional, and indeed lay, ideas
about childhood, and emphasis on the responsibilities of parenthood.
Kagan (1998) writes of the three 'seductive ideas' which inform the
developmentalist belief system. The idea that the first couple of years
or so predetermine the rest of life is the foundational belief. The
allure of 'infant determinism' rests on the metaphysical conviction that
'every experience produces a permanent change somewhere in the
central nervous system and therefore the earliest experiences provide
the scaffolding for the child's future thought and behaviour' (p 86).

> Every society speculates about the causes of variation
> amongst its members. Some attribute special power to a
> person's date of birth or sorcery. A much smaller number
> have decided that experience during the early years
> (especially the biological mother's affectionate care) are
> the most potent force in shaping a life. (Abridged from
> Kagan, 1998: 83)

Kagan traces the provenance of this preoccupation with parenting to the lifestyle of the 18th-century European bourgeoisie, where:

> a growing number of wives of merchants and skilled artisans were gradually freed of the responsibility of gathering wood, picking berries ... Society assigned to these women, idled by historical change, the task of shaping the future of their infants. A perfectly nurtured child who married well or mastered the skill that led to a position of prestige would enhance the family's status. (Kagan, 1998: 85)

The child, also freed from the drudgery of the domestic round, was in a complementary position, dependent on signs of affection that assured him of his beloved place in his parents' eyes. The logic that early childhood represented a 'critical period' for the development of affectionate bonds, and the need for intervention to ensure the child's optimum progression, naturally fell into their allotted place. They were held there not yet by the science, but by class politics and an emergent project of moral regulation.

> Many children of poor urban families arrive in school minimally prepared for academic instruction ... many of these children have great difficulty learning to read. Everyone agrees on the necessity of benevolent intervention to persuade the mothers of these children to adopt the regular practices of middle class parents, playing with and talking to their children. (Kagan, 1998: 89)

Through the 20th century, the significance accorded to early childhood in psychological thought was amplified, forming the bedrock of infant determinism (see inter alia Rose, 1989). Donzelot (1979) identifies child psychiatry in particular as central to the process by which the surveillance of family life became legitimated by both medicine and the law in the name of public health. 'Object relations' theory (Klein, 1952; Winnicott, 1973), for instance, placed considerable emphasis on the early relations between the infant and the *primary object* (usually the mother). The emergence of this school of thought gave a significant boost to the preoccupation with a child whose very normality was seen as fragile. Within Freudian psychoanalytic theory, neurosis had been accepted as an inescapable part of human existence. But in object relations theory, a psychologically secure and healthy adult life becomes theoretically achievable, through the idealised mother–infant relationship in which the mother becomes lost in her infant, in a state of maternal reverie (Bion, 1962).

With this theoretical turn, professional assessment of the mother–infant dyad increasingly came to involve the surveillance of intimate relations. Being 'unhealthy' no longer required the identification of major deficiencies in parenting, such as failing to provide nutrition, or acting cruelly. Rather, by scrutinising the minutiae of interactions, smiling, eye contact and so forth, the child health professional became charged with spotting those at risk of developing social and emotional maladjustments. And when risk was spotted, it must be pre-empted, giving impetus to professional intervention and the preventive project in general. Maternal style came to be seen as crucial to infant 'regulation', and in turn a range of 'infant regulatory disturbances' was spawned, such as 'excessive crying, feeding or sleeping difficulties, and bonding/attachment problems'. These came to 'represent the main reasons for referral to infant mental health clinics' (Barlow et al, 2015), and continue to do so in present times.

Alongside psychodynamic ideas, stressing the spectre of emotional 'damage', the certainties of developmental testing duly took their place:

> It was the child of the twentieth century that became the first target of the full deployment of the concept [of precarious normality]. The significance of the child was that it underwent growth and development: there was therefore a constant threat that the proper stages might not be properly negotiated. (Armstrong, 1995: 396)

Behavioural norms of development were also psychologised to include indices designed to *measure* socio-emotional adjustment. Armstrong continues:

> As with physical development, psychological growth was construed as inherently problematic, precariously normal. ... The nervous child, the delicate child, the eneuretic child, the neuropathic child, the maladjusted child, the difficult child, the neurotic child, the oversensitive child, the unstable child, and the solitary child, all emerged as new ways of seeing a potentially hazardous childhood. (Armstrong, 1995: 396)

In the United Kingdom, this mass surveillance would have been inconceivable without the clinics, nurseries, health visitors and the School Health Service of the post-Beveridge welfare state. Developmental assessments came to be routinely administered to all children at the ages of 6–8 weeks, 6–9 months, 18–24 months, 3 years and at school entry. This surveillance axiomatically depends upon the notion of the standardised child as the universal yardstick; having so-defined normality, any deviation from these developmental markers is thus rendered problematic and must be accounted for. Such accounting, Stainton Rogers and Stainton Rogers argue, relies on the 'alembic myth', the alembic being the distilling apparatus used by medieval alchemists:

> This supposes a child to be grown out of an alchemical transformation of two kinds of substance: a semi pre-programmed, vital, material frame (nature) and an impinging and pro-active cultural medium (nurture). Each is accorded some leavening power, each some ability to engender personhood. ... Each may also be accorded a qualitatively variable productive role ... in a child's developing personhood. Finally, each may also take on a moral condition as a source, in a way we account for an individual's goodness or badness as a person. (Stainton Rogers and Stainton Rogers, 1992: 40–1)

This 'alchemical relationship', with its balance of nature and nurture, seems to be wholly plausible, and its foundational assumptions are reinforced in contemporary biological sciences. Yet, notions of causation linked to the alembic myth have profound significance because, although science purports to be concerned with the discovery of the causes which precede certain effects, in practice, it often *constructs* effects for which it then prescribes a cause.[3] Dividing childhood into a number of defined and predictable, age-based stages has a number of consequences for professional intervention and decision making. The passage of the child through time comes to be seen as a sequence of 'milestones' demarcating critical, or sensitive, periods. In developmental thinking, the past is accorded a special significance in predicting the future, particularly, as we have seen, the early years of life. This is further illustrated in the following maxim from influential child psychiatrist Arnon Bentovim:

> The period of maximum sensitivity for attachment ... is generally accepted as between four months and up to the end of the third year of life. This is the period when the

child has least capacity to understand what is happening, has most need of secure attachment figures and is most prone to develop insecure attachments which can have long lasting effects. (Bentovim, 1995: 41)

The first three years continue to carry deep, indeed mythological, significance in the mindset of contemporary policy and practice. The notion of irreversibility is built into such thinking, having the effect of amplifying danger (and hence *urgency*) particularly in relation to young children, who not only are at greater risk of physical injury, but are fragile vessels who must be filled with the appropriate quantity of adult attention in order to avoid psychological damage. In this context, attachment theory has become a cornerstone of policy and practice. This theory, popularised by Bowlby during the 1940s and 1950s, is a synthesis of object relations theory and ethological developmental psychology. We will devote the next section to analysing the key ideas and the influence of this theory which cements the story of the symbiosis of nature and nurture, achieved through the ministering of the mother:

> The new psychological social workers combined with the psychologists of the clinic in writing narratives of love gone wrong ... Abnormality had its roots in the interplay between the desires of the parents and the desires of their children, in the medium of love itself. (Rose, 1989: 155)

Attachment theory: setting the biological stage

In the mindset of modern child welfare, 'secure attachment', a strong bond between offspring and mother, has come to be seen as one of the child's most basic needs. This has led to the proliferation of classification for different attachment patterns, some ideal and some defective, facilitated by a range of experimental methods based on observation of parent–child interaction. The most famous of these is the Strange Situation Test (Ainsworth and Wittig, 1969). This is the 'gold standard' (Bernier and Meins, 2008: 969) for assessing attachment behaviours, in which a child's behaviour on the departure and return of her primary caregiver and a stranger are observed over eight episodes.

Typically, two thirds of infants in a nonclinical sample (of 'middle class' children) will be categorised as showing 'secure attachment' (Ainsworth and Wittig, 1969). This group, while showing some separation distress, can be comforted quickly by a caregiver on return.

About one fifth will show little sign of distress, which Ainsworth attributes to learned behaviour in response to caregivers who tend to discourage displays of distress. These infants are classified as 'insecure-avoidant'. Children who exhibit distress before separation, and who were difficult to settle on return, are classified as 'insecure-resistant/ambivalent'. Strong claims have been made about the predictive validity and inter-rater reliability for these attachment categories (Solomon and George, 2008; Duschinsky et al, 2015).

We are not disputing the intuitive 'truth' and the commonsense reality that relationships matter greatly to infants and, for almost all of us, form the basis for our sense of ourselves (Duschinsky et al, 2015). That said, these attachment styles (generated, we should note, in 'normal' nonclinical populations) have undergone such revision and fine tuning, and have such prolific malleability, that almost any permutation of infant (and indeed adult) behaviour can be thus explained, and hence made subject to expert scrutiny. For those subject to professional surveillance, this creates the conditions for polar opposites of behaviour to be read as pathology. The theory is used ubiquitously in child welfare, particularly social work, and can make it devilishly hard to hang on to normality. Children who appear to be 'excessively' independent may, for instance, be pathologised as having an 'anxious-avoidant' attachment, those who are merely a little demanding, an 'ambivalent' attachment, and so forth.

> If the child will not settle to play some distance from her mother while she is there, the attachment is considered insecure. Conversely, this conclusion is also drawn if the child fails to protest at his or her mother's departure. (Burman, 1994: 83)

If one were a parent being professionally observed this is clearly a problem. For the professional observer in search of a diagnostic category, it is potentially a case of 'heads I win, tails you lose'. To the original trio of canonical patterns, which in their differing ways are referred to as 'organised' attachments, has been added a fourth dimension, known as 'disorganised attachment'. This is used to describe infants who do not display a consistent response in dealing with the scenarios in the strange situation test. Behaviours included in this category are diverse, and include the infant 'freezing', averting their gaze, hitting the parent after seeming pleased to see them, and so forth. In short, they embody some sort of contradictory response. The hypothesis of choice to explain the means of transmission of these contradictory responses is as follows:

The basic assumption is that if caregivers appear fearful or display frightening behavior, this not only will alarm and frighten their infants but will present them with an unsolvable paradox: The person who can alleviate their fear and alarm is the very source of these negative emotions. The infant can therefore neither flee from nor approach the attachment figure. This 'fright without solution' is postulated to result in the anomalous behaviors that are the hallmark of disorganized attachment. (Bernier and Meins, 2008: 970)

There is considerable debate in the domain of academic research journals about the 'transmission' mechanisms of disorganised attachment, and indeed the category itself. Disorganised attachment was not sitting out there, like a tree or a rock, easily and unambiguously identifiable, just waiting to be found. Rather, it is an artefact which had to be filled in and fluffed out with considerable intellectual labour. It is worth tracing something of its history. Van Ijzendoorn et al note:

Although disorganized attachment behavior is necessarily difficult to observe and often subtle, many researchers have managed to become reliable coders.... In normal, middle class families, about 15% of the infants develop disorganized attachment behavior. In other social contexts and in clinical groups this percentage may become twice or even three times higher (e.g., in the case of maltreatment). Although the importance of disorganized attachment for developmental psychopathology is evident, the search for the mechanisms leading to disorganization has just started. (van Ijzendoorn et al, 1999: 225)

In the paper's discussion section, the authors note that, for diagnostic purposes, the coding system for disorganised attachment is complicated, and the intercoder reliability only marginal: in nontechnical argot, not all observers can agree when they have seen a case of disorganised attachment behaviour. A notably egregious example is a case in which the 'detection' of disorganised attachment in a child's home took almost 4 hours of videotaped observations, with the further frustration that the disorganised response was inconsistently triggered! This might lead some to question the validity of the category, but the authors see only a challenge, urging a search for 'ethically acceptable ways of inducing these triggering behaviours in the parent' (van Ijzendoorn et al, 1999:

242). This is a somewhat troubling idea in itself, and a clear indication of the incertitude of the knowledge reviewed, but such considerations do not seem to trouble the authors. Calling for further research, the paper concludes:

> We should be cautious, however, about the diagnostic use of disorganized attachment … the meta-analytic evidence presented in this paper is only correlational and the causal nature of the association between disorganized attachment and externalizing problem behavior still has to be established. (van Ijzendoorn et al, 1999: 244)

A more recent, thorough review by Bernier and Meins reiterates the difficulties in establishing the facts of disorganised attachment:

> Any explanatory framework for the antecedents of disorganization will thus need to speak to two major anomalies in the extant literature. First, it must account for why different aspects of parenting—insensitivity, fearful behavior, and frightening behaviour—can result in disorganization depending on the prevailing social–environmental conditions. Second, it must explain the fairly large portion of variance in disorganized attachment that is not explained by the (parental) mediation model … the magnitude of the relations found thus far suggests that some children manage to establish organized attachment relationships in the face of exposure to atypical parenting behaviors and a high-risk environment, whereas others form disorganized attachments in the absence of putative risk factors. (Bernier and Meins, 2008: 971)

But as we move away from the original science, these carefully worded observations quickly begin to lose their equivocation and establish themselves as facts. In an 'evidence review', recently produced for the UK Department of Health for the purposes of training the family judiciary in England, Brown and Ward assert: 'There is *consistent* evidence that *up to* 80% of children brought up in neglectful or abusive environments develop disorganised attachments' (Brown and Ward, 2013: 29, emphasis added). For the critical reader, the first point of note is the use of the expression 'up to' which may refer to anything from zero to 80%; the second is the unequivocal causal association of disorganised attachment with child maltreatment. Nonetheless, the currency of the category 'disorganised attachment' in the child protection field is indeed considerable, with some going further and claiming it as a key diagnostic marker of maltreatment:

> Disorganised attachment behaviour is 'indicative' as distinct from 'predictive' because its presence does not imply that a child will be or even is likely to be maltreated in the future, instead it suggests they may well have been abused already and are still experiencing the consequences of maltreatment, as shown by the way they react and respond to mild activation of their attachment system. (Shemmings and Shemmings, 2014: 22)

The important point here is that different accounts of the same phenomenon coexist; they are associated with different worldviews. The domain of psychological science, occupied by Bernier and Meins, reflects (and indeed requires) a different style of thinking to that occupied by child welfare or child protection specialists and campaigners. The confident proclamations of the latter belong to the world of professional handbooks rather than research papers. This, as we see in the next chapter, is a simplified world in which the inconvenient quandaries of the original science are effectively airbrushed out. For all practical purposes they do not exist. This has an effect on what professionals 'see' when they 'observe'. Attachment style and the 'attachment system' become mythologised; they form a normative belief system which configures the world in a particular way, presenting what is a cultural artefact as the natural order.

Imagine the following situation: a social worker has been asked to observe the relationship between a three-year-old child and his father, with a view to deciding whether the father should be allowed to have the child come to stay with him each week. The child arrives tearful, distressed and clinging to his mother. The father appears embarrassed and becomes slightly irritated with the child and the mother. He protests that this has never happened on previous contacts. All his somewhat clumsy efforts to comfort the child are rejected; they only seem to increase the child's distress, and anger the mother. The mother looks at the social worker with an 'I told you so' expression.

How would one make sense of these events? How would one impose some sort of order on this fast-flowing continuum of interaction? In imposing order, what inferences would need to be made about the dispositions and characters of the participants and their relationships? First, for professional purposes, one has to assume that the observed behaviour is typical; second, categorisation becomes easier and the situation less 'noisy' if we make use of the pre-existing vocabularies of attachment theory. The latter is used to make an inference about a covert, underlying theoretical construct: an insecure, or disorganised attachment, disorder. This style of thinking, of discrete pathological conditions with underlying common causes, very much reflects, as we shall see in the next chapters, that of modern medicine.

In sum, the questionnaires, checklists, indeed all 'technologies' of professional assessment are the handbook implementations of theoretical positions, operational tools that put these theories into practice. As such, they can construct versions of reality and affect what we 'see'; as John (1990) notes:

> Just as theories are underdetermined by facts, so facts are overdetermined by theory, which means that situations may be capable of a range of factual interpretations depending on the theory selected. Furthermore, individual psychological theories have been shown to be capable of such a degree of interpretive flexibility as to be virtually incorrigible; it has sometimes been difficult to find situations, even when they involve quite contradictory outcomes, which they could not plausibly explain. (John, 1990: 127)

We have observed that biology tacitly underlies much of the developmentalist mindset. As such, it occupies an ambivalent and ambiguous status. The notion of development as a highly predictable and pre-programmed phenomenon is clearly a materialist concept, relying on the assumption that universal neurological and organic structures exist. However, while biological pre-programming may be implicitly accepted as a valid framework in understanding 'normal' development, for much of the latter part of the last century it was unfavoured as an explanation for deviance: instead, parent and environment were seen culpable. Under the influence of this latter form of developmentalism, the child's body was seen as a malleable beneficiary of 'good enough' parenting.[4] But good enough is arguably no longer good enough: the body is now big business, with science promising to map the mechanisms whereby the parent is etched indelibly on the infant's brain and written into the molecular activities of its cells. If we can only find the basic building blocks of disorder, we can fix people for good. Moral biology takes its place on the stage.

Moral biology?

Writing originally in 1944, the physicist Erwin Schrödinger asked the simple question: 'What is life?' (Schrödinger, 1967: 1). Reflecting on the work of geneticists in the early part of the 20th century, and seeking to apply and infer applications from physics and chemistry to the events taking place at the molecular level of cells, Schrödinger is credited with influencing the discovery and interpretation of DNA and spurring the beginnings of 'quantum' biology, now gaining faddish traction. In so doing he was portentous in raising a number of philosophical and moral questions on mind and matter, on free will and determinism, and on the role of the State in the amelioration of social ills. Like his contemporary C.H. Waddington (who coined the term 'epigenetics' in 1942), Schrödinger was concerned about the social consequences which potentially flow from the possibility that the results of one generation's interaction with its environment may be passed on to its progeny.

Longstanding debates about the precise nature and mechanism of these changes, and their durability over generations, still feature in contemporary biology, ranging between the *neo-Lamarckian* pole (an organism can pass on characteristics that it has acquired during its lifetime to its offspring) and its *neo-Darwinian* opposite (heredity is hard wired, and once fixed at birth cannot be changed). The allure of an escape from the straitjacket of Darwinian (hard) heredity beckons with both the promise of a utopian future and the threat of impending degenerative catastrophe. Based on the science available in his day, Schrödinger argued that behavioural choices can confer advantages leading to piecemeal improvements, or their opposite, from generation to generation. That is, there are possibilities for both social improvement and degeneration of the germline. In freeing us from determinism, this form of genetics creates a space for benignant social engineering. Schrödinger refers to its possibilities as 'beautiful, elating, encouraging and invigorating' (p 107), but these enticing prospects may also create minatory moral hazards:

> We are, I believe, at the moment in grave danger of missing the path to perfection ... I believe that the increasing mechanization and 'stupidization' of most manufacturing processes involve the serious danger of a general degeneration of our organ of intelligence ... the unintelligent man, who naturally finds it easier to submit to the boring toil will be favoured; he is likely to find it

easier to settle down and to beget offspring. (Schrödinger, 1967: 116–17)

Once the mechanisms of life appear to be tractable to human endeavour, and once behaviour is moralised through 'choice' and 'responsibility', the State arguably has no option but to act: to act in new ways, on old problems. For Schrödinger, some of its actions create undesirable effects of their own: welfare institutions, for example, might mitigate poor choices, sustaining the proliferation of the 'unintelligent'. This is remarkably eugenicist in tone, especially given contemporaneous events in parts of Europe, but Schrödinger surely meant well. His main critique is of the distorting effects of global capital. His aim is to replace these with interesting and intelligent 'competition' between single human beings in the service of the species, through fruitful and rewarding work. Schrödinger is ultimately modest about what can be known, arguing that, however far the science advances, it will never:

> meet the personality … The dire pain, the bewildered worry within this soul … our skulls are not empty. But what we find in there is truly nothing when held against the life and the emotions of the soul. (p 124)

Since then, the technologies and aspirations of the biological sciences have moved on apace and religion has been assigned a back seat. Emerging epigenetic explanatory frameworks carry with them a mandate for the State to act on the stuff of life. Developmental biologist, Vincent Cunliffe, recently reviewed work on experience-sensitive, epigenetic changes in gene expression across a range of animal and human studies, arguing:

> The possibility that epigenetically programmed diseases are induced by avoidable environmental factors raises important ethical questions about collective and individual responsibilities to minimize known health risks, develop human capabilities, and apply principles of distributive justice for current and future generations. (Cunliffe, 2015: 67)

Though expressed in different terms by Cunliffe, such sentiments have proved durable and are wholly understandable aspirations of the sciences and social sciences. They absolutely reflect and present anew the norms of European modernity through which 'the state and the individual embarked on an unprecedented quest for the renewal of an idealised national community' (Turda, 2010: 120).

However, the axes which perpetually shape the social engineering project are the control of deviance and the management of madness and disorder. The goals of human and social betterment seem to lead inexorably, when articulated in biological terms (as we saw in Schrödinger's preoccupations), to the 'germline' of human reproduction, ensuring good stock, and psychologically to the parent–child relationship. It is in this intimate environment that exploiters of developments in neuroscience and biology seek to optimise conditions in the cause of preventing disease and promoting social progress. As we have noted, none of this is new.

For much of the 20th century, debates raged about whether the causation of deviance, 'abnormal' development, social inequality/disadvantage could be found in biology, inadequate or deficient parenting, society, culture or chance. A seminal paper, written in 1975 by anthropologists Valentine, Valentine and others, critiques the theory of 'socio-genic brain damage' put forward at the time by the distinguished anthropologist Ashley Montagu. Forty years ago, the Valentines rehearsed many of the arguments we shall be making in this book. Montagu was a progressive thinker attempting to find ways to ameliorate intergenerational disadvantage among socially deprived communities. In the US these communities were disproportionately African American. The Valentines' argument was that:

> A consensus has been developing that low-status groups suffer from organic damage and dysfunction of the *central nervous system. This consensus is approaching orthodoxy with the construction of theoretical* formulations such as Montagu's 'sociogenic brain damage'. (Valentine et al, 1975: 117)

An impressive and liberal-minded scholar-scientist, Montagu's argument was:

> Social malnourishment, both structurally and functionally can be just as brain/mind damaging as physical malnourishment … it constitutes an epidemic problem of major proportions … it can only be solved by those improvements in the environment which will assure any new-born baby the realization of his birth right, which is the development of his potentialities to the optimum. (Montagu, 1972: 1058)

In a forensic critique of both the argumentation and the science, Valentine et al draw on the considerable evidence from cultural anthropology to argue that the human organism develops normally under astonishingly different, and often very challenging, environmental conditions. They caution against extrapolating from studies charting the organic effects of non-stimulating environments in the brains of rats and salamanders in laboratory conditions, and point to the adaptive nature of many of the behavioural traits of the poor who, at the time, were being pathologised by bourgeois commentators of both conservative and liberal persuasions. Social engineering requires an infrastructure of technology and bureaucracy. This seems to lead inexorably to surveillance and interference in the lives of disadvantaged communities, frequently with little, or highly conditional, practical help. Genetic determinism (through 'bad genes') and theories of environmental intergenerational disadvantage, associated with either political polarity, for Valentine et al lead inevitably in the same direction: 'Despite enormous amounts of data and highly elaborate specialised technical procedures, the experts are conspicuously failing to integrate available information and knowledge into useful insights' (Valentine et al, 1975: 130).

Conclusion

In this chapter, we have reviewed the history of attempts at social improvement and highlighted the role of developmental thinking in the contemporary mindset, including addressing what to do. Attempts at improvement, fuelled by a potent desire for a better world on the one hand, or by fear of the mob and moral degeneracy on the other, have since the Enlightenment relied on Science and Reason. Who benefits, and who is controlled in the service of a better world, represent fundamental dilemmas (and contradictions) freighting the utopian project, which we argue in the chapters that follow are not easily resolved by technical means. At present, the contradictions are being obscured by a high-tech turn in the biosciences which renders our cells and brains in molecular technicolour. But the ethical complexities have not gone away. Indeed, as we have noted, they were embedded in the project of technological biology explicitly at its outset, and they can add considerably to the moral maze. Utopians, like circus horses smelling the sawdust, cannot help but dance. The tune may be different but the steps are well rehearsed.

So, what to do? For us, the counterargument and the needed moral debate should take as the starting point the reality that science is not nature, it is knowledge made by people and that people, including scientists, are embedded in culture. As Khan (2010) notes: 'Science is not an anthropomorphic being, it does not "tell" anything. Scientific data has no meaning until one interprets it and such interpretations are inevitably packed with qualitative judgements' (Khan, 2010: 311).

We will be discussing a good deal of laboratory science in the chapters that follow. In order to understand the status of extant knowledge in the relevant fields, it is important to read the original sources. As we saw with the example of disorganised attachment, it is only through examining the ways in which knowledge is elaborated in laboratories, and other research settings, that we can make informed sense of its potentialities and limitations. Throughout the book, we will explore the intersections between biological science and public debate, examining the capacities of both to turn enduring moral issues and social problems into technical fixes. We request that the reader persevere with the detail and the argument, for gaining some sense of the underlying science is essential. Science is a social activity, with its own vocabularies. Citation practices, that is, what work gets cited and becomes seminal within the scientific community, critically affect what is asked in subsequent research, and some contestable findings become rewritten as fundamental truths. Thus, research becomes 'path dependent' and the commitment of the scientific community to a particular knowledge quest escalates. The research funding follows, and the 'facts' reproduce themselves, gaining the status of incontrovertible truths. In the next chapter we will examine how knowledge gets made in neuroscience and molecular biology, and in epigenetics in particular.

Notes

[1]   http://www.tribune242.com/news/2015/nov/16/caribbean-reparations/
[2]   We should note that these also often demand a great deal of conformity and ideological purity from individual people.
[3]   As Nietzsche put it with some élan: 'Cause and effect: such a duality probably never exists; in truth we are confronted by a continuum out of which we isolate a couple of pieces' (Nietzsche, 1974: 112).
[4]   In common parlance since the mid 1980s, originally deriving from Donald Winnicott.

TWO

How knowledge gets made in neuroscience and molecular biology

In the preface and opening chapter of the book, we outlined the ways in which technological biologies have joined forces with the enduring project of human improvement. We have hinted that the way biology has flourished of late has been, to a significant degree, a product of a mutually reinforcing configuration of alliances and networks which buttress the biotechnological research agenda, and which also serve to fuel particular ways of thinking about deviance and risk. This chapter provides an introduction to some key concepts from the philosophy and sociology of science, and proceeds to examine two biotechnologies in depth to reveal how the underlying sciences 'think' and construct knowledge. We review two exhibits, 'neuroscientism', a form of thought affording neuroscience a privileged worldview, and the 'epigenetic' thought style. We begin with a brief excursion into the philosophy and sociology of science which will help us understand how science gets made within scientific communities. This will enable interrogation of the presuppositions and supporting assumptive bases of our two principal exhibits, which are exerting a foundational influence on social policy.

Facts and thought styles

The idea that science is a human and social matter, progressing through episodes of settled thinking, punctuated by fundamental change, is well established. The work of the influential philosopher of science, Thomas Kuhn (1962), may be familiar to many readers. Kuhn conceived of science in terms of 'paradigms' (ways of thinking and doing science) that, at any one historical period, define what counts as 'normal science' for that epoch. He saw scientific change in terms of 'revolutions', or major shifts in ways of thinking, which Hacking describes as follows:

> Normal science ... proceeds in a rather inevitable way. Certain problems are set up, certain ways for solving them are established. What works is determined by the way the world collaborates or resists. A few anomalies are bound to

persist, eventually throwing science into a crisis, followed
by a new revolution. (Hacking, 1990: 97)

By putting thinking in its historical context, Kuhn is widely proclaimed
as one of the pioneers in the social study of science. Yet, as Hacking
(1990) notes, he had very little to say about the detail of social
interaction in scientific communities, and its role in the production
of either paradigms or revolutions. This is precisely the concern of
Ludwig Fleck. Fleck, himself a physician and biologist, began his
seminal book, *Genesis and development of a scientific fact* (1979), with
the blunt question 'What is a fact?'. He begins his treatise with the
first appearance of the concept of syphilis in the 15th century, tracing
its progressive development from an 'ethical-mystical disease entity of
"carnal scourge"' (p 5) to its well-defined modern status as a specific
medical condition. In parallel, he outlines developments in medical
science leading to the emergence of bacteriology and serology in
the 19th century, which made possible diagnostic tests such as the
Wassermann test, which finally established the medical 'factuality'
of the condition. Even then, its birth was a difficult one: 'From false
assumptions and irreproducible initial experiments an important
discovery has resulted after many errors and detours' (Fleck, 1979: 76).

The concept of the 'thought collective' (*Denkkollektiv*) is central to
Fleck's thinking:

> If we define 'thought collective' as a community of persons
> mutually exchanging ideas or maintaining intellectual
> interaction, we will find by implication that it also provides
> the special 'carrier' for the historical development of any
> field of thought, as well as for the given stock of knowledge
> and level of culture. (Fleck, 1979: 39)

Fleck designates the set of beliefs and values common to members
of a given collective as its 'thought style' (*Denkstile*). We have already
encountered our first thought collective and its attendant style, namely
that of developmentalism. As we saw, such mindsets exert a potent
influence on how we see the world and set priorities for action.
Crucially, the individual within the collective is never, or hardly ever,
conscious of the prevailing thought style which exerts a compulsive
force upon their thinking. It is not merely that the thought collective
constrains what can be thought, but that without such structures,
there can be no knowledge: 'The true creator of knowledge is not an
individual but the thought collective' (p 123).

Fleck devotes much space to the analysis of the social structure of thought collectives, making the key distinction between small 'esoteric' circles (the expert elite of scientists directly engaged in the research) and wider 'exoteric' circles (of teachers and practitioners). He also distinguishes between journal science, published by the original scientists, and the sort of science represented in manuals, handbooks, textbooks and the like. 'Journal science' is tentative and provisional (typified by modal phrases, 'it appears possible that', and so on, which invite the collective to adjudicate on the rightness or wrongness of the claims). Over time, journal science is moulded and distilled into a simplified vade mecum form, an expression which has come to mean the kind of 'take-away knowledge', or 'knowledge to go' we find in handbooks, encyclopaedias, and so on. Once assembled, this new, more certain science appears to be self-evidently right; it is characterised by orderliness, consistency and certainty, traits which also tend to characterise public accounts of science. In their research on the professional socialisation of scientists, Delamont and Atkinson observe that each generation of scientists, once they enter postgraduate study:

> learn that everyday research in the field of the laboratory does not necessarily produce stable, usable results until they have mastered tacit craft skills. In turn they then learn to remove all mention of those tacit, indeterminate aspects from public accounts of their research. (Delamont and Atkinson, 2001: 87)

As handbook science travels further away from its sites of production, via the media into the domain of popular science, its status becomes even more simplified and 'certain'. Popular science is characterised by the omission of detail and of dissenting or controversial opinion. This transforms knowledge into something 'simplified, lucid, and apodictic' (Fleck, 1979: 112). It is this kind of knowledge that often appeals to policy makers seeking solutions to pressing problems. It is tempting to think that the journey from journal to handbook and thence to popular science takes place on a 'survival of the fittest' basis. The best ideas thrive and are available to be disseminated in pared-down, user-friendly form. This is obviously part of the story; however, the potential for current handbook knowledge to limit what can plausibly be claimed means the process is a good deal more contingent than that.

When policy makers look for evidence to support their proposed interventions they frequently draw on intermediate sources, where research findings have been translated, summarised, simplified and, at times, quite fundamentally redrawn. Complex and often contradictory scientific claims become axioms, their origins obscured. This 'translational imperative' (Rose and Abi-Rached, 2013: 228) operates upon researchers too. Funders demand that research has rapid impact and direct applicability to pressing human problems. Thus, there are many incentives for researchers to suggest:

> that the outcome of a series of experiments on fruit flies or feral rats has something to tell us about human violence, or that brain scans of individuals when they are exposed to differently coloured faces in an fMRI machine has something to tell us about the neurobiological basis of racism. (Rose and Abi-Rached, 2013: 228)

Another useful framework for understanding the relationship between science, policy and practice is actor network theory (ANT). ANT is an approach to social theory and research, originating in science and technology studies, which treats objects and facts as part of, and substantially a product of, social networks. We do not intend here to undertake an ANT analysis of the technological biologies and their relationship with policy and practice, so our summary of the concepts is necessarily brief and selective. We have drawn on a number of concepts from ANT to describe and analyse how some ideas have flourished and are sustained and it is important to understand some of the terminology. With its origins in social anthropology and the sociology of science, in particular the work of Callon (1986a), Latour (1987, 1993) and Law (1994), ANT is concerned with the creation of facts (claims, machines, innovations), through a translational process known as 'blackboxing'. The idea of a black box comes from engineering, denoting a system which can be viewed purely in terms of its external function, that is, without any knowledge of its internal workings, which are opaque and taken for granted. Through blackboxing an 'assembly of disorderly and unreliable allies' (the assembly includes human actors such as the scientists themselves and their technicians, and nonhuman 'actants', that is, the objects of their research, laboratories, technologies, and so on) slowly evolves into 'something that closely resembles a black box' (Latour, 1987: 130–1). Each new ally strengthens the actor network, making the box blacker, the fact harder, obscuring its historical and contingent nature: 'scientific and technical work is made invisible by its own success. ... paradoxically, the more science and technology succeed, the more opaque and obscure they become' (Latour, 1999: 304).

When we look at how biology has merged with longstanding notions of human improvement we can trace such networks of association, in which diverse communities (of politicians, scientists, lobbyists, commercial interests, funding bodies), by virtue of the strengths of their aligned interests, create those black boxes that eventually come to be seen and accepted as the facts of everyday life. If we are to engage effectively with the complexities involved in the translation of laboratory biological science in the service of utopias, the black box must be opened, to reveal 'a swarm of new actors' (Callon, 1986b: 30). The following extract from a review paper on the effect of stress on the developing foetus provides an illustrative example of such a 'black box':

> Meaney and his group have shown how variation in maternal care can have long-lasting effects on both the behaviour and function of the HPA axis of the offspring. Offspring of mothers showing more maternal care are both less anxious and have a less pronounced corticosterone response to a new stressor. This [Meaney's] group is also uncovering some of the epigenetic changes in the brain, altered methylation … which underlie this. (Glover et al, 2010: 18)

Michael Meaney is an influential researcher whose teams have investigated the behaviour of maternal rats and its impact on their pups; we will be examining the complexities of the rodent work in chapter seven. In the quotation, he is said to be 'uncovering' epigenetic changes in the brain, but as we shall see in due course, he needs a number of allies and a particular way of thinking to achieve this revelation. Similar assertions can be found in the mainstream press:

> The biggest excitement … surrounds growing research that suggests it's not just physical characteristics or illnesses we might be passing on to future generations. Instead, our DNA might be affected by behavioural epigenetics too. Research on rats by Prof Michael Meaney of McGill University, Montreal, and Frances Champagne, a behavioural scientist at Columbia University in New York, have identified changes in genes caused by the most basic psychological influence: maternal love. The 2004 study showed that the quality of a rat mother's care significantly affects how its offspring behave in adulthood – that rat pups that had been repeatedly groomed by their mothers during

the first week of life were subsequently better at coping with stressful situations than pups who received little or no contact. (Bell, 2013)

Here we see introduced some other important actors in our emerging story. The HPA axis[1] (hypothalamic–pituitary–adrenal axis) is a key player in the stress response in humans and other animals. With the steroid hormone cortisol (another nonhuman player) it is ubiquitous and will become familiar to the reader as we progress. Methylation (of parts of the DNA sequence) is a key epigenetic mechanism, and animal work is routinely invoked as epigenetic evidence of foetal stress *in utero* and the effect of 'parenting style' on infants' stress responses. It is frequently not made clear, in papers developing implications for policy and practice, that much of this research derives from laboratory work on rats, not people in real environments. Although Glover et al (2010) conclude that animal studies 'show convincingly' a long-term effect on the HPA axis of prenatal stress, they also acknowledge that 'equivalent work in humans is only just starting' (p 21). Such reticence is not always so explicit. Writing some 10 years earlier, and making what appears to be a clear extrapolation from rat work, seamlessly merging this with psychological literatures on humans, Michael Meaney himself asserts: 'Cold, distant parent-child relationships are associated with a significantly increased risk of depression and anxiety in later life ... warm, nurturing families tend to promote resistance to stress and to diminish vulnerability' (Meaney, 2001: 1162).

We have noted, in the last chapter, the potency of the aspiration for human perfectibility, and its association with curing social problems and preventing moral degeneracy. Thus the first phase of blackboxing is easily accomplished for the neuro-bio-social policy project. The 'developmental' nature of the problem is easily defined and recognisable to all. Key actors like Michael Meaney, child welfare campaigners and charities establish themselves as indispensable to the solution to the problem. They entrench themselves as 'obligatory passage points' (Callon, 1986a). Once the actor network has been effectively created, it is easily mobilised and whatever (policy) solution the actors propose is carried into effect.

Thus the stage and process of production of the fact '*maternal care can have long-lasting effects on both the behaviour and function of the HPA axis*' is blackboxed. The activities of Meaney's laboratory and its technicians, its ecology and inevitable artifices, the ways animals are selected, bred and handled, and how all these shape the data and its interpretation (Rose and Abi-Rached, 2013), are no longer accessible.

Neither are they relevant for those acting subsequently. For example, an 'evidenced-based review' commissioned by the UK government to guide judgement in child protection cases argues without equivocation:

> A baby's stress response system is unstable and reactive; it will produce high levels of cortisol if the baby's needs are not being met, or if the baby is in an environment which is aggressive or hostile. Persistent and unrelieved chronic stress in infancy results in the baby's brain being flooded by cortisol for prolonged periods. This can have a toxic effect on the developing brain, with detrimental consequences for future health and behaviour. (Brown and Ward, 2013: 44)

In 2015, 40 years after Valentine et al made their case, Adam Perkins, a neurobiologist of personality, wrote *The Welfare Trait: How State Benefits Affect Personality*. The book's central argument is encapsulated below:

> Childhood disadvantage has been shown in randomised controlled experiments – the gold standard of scientific proof – to promote the formation of an aggressive, antisocial and rule breaking personality profile that impairs occupational and social adjustment during adulthood … A welfare state that increases the number of children born into disadvantaged households therefore risks increasing the number of citizens who develop an aggressive, antisocial and rule-breaking personality profile due to being exposed to disadvantage during childhood. (pp 2–3)

Perkins' road is paved with good intentions: preserving the welfare state for the worthy by ridding it of the burden of the employment-resistant personality type. In support of this bold thesis, Perkins marshals a series of human and nonhuman witnesses, the randomised controlled trial, mouse genetics, and the equations of the economist James Heckman[2] among them. Epigenetic changes are in Perkins' cast of witnesses too. Indeed, all of our star players make an appearance – though we have a different take on what they say and what they mean.

So, throughout the book, we have a number of detailed exhibits from the primary science and elsewhere which will serve to introduce a number of influential actors, both human and nonhuman 'actants'. These include influential scientists and persuasive clinicians, lobbyists, campaigners, politicians, economists, research funders and commercial interests, quite a number of laboratory rats, brains, cells, genes, neurones and hormones, technological equipment, data repositories. And of course, ordinary people who need to be fixed.

Having outlined this broader social context of science, we must now turn our attention to understanding in detail the thought styles embedded within two of the 'new biologies' which are exerting an influence over current policy and practice, and beginning to transform our sense of human identity. As we shall see, there is a natural alignment between these biologies and the developmental 'thought style' of the previous chapter, which emphasises the child's gestation and early years as foundational for all other experience. It is a time of great potential, but is pregnant with risk that the next developmental stage might not be successfully negotiated. Throughout the book, we shall show that this thought style is seminal to the development of the applied techno-biological project. In explicating this way of thinking, we are not minimising the importance of early childhood, or making an apology for child neglect. Rather, we will focus attention on the 'now or never' nature of the arguments, which usher in particular consequential effects. It creates the parameters through which the State fixes its gaze on fixing people and fixing the future.

Contemporary neuroscience has played a pivotal role in this emerging settlement, furnishing much of the biological case for preventive early action. In the following section, we present an extended critical exposition of this thought style, which aligns so naturally with the developmental paradigm. We will look in depth at the journal science, highlighting the uncertainties it presents. In subsequent chapters, we will contrast this with the handbook (vade mecum) version that has been inveigled into the world of policy and practice. We will conclude with a short example how the two styles have come together in providing a neurodevelopmental model of an important cognitive process; another important biological actor, the genome, will make its first appearance in this vignette. This sets the scene for an overview of the second of our new biologies in the latter part of the chapter: epigenetics.

The neuroscientific thought style: neuromania at large

In 2013, the International Society for the Prevention of Child Abuse and Neglect held its annual conference in Dublin. The gathering of researchers was a large one, with hundreds of contributions in the form of papers and poster presentations, studded with keynote speakers of international renown. Yet one piece of research really caught the attention of the local press; the *Irish Times* ran the eye-catching headline: 'Researchers find key differences in brains of abused and neglected young people'; the gist of the story was as follows:

> The brains of some children who have been abused or neglected are structurally different from those of young people who have not been exposed to ill-treatment. ... Researchers speculate that these structural abnormalities may be biological markers of vulnerability as a result of early exposure to mistreatment. ... A growing body of research has demonstrated a strong association between childhood abuse and increased vulnerability to psychiatric disorders.

The work in question was attributed to 'a team of experts at University College London [who had] scanned the brains of more than 20 children aged between 10 and 14 years of age who were referred to social services following documented experiences of mistreatment'. The research highlighted the reduction in brain size (grey matter, that is, nerve cell bodies) revealed by brain scans in two regions of the cerebral cortex (the medio-orbital frontal cortex and the left middle temporal gyrus) which are 'implicated in decision making, emotion and autobiographical memory, processes that are impaired in a number of psychiatric disorders associated with maltreatment' (De Brito et al, 2013: 105). What seemed to draw less interest from the journalists, and indeed perhaps the authors, judging by the content of the paper's abstract, was that the study had failed to find any significant differences between the maltreated children and the controls in terms of IQ, mood, anxiety, depression, anger, post-traumatic stress, peer problems, social problems and emotional problems. There were behavioural differences in only two areas: conduct problems and hyperactivity.[3] In fact, there were remarkably few differences between the children, except in small areas of their brains. There is no doubt about it; brains pack a punch! We shall see more of this in the succeeding chapters; especially punchy are images purporting to show brains shrunken by neglect.

Brains, or their proxies, have featured from the start of the project of social improvement. Way back at the end of the 18th century, the German physician Franz Joseph Gall founded the discipline of phrenology. Phrenology is based on the belief that the human mind has a set of faculties, located in different areas of the brain, and manifest in the shape of the skull. Areas of the cranium were believed to be proportionate in size to 'propensities', good and bad! These character traits may be as vague and esoteric as 'love of life', 'wit' or 'mirthlessness'. According to Wikipedia, phrenology took a powerful hold of the public imagination during its 19th-century heyday:

> The popularization of phrenology in the middle and working classes was due in part to the idea that scientific knowledge was important and an indication of sophistication and modernity. Cheap and plentiful pamphlets as well as the growing popularity of scientific lectures as entertainment also helped spread phrenology to the masses.

The principal British centre for phrenology was established in Edinburgh in 1820, and a book by George Combe (*Constitution of man and its relationship to external objects*, 1847) apparently sold over 200,000 copies through nine editions. Although largely discredited as a scientific theory by the middle of the century, Pustilnik (2009) documents how the idea that a disordered brain is responsible for behavioural abnormalities took tenacious hold. Thus transformed into a medical condition, the stage was set for the 'emergence of psychiatric medical intervention in the never-ending project of improvement or morals' (Rimke and Hunt, 2002: 61) with this project reaching its inglorious apogee in the 20th century, with the rise and fall of frontal lobe surgery (lobotomy). During its heyday, nearly 70,000 people were subjected to this intervention, 'sedative psychosurgery' as its advocates called it. Though discredited, the underlying phrenological logic is still with us:

> Psychointervention is easy to dismiss as horrifying but irrelevant ... [yet it] has immediate lessons now. Whilst we now know that the claims of psychointervention were inflated and we reject its abuses, its logic – like that of phrenology – is both elegant and fully consistent with prior movements in understanding violence entirely internal to the brain. The investigator then tries to solve what he or she has defined as the brain's violence problem through brain intervention. (Pustilnik, 2009: 204)

The 'sticky' hold on the imagination that phrenological thinking exerts, and continues to exert, is eloquently attested in the contemporary fascination with brain imaging, for the public and professionals alike. Brain scans embody the simple idea that different parts of the brain do different things. Naturally, we tend to believe this must be so, after all this is a characteristic of all the complex technologies devised by humankind, be they mechanical, electronic or indeed social (bureaucracies). However, although it is meaningful to consider the brain, as a physical object, in this way, the idea of physically localised functions does not easily apply to psychological processes, such as learning and memory: 'the mind is not the sort of entity that resides anywhere in space' (Miller, 2010: 718); or, as Descartes put it, mind has no extension.

It is arguable that the development of neuroscience over the last hundred years or so has more to do with technology than brains. This is true in two ways: technology as an instrument for investigating the brain, and as a metaphor for how the brain works (be it telephone exchange, digital computer, hologram – all have been used as models at some point). When the first author commenced his PhD in the late 1970s, the technology of choice for exploring brain function in humans was the electroencephalogram (EEG). The EEG provides an ongoing record of electrical activity inside the brain ('brain waves') from electrodes placed on the scalp. At that time, the dominant model of human cognition was to see the 'brain' as a computer-like information processing system, involving a number of interacting modules for perception, attention, memory and so on, often represented as a block diagram (see appendix A). The typical psychology experiment, then as now, involved presenting the 'subject' with a discrete stimulus of some sort (sound or image) to which a response was required, that is, some form of 'information processing'. Considerable excitement was stirred by the EEG response to such stimuli (the so-called event-related potential, ERP), which consisted of a series of waves unfolding over the half second or so after the stimulus. It was tempting to think that the orderly progression of peaks and troughs reflected the sequential activation of 'cognitive modules' in the brain, and to see changes in the configuration of the waveform as saying something deeply meaningful about brain function, such as that 'bigger peaks' mean more intense 'information processing'. An industry of research was thus spawned looking for such correspondences, which continues to this day.

Although seductively plausible, the morphological similarity between a conceptual model on the one hand (the block diagram of cognition) and an electronic trace on the other is necessarily no more than that, a suggestive correlation. Empirically, there have been inconveniently contradictory results: appendix A presents one such cautionary tale from the first author's PhD research, namely the finding that larger amplitude waves can be associated with less, not more, mental work. There are a number of important lessons here. First, that electronic signals recorded from the brain can often look as if they mean something, when all they represent is a plausible correlation with *inferred* psychological processes. And it is the inferred processes that are framing the interpretation: without the information processing model of cognition, the waves would be meaningless squiggles. Second, that psychological models themselves are very often simply crude metaphors. The idea, for instance, that the brain (mind) is an information processing machine was inspired by analogy with the digital computer.[4] In earlier times, other technological metaphors have been invoked, such as the telephone switchboard (Roy John, 1972) or the hologram (Pribram, 1991). Nowadays, as we shall see, we think of the brain as a type of macro-network; partly this is inspired by its internal structure of various apparently discrete areas somehow working together, but it is also buttressed by the ubiquitous nature of the idea of a 'network' as a form of functional organisation, equally applicable to people, organisations or indeed technology.

Mind–brain correspondences

Although technologies for investigating the brain have become more and more sophisticated, the underlying experimental paradigm remains the same. On the one hand, we have psychological models which depict important causal relationships among psychological states and behaviours, and on the other we have some technology for recording neurophysiological activity. A correspondence between these two realms is then sought, typically proceeding from the former to the latter: the psychological state of the 'subject' (be it rodent or human) is varied and some change in the brain state is registered:

> Our understanding of neural information processing is founded on the conceptual assumption that, if two or more sensory stimuli can be discriminated, or two or more behavioral responses are different, their associated patterns of neural activity must be readily discriminable. (Panzeri et al, 2015: 162)

In drawing such correspondences, Uttal (2016) makes an important distinction between signs and codes:

> A sign is any neurophysiological signal that correlates with a cognitive process. A code is the actual neurophysiological action or mechanism (the psychoneural equivalent) that IS the cognitive process … All that a sign does is to tell us that there is a recordable brain response to some stimulus

> or state … it does not necessarily explain or represent the
> mechanism by means of which brain activity is transmuted
> into mental activity. (Uttal, 2016: 106)

For an extended discussion of the sign/code distinction, the reader is referred to appendix A.[5] Here we merely note that the principles of neural coding are not fully understood, even in the peripheral sensorimotor systems (systems relating to perception and movement) and the study of higher-level cognitive processes (planning a trip to Bali, recalling sitting by a river on a summer's day in 1986) remains virtually untouched by such progress, even at a crude level (Uttal, 2011: 24). In the visual system, for instance, it is believed that the encoding of optical inputs involves a hierarchy of increasingly sophisticated feature detectors (single neurones) in the visual cortex, which increase their firing rate in response to the presence of the feature to which they are 'tuned'. The existence of such detectors for simple features (lines, edges) has been known for over 50 years (Hubel, 1963), and it has been suggested that more complex detectors subserve the identification of whole objects, giving rise to the surreal concept of the 'grandmother cell', which fires when a person perceives a specific entity, such as one's grandmother. But, although variations in firing rates are consistently correlated with particular stimuli, this does not mean that this is the coding mechanism used by the brain, however intuitive this scheme may seem. As a coding scheme it is both slow and inefficient, and alternative mechanisms have been proposed, based on the patterned response of ensembles of neurones rather than singletons (see appendix A). The concept of the grandmother cell is also something of a lampoon, and although there have been eye-catching studies which appear to show the existence of cells with such behaviour (for example, the 'Halle Berry' neurone described by Quiroga et al, 2005), the mainstream view is that information is processed in the brain through the patterned activation of populations of neurones, rather than specialised feature detectors.

The interested reader is referred to appendix A for further details. Here, we limit ourselves to the general point that neural coding remains a contested issue. Establishing a sign as a code demands a high level of proof (Uttal, 2011). The existence of a stable and well-defined repertoire (taxonomy) of both psychological and brain states is a sine qua non for establishing correspondences between the two domains, and it must be shown that the brain states stand in a one-to-one 'necessary and sufficient' correspondence with the psychological states. In the extreme, this requires that whenever such-and-such a brain state is manifest, the psychological state must always be present, and vice versa. But even this is not enough to move beyond the merely correlational. As Miller writes, a mechanism bridging the two 'ontological domains' is needed:

> We know that, given a gas in a fixed, closed space, heat will increase the pressure. That observation can be seen as providing circumstantial evidence of heat playing a causal role in pressure, but it does not provide a mechanistic account of how it does so. Based on additional work, we can spell out the relevant mechanism at various degrees of granularity, and as a result we are quite satisfied that there is a causal relationship between heat and pressure. (Miller, 2010: 717)

The 'additional work' here was the breakthrough in our understanding of heat as the aggregated kinetic energy of the molecules making up the gas. In molecular biology, it is our detailed understanding of the cellular mechanisms which lead from DNA sequences through RNA to the synthesis of proteins by ribosomes that gives confidence that DNA provides the code, and that it has been cracked. But for mind–brain relationships: 'Such a thoroughly worked out story of the causal mechanisms is lacking for events we view as involving both psychological and biological phenomena ... The "how" of those causal relationships—the mechanisms—remain a mystery' (Miller, 2010: 717).

There are further complications arising from the sheer complexity of the brain, with billions of neurones and uncountable connections, making the characterisation of its 'state' at any time a formidable, if not an insuperable, computational challenge:

> Because of their great complexity and number, it is not possible for us to analyse the great neuronal networks of the brain in a way that would permit us to identify the neural equivalent of any kind of mental activity at this microscopic level of analysis. (Uttal, 2011: 19)

Macroscopic mapping: what do brain images really tell us?

While studying detailed patterns of neural activity at the microscopic level (the level of individual neurones) is a formidable challenge, valuable technologies have emerged for studying the aggregated activity of (very) large numbers of neurones across wide 'geographical' regions of the brain 'macroscopically'. The EEG is one example; brain imaging is a more recent instance. The latter has led to a burgeoning of neuroscientific research in many increasingly exotic domains: just about every conventional field of study now has its neuro-prefixed version, neuro-economics, neuro-law, neuro-philosophy, neuro-politics to name but a few, inspiring Tallis (2011) and Legrenzi and Umilta (2011) to coin the neologism 'neuromania'. But brain images suffer from the same limitations as all macroscopic techniques; they measure aggregated activity, and lose critical detail. In the case of functional MRI (fMRI) brain images, what they measure (glucose metabolism[6]) is only indirectly related to the brain activity thought to be functionally important (the firing of neurones). The relationship may be plausible, but we have already witnessed two cautionary tales on this point: both the amplitude of the ERP and simple frequency coding seemed plausible indicators of how the brain worked, but both have proved somewhat questionable when subjected to more searching interrogation.

The risibility of much of contemporary research with brain images is ruthlessly lampooned by Tallis (2011). Such research plays well with the media. A study cited by Tallis, for instance, led its authors to propose a 'speculative model of the neurobiology of wisdom'. In a press release this was translated by journalists into an article entitled 'Found: the brain's centre of wisdom'. Tallis mocks these studies: 'They seem like brochures from the Grand Academy of Lagado in *Gulliver's Travels* ... as manifestations of neo-phrenology' (p 75). He gives other examples, including the following study entitled 'The neural basis of unconditional love':

> Care assistants were invited to look at pictures of people with intellectual difficulties first neutrally then with a feeling of unconditional love. By subtracting the brain activity seen in the first situation from that seen in the second, the authors pinned down the neural network housing unconditional love. (Tallis, 2011: 74)

The paper names the following brain regions as making up this network of activation: 'the middle insula, superior parietal lobule, right periaqueductal gray, right globus pallidus (medial), right caudate nucleus (dorsal head) ...' (Beauregard et al, 2009). And how impressive is the list of Latinate names – they 'shout science' (Poerksen, 1995)! But let us examine the experimental logic of the typical fMRI study more closely. It depends on the idea that that there is some discrete psychological state (of unconditional love, as opposed to other kinds of love) that can be magically brought into being just by thinking about it, or engaging with a task that involves the state/process in some way. It further assumes that we can isolate this psychological quality by also producing a state of mind that does not involve the quality and subtracting one from the other. The difference between the two mental states is held to reflect the quality in question, from which it is inferred that any difference in the brain image must be the biological embodiment of the psychological state/process. Such logic of 'cognitive subtraction' is as tortuous as it is unconvincing (Legrenzi and Umilta, 2011). It relies on the untested and somewhat implausible assumption that both brain and mind can be decomposed into robustly defined, discrete states which can simply be added and subtracted. But we are far from understanding what constitutes a brain state, or indeed a mental state such as unconditional love, let alone showing that they are susceptible to simple arithmetical manipulation.

But despite the crudeness of the experimental procedures, brain images are rhetorically powerful. It feels as if we are really seeing what is going on in the brain. Ramani (2009) describes neuroscience information 'as a marker of good explanation, regardless of the information content' (p 5). A notorious study by McCabe and Castel[7] demonstrates the rhetorical potency of such images. A group of undergraduate students were asked to evaluate some fake news articles on brain imaging research. The reports were clearly fictitious, for example, an article entitled 'Watching TV is Related to Math Ability' concluded that, because watching television and completing arithmetic problems both led to activation in the temporal lobe, watching television improved math skills. When asked to rate the credibility of the reports, those including brain images were rated consistently higher than those without. Brain images would appear to be treacherously seductive; as Tallis acidly observes, a brain scan is 'a fast acting solvent of critical faculties' (p 280). This is especially so for those produced by functional MRI scans which portray brain activity in compelling technicolour maps. Uttal attributes the appeal of brain images to the 'illusion of inferential proximity' that makes us feel we know something when we don't ... 'pictorial splendour overwhelms critical considerations' (p 21). That different parts of the brain seem to 'light up', to use a favoured phrase of Tallis, when certain mental activities are in train is so very convincing. That these images are the result of very complex processing and provide but crude information about the brain (as we shall see) is of no concern to the viewer, so potent is the spell cast.

A more general limitation to the explanatory potential of such topographic maps of aggregate activity[8] may be illustrated by reference to figure 1, which shows a heat map for a game of football between Barcelona and Real Betis. Superficially, by presenting a coloured 'map' of the game it resembles a brain image; more fundamentally, brain images and heat maps are technically equivalent in that they both represent spatially distributed patterns of energy expenditure. The limitations of such heat maps are easily pointed up by pondering the football version. How much information about the game does the image convey, one might ask? Very little, is the obvious answer. Not zero though, as some appreciation of the match and the pattern of play may be gleaned. It is hard to make out for certain who was dominant, though the map suggests that Barcelona were stronger along the wings, the right in particular. But that is about as far as one can go without having been at the game, or read a match report. In fact, the game was won impressively by Barcelona 6-2, with three goals from Luis Suarez. There is little in the heat map, even at the crudest level, to suggest such a one-sided contest.

The poverty of reducing a game of football to a heat map is clear for all to see. Heat maps of the brain, like heat maps of football, provide only a rather impoverished account of what is really going on. But there is a more fundamental point to be made. We can only make something of the football example because we already understand football. We know the code, and we can elaborate an account of the game in as

Figure 1: Heat map of a game of football in the Spanish Liga between Barcelona and Real Betis; Barcelona are playing right to left (Image used with the permission of Squawka Ltd, London).

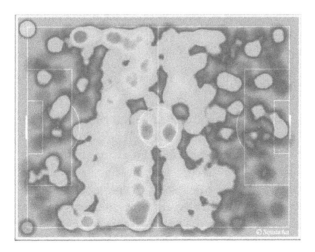

much detail as we choose (for example, a match report, or a more detailed narrative), adopting whatever pet theory we hold about the right system of play, the form of key players, and so on. In the case of the brain, we do not know the code; we have only a correlation. Our prior knowledge of football is critical to understanding the heat map, and in this very real sense, the psychosocial phenomenon of football is more fundamental than its thermodynamic properties. By analogy, we may say that the psychological level of description of the mind is more fundamental than the neurophysiological description of brain states. Brain states will never provide an explanation of psychological states, simply because psychological states always provide the frame of reference for identifying and interpreting the brain states.

Self-evidently woolly notions abound as the neuro-disciplines proliferate. One of us has recently edited a Special Issue of the *Journal of Organizational Behavior*,[9] entitled 'Can neurones manage?' Part of the inspiration came from the recent burgeoning of interest in the neuroscience of leadership within the field of organisational studies, with a small but growing corpus of research articles. There are, needless to say, as many theories of leadership as there are theorists. Which, of course, does not provide an auspicious starting point for building a coherent and stable body of knowledge! Another example from cognitive psychology is the addition of an 'episodic buffer' (integrating information from multiple sources relating to a meaningful episode of human experience) by Baddeley (2000) to his original model of working memory (Baddeley and Hitch, 1974). Doubtless this will lead to the search for its embodiment in the brain, if it has not already done so. But it will have been the psychological breakthrough which led to the search for brain mechanisms, again showing which domain is primary. It is difficult to see how brain science could ever lead to innovations in psychological theory, that the equivalent of an 'episodic buffer' would be discovered merely by looking at brain imagery.

Macroscopic network theories

Despite the foregoing critique, the phrenological idea that there are specialised centres in the brain for different psychological functions continues to exert a strong hold in brain theory. Increasingly, it is the operation of networks of such centres in concert which has become the dominant idea. Regarding the perception of complex objects, for instance, it used to be believed that a discrete brain centre (the fusiform face area, FFA) in the temporal lobe was responsible for the recognition of faces. Writing in 2006, Grill-Spector et al described the debate on the FFA's role as typifying more general controversies regarding how the brain processes information. In contrast to the view that the FFA is a cortical area specialised for processing faces, the 'distributed view' suggested that it was part of a multicentred object recognition system spanning the visual cortex and other areas of the brain, including parts of the temporal lobe (the so-called 'ventral stream'). The latter perspective prevails today, and the area is now seen to play a more general role in object recognition, with some interesting gender specialisations, such as an association with car recognition in men (McGugin et al, 2016)!

Uttal also uses violence to illustrate the distributed nature of brain activity, drawing on a review study of 17 brain imaging studies of aggression (Bufkin and Luttrell, 2015). The review concluded that a system of brain structures was implicated, with both decreases and increases in activation associated with increased aggression. Over 30 different structures are named as being abnormal in aggressive patients: the amygdala (2 times), anterior frontal cortex (1), anterior medial frontal cortex (2), hippocampus (1) and so on. To the question, which brain regions subserve violence, it is impossible to disagree with Uttal's answer: 'Pretty much the whole brain' (Uttal, 2011: 173). He concludes: 'Brain activity associated with mental activity is broadly distributed on and in the brain ... The idea of phrenological localisation must be rejected and replaced with a theory of broadly distributed neural systems accounting for our mental activity.'

Contemporary neuroscientific theory is 'mainly driven by the metaphor of macroscopic nodes interconnected by signal bearing tracts' (Uttal, 2016). This idea has a long history; the archetypical macroscopic network is the Papez circuit, elaborated in 1937 by Papez. It is described in the paper's summary as follows: 'It is proposed that the hypothalamus, the anterior thalamic nuclei, the gyrus cingula, the hippocampus and their interconnections constitute a harmonious mechanism which may elaborate the functions of central emotion, as well as participate in emotional expression' (Papez, 1937: 743).

Of note is the fact that the circuit was identified primarily on the basis of anatomical evidence regarding brain structures and their connectivity. At the centre of the circuit is a cortical region in the middle of the brain known as the cortex of the cingular gyrus (*gyrus cingula*) which: 'may be looked on as the receptive field for experiencing emotion ... Radiation of the emotive process from the gyrus cingula to other regions in the cerebral cortex would add emotional coloring to psychic processes occurring elsewhere'[10] (Papez, 1937: 728).

Over the years, this basic circuitry has been substantially elaborated. In particular, the amygdala is seen as playing an important role in the generation of strong emotions, including aggression, and the role of the hippocampus has been downplayed (Uttal, 2011). It is noteworthy that the hippocampus (seahorse in English) and amygdala[11] (almond) are adjacent structures, forming part of the brain known as the limbic system.[12] The frontal cortex is also seen as playing key role in the regulation of emotion; anatomically, it is heavily interconnected with several elements of the Papez circuitry (the amygdala, hypothalamus and hippocampus in particular) and has a widely acknowledged role in decision making, planning and executive control. To give a flavour of contemporary research on the (extended) Papez circuit, the reader is referred to appendix B. This summarises a recent review article by Hermans et al (2014), focusing on a particular region of the amygdala, the basolateral complex (BLA), which is believed to play an important role in emotional regulation. Here in the main text, we shall simply draw attention to a number of key points which highlight typical lineaments of the neuroscientific thought style.

First we note the sheer industrial scale of the research on this tiny brain region; over 300 papers are covered by the review, and we may consider this as but the iceberg's tip. We further note that the bulk of the research involves laboratory experiments mainly on rodents. Second, these experiments typically involve 'training tasks', such as an animal analogue (model) of learning, and a degree of stress is involved, for example, fear conditioning. Third, the general finding from such studies is that stressful tasks stimulate the release by the BLA of a neurotransmitter, norepinephrine.[13] Fourth, this secretion indirectly promotes 'memory processing in regions elsewhere in the brain', especially key elements of the Papez circuit involved in learning and memory, such as the hippocampus and the anterior cingulate cortex. Fifth, pharmacological interventions are often deployed in the reviewed studies to provide confirmatory evidence of this role, for example, blocking the secretion of norepinephrine by the BLA suppresses the animals' retention of learning. Sixth, human studies of patients with lesions to the amygdala are invoked to confirm the role of the amygdala in 'successful memory formation for emotional items' (Hermans et al, 2014: 7). Next, the participation of the amygdala in a distributed brain network (known as the salience network) is noted, which mediates attentional responses to salient external events; it is noted that more research is needed to explicate the role of the BLA in this network. The more research we have, the more we need, it would appear!

Two further dimensions of the neuroscientific thought style are worth noting. The hope invested in technology is one: the review article laments the limitations (either in time or anatomical location) of current imaging technologies for capturing the fine detail of neural information processing. Nonetheless, it has firm faith that new technologies, such as optogenetics, have great promise in overcoming these shortcomings. Finally, although the authors concede that 'our understanding of the dynamics of amygdala ensembles and their role in memory ... remains limited' (p 11), nonetheless they are optimistic that research 'might provide a mechanistic account of mental disorders linked via mnemonic traces to stressful life events that enables *mechanistic and individualized treatment*' (emphasis added, p 11).

Macroscopic networks meet developmentalism

We end this overview of neuroscience with a pertinent example of such a Macroscopic Network Theory as provided by Posner et al (2006, 2014). The study is of added relevance as it brings genes into the equation, and addresses developmental issues. The theme of the paper is human attention, and three modes are distinguished: alerting, orienting and executive control; the latter is the focus, defined as 'the resolution of conflict between neural systems and regulating thoughts and feelings' (Posner et al, 2006: 1422). The Attention Network Test, which involves detecting whether all the arrows in a sequence consistently point in the same direction (congruent) or not (conflict), was used to measure this form of attention. The reader will note that the cingulate gyrus (the lynchpin of the Papez circuit) is a key actant in their macroscopic network: 'conflict tasks show that the more dorsal part of the anterior cingulate [ACC] is involved in the regulation of cognitive tasks, while the more ventral part of the cingulate is involved in regulation of emotion ... the dorsal part of the ACC shows connections to cortical areas of the parietal and frontal lobes, while the ventral part of the ACC has strong connections to subcortical limbic areas' (Posner et al, 2006: 1424). Functional MRI scanning, while subjects performed the Attention Network Test, allowed the network to be mapped out, as depicted in figure 2: the focus was the dorsal ACC, with nodes in the prefrontal lobe (BA6, BA10), superior parietal gyrus (BA7) and temporal parietal junction (BA22).

The numbers on the diagram represent cortical areas defined according to the widely used Brodmann coding scheme.

Figure 2: Schematic side view of the brain showing Posner et al's macroscopic brain network, adapted from figure 3 of their paper.

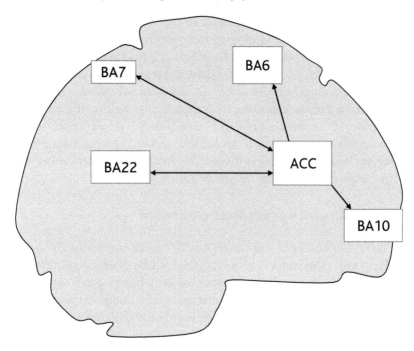

Using age-related tests of executive attention (for example, tests of anticipatory looking for very young children), the authors go on to track the development of this mode of attention in children. Their data suggest 'the possibility that rudimentary executive attention capacities may emerge during the first year of life but that more advanced conflict resolution capacities are not present until 2 years of age':

> Results suggest that executive attention continues to develop throughout childhood but may stabilize at near-adult levels of performance by about eight years of age. There is considerable evidence that the executive attention network is of great importance in the acquisition of school subjects such as literacy, numeracy and in a wide variety of other subjects. (Posner et al, 2006: 1425)

The authors go on to explore whether executive control can be enhanced by training, using a five-day training programme targeted at 4- to 7-year-olds, 'the period of major development of executive attention according to our previous results'. Improvements in both executive control and intelligence were found. Interestingly, evoked potentials formed part of this evaluation.[14] Regarding the efficacy of training, the authors observe that not all children need or benefit from attention training. The authors claim to have found a 'biomarker' in the 6-year-old children participating in the training study: 'a genetic polymorphism ... of the dopamine transporter (DAT1)' which was associated with more efficient conflict scores. We will hear more of dopamine[15] later. They end with the noteworthy speculation that:

> it is expected that attention training could be especially beneficial for those children with poorer initial efficiency. These could be children with pathologies that involve attentional networks, children with genetic backgrounds associated with poorer attentional performance, or children raised in different degrees of deprivation. (Posner et al, 2006: 1427)

We shall see more of such 'genetic targeting' in chapter six: it is integral to the thought style in the world of policy and practice.

Neuroscience: concluding comment

> Suppose that there be a machine, the structure of which produces thinking, feeling and perception ... This being supposed, you might visit its inside, but what would you observe there? Nothing but parts which push and move each other, and never anything that could explain perception. (Leibniz, *Monadology*, 1714)

Judging by the burgeoning of research, neuroscience, spurred on by the allure of new technologies, has seemingly made great progress. We have witnessed its thought style to be profoundly technological. It is characterised by machine metaphors for understanding brain function, which come and go as technologies evolve, and by a dogged faith that ever more powerful technologies will ultimately resolve any encountered impasse. Neuro-theory and neuro-technology mutually shape and reinforce each other, in an enabling but constraining duality (Giddens, 1984). Macroscopic imaging begets the idea that the brain functions as a distributed network; and in turn, such a conceptualisation reinforces the validity of macroscopic technology as the right investigative tool. This mindset also tends to lead to technical remedies, such as pharmacological interventions, which also characterise much of the experimental work on animals.

Contemporary neuroscience is a powerful industry, with enormous investments of human and financial capital. As neuro-technologies evolve, the army of neuroscience researchers around the world grows exponentially, as does the volume of research. Though burgeoning, it is an industry characterised by a disproportionate lack of dissent, although, as we saw in the signs versus code debate, there is much of a profound nature to dissent about. The dominance of neo-phrenological thinking is one such problematic. Another is the ubiquitous use of animal models and the inherent problems of generalising from such constrained, experimental analogues, a topic to which we shall return at various points throughout the book.

How well is the field doing?, one may (im)pertinently ask. We hope that through this brief overview we have done enough to at least raise some critical questions. We have seen, for instance, that consistency of findings across studies in terms of brain locations remains elusive,[16] as in the case of aggression, where different studies have identified a wide range of correlated loci. Settled knowledge in the realm of the journal science seems far off; research seems only to beget the imperative for more research. We hope we have shown the state of current knowledge to be at a very early and provisional stage. As Bruer avers, after a century of neuroscience, we are still closer to the beginning than the end of this quest. We leave the final word to Andrew Scull, in a recent book to which we will return in the next chapter:

> Despite important advances in our understanding, we are very far indeed from being able to connect even very simple human actions to the underlying structure and function of people's brains. We are decades away after all, from successfully mapping the brain of a fruit fly. (Bruer, 1999: 409)

The epigenetic thought style

We now turn to the second area of technobiology with which we are concerned, namely, epigenetics. As with neuroscience, there is a strong alignment with developmentalism, and we shall focus on this in considerable depth in chapters seven and eight, although we realise that this is some distance away. What follows is an overview of the cellular mechanisms involved in genetic and epigenetic processes, aiming to give the reader the opportunity to immerse themselves in the central ideas and vocabulary of the astonishingly busy realm of cell biology. This is vital in providing the context for some of the wilder 'translational claims' we will encounter in chapters seven and eight in particular. At this point, we recognise that not everyone will want to read the book in strict sequential order; some readers, for example, may prefer to read chapters seven and eight first, and return to this section equipped with their own questions from the policy and practice domains.

To recapitulate, the term epigenetics was first coined by the British biologist, Conrad Waddington, in 1942; it refers to the study of the ways in which the expression of heritable traits is modified by environmental influences, or other mechanisms, without a change to the DNA sequence. The field has expanded rapidly over recent years as technology has facilitated the examination of these mechanisms at a molecular level. Here we shall attempt to summarise some of the main technical concepts in this nascent field, enough we hope for the subsequent argumentation to make sense to the nonspecialist reader. By necessity, what follows is a somewhat selective and superficial overview. There are many introductory books on epigenetics which provide a somewhat more comprehensive grounding (for example, Carey, 2012) to which the interested reader is referred.

The regulation of gene expression

The hereditary substrate of all multicellular organisms is the well-known double helix of deoxyribonucleic acid (DNA), containing all of our genes distributed across, in humans, 23 pairs of chromosomes. In abstract terms, DNA comprises a code, made up of four molecules (so-called 'nucleotide bases'): the four bases are: adenine, cytosine, guanine and thymine, abbreviated to A, C, G and T. DNA itself is analogous to a twisted zip with two backbones; the teeth of the zip are made of up two types of base pair, either A on one strand linked with T on the other, or the combination C–G. No other pairings are possible. The basic code is formed from sequences of three such base pairs, known as 'codons': amino acids, the basic constituents of proteins, are specified by these codons. Genes are regions of DNA responsible for the synthesis of proteins encoded by the codon 'script'. Throughout this book, will follow the usual convention of labelling the gene for a given protein in *italics*, and the protein itself in normal typeface.

Not all human cells are alike and, over the process of embryonic development, cell differentiation from the original fertilised egg gives rise to myriad cell types. These differ widely in both structure and function, from the long branching neurones of the brain, specialised for conveying nerve signals, to the blob-like red blood corpuscle, specifically designed for transporting oxygen around the body using haemoglobin. All these cells contain identical DNA; their specialisation is accomplished via control of the 'expression' of their constituent genes. Gene expression denotes the process by which the gene's protein is synthesised: it is estimated that of the 21,000 protein-coding genes in the human organism, between 5,000 and 15,000 are expressed in a typical specialised cell. It is the collage of gene expression specific to each cell type which gives rise to the wide variation in the size, shape, behaviour and function of different cells.

Various mechanisms regulate gene expression, which is achieved, in crude terms, by switching the gene on or off. The production of proteins from the DNA script involves an intermediary molecule, RNA, which replicates the DNA template in a process known as transcription. Transcription of RNA is initiated in a region of the gene known as the promoter, and is accomplished by an enzyme[17] which 'unzips' the gene's code, making the RNA copy of the gene. Although the on/off dichotomy suggests gene regulation to be a simple process, this belies its complexity. Multiple DNA sequences outside the promoter region are involved in gene expression; these 'regulatory sequences' respond to proteins called *transcription regulators*, which may either turn genes off (transcriptional repressors) or on (transcriptional activators).

Working in concert, these regulatory mechanisms act as 'molecular microprocessors integrating information from a variety of signals into a command that dictates how often transcription of the gene is initiated' (Alberts et al, 2014: 265–6). This statement gives a sense of the complexity of gene regulation, even at the level of the individual gene. But metabolic processes involve rather more than single genes operating on their own. Even in very simple bacterial organisms, multiple genes work in a complex, coordinated manner to regulate metabolic activity.[18] In the more complex 'eukaryotic cells' (cells with a distinct nucleus and cytoplasm) of multicellular organisms, the general mode of operation is yet more sophisticated. The concept of 'combinatory control' refers to the committee-like operation of groups of regulators 'all of which are necessary to express the gene in the right place, at the right time and in the required amount ... a typical gene is controlled by dozens of transcription regulators' (Alberts et al, 2014: 272).

A pertinent example of coordinated regulation in humans is provided by the hormone cortisol, of which much more in later chapters. Cortisol (a steroid hormone in the class known as glucocorticoids) has a range of systemic effects, including the elevation of blood sugar, suppression of the immune system, as well as aiding in the metabolism of fat, protein and carbohydrate. An important property of steroid hormones is that they can pass directly through the cell wall to activate 'glucocorticoid receptors' (GR) inside the cell; these act as *transcription regulators*, promoting or inhibiting the transcription of not one but multiple target genes. The particular patterning will depend on the type of cell: in response to cortisol, for instance, liver cells increase the expression of many genes, including those encoding the enzymes involved in glucose synthesis; when cortisol concentration falls, expression of these genes reverts to normal. Thus a single transcription regulator, responding to a signal from outside the cell, can orchestrate the expression of many different genes.

Epigenetic mechanisms

Returning to our epigenetic narrative, we have noted that the cells of a multicellular organism are highly specialised. It is clearly necessary that once this specialisation has occurred, this identity must be maintained throughout the life of the cell, and throughout subsequent generations of daughter cells produced by cell division (mitosis). This phenomenon of *cell memory* is essential for the maintenance of the stability of different cell types, otherwise your heart might become your liver over time! The mechanisms by which it is achieved are referred to as epigenetic, the prefix 'epi' stressing that these mechanisms do not alter the structure of DNA itself, which remains the same. Several mechanisms mediate these modifications to the chromatin (that is, the overall complex of DNA, proteins etc. which make up a chromosome).[19] We shall consider these in turn.

The most familiar of these mechanisms to the lay audience is DNA methylation. This refers to the attachment of the small methyl molecule (one carbon and three hydrogen atoms) to cytosine bases. For the most part, this only occurs when the cytosine node is followed by a guanine base. Such binary sequences are denoted CpG, and regions of DNA containing a large concentration of such sites are called CpG islands. Methylation controls genes by binding proteins[20] to the methylated CpG node, which have the effect of switching off the gene. Methylation has achieved something of celebrity status in popular writings. Carey (2012) recounts laboratory studies of mice, in which a certain gene (the *agouti* gene) is switched on and off through a methyl-rich maternal diet during gestation. This engenders lasting effects on coat colour, weight and susceptibility to disease which seemingly persist into the following generation: 'you are what your grandmother ate' it would seem (Meloni and Testa, 2014: 442). But more of this later.

Histone modification provides another well-known epigenetic mechanism. The histones are a group of proteins abundantly present in chromatin. DNA wraps itself around these nodes, enabling lengthy DNA strands to be packed into tiny cell nuclei. Histones can become physically modified in various ways. The first discovered mechanism was lysine acetylation, involving the addition of acetyl groups to one of the amino acids (lysine) making up the histone. Lysine acetylation *increases gene expression* in adjacent genes, but since its discovery a wide range of other histone modifications have been identified, some of which augment gene expression whereas others have a depressive effect.[21]

Gene regulation via RNA provides another epigenetic mechanism. In addition to protein synthesis (encoded by so-called messenger RNA), RNAs perform other critical tasks. One of the noncoding functions of RNA is the regulation of gene expression. MicroRNAs, for example, are tiny molecules (a score or so of nucleotides in length) which are 'packaged with specialized protein to form an *RNA-induced silencing complex* (RISC)' (Alberts et al, 2014: 282). These complexes 'patrol' the cytoplasm, seeking out complementary messenger RNAs which are then either destroyed or their translation otherwise blocked. A single microRNA can inhibit the transcription of multiple RNAs, which makes them very effective regulators of gene expression. There are considered to be roughly 500 microRNAs encoded by the human genome, and they are thought to regulate the expression of at least one-third of all protein-coding genes (Alberts et al, 2014: 282).

Methylation and the myth of permanence

Of these various epigenetic mechanisms, methylation has, as we have noted, attracted particular interest, especially in the popular literature. Carey (2012) articulates an important claim regarding methylation, that 'heavily regulated' genes can become *'shut down almost permanently*. The DNA gets incredibly tightly coiled up and the gene transcription machinery can't get access to the base-pairs to make mRNA copies' (Carey, 2012: 59, emphasis added). This association between methylation and permanent change is an important one in the epigenetics literature; it bespeaks a fundamental shift from flexibility to fixity. In chapter seven, for example, we will see that correlations between increased methylation of the *NR3C1* gene (responsible for GR synthesis, see earlier) have been found in several studies associated with child maltreatment. There is a tendency in such work to link methylation with permanency. For instance, Perroud et al (2011) argue 'that excessive methylation of the *NR3C1* promoter region as a consequence of childhood maltreatment permanently disturbs the expression and thus the availability of GR in the brain'. But how excessive is excessive? Actually, the increase in methylation as a result of sexual abuse was only 10% in the subjects studied (sufferers of borderline personality disorder and major depression). Intuitively, this hardly sounds like the degree of 'heavy regulation' Carey has in mind. The overlap in methylation levels between the various groups in the study was actually substantial, and indeed severely abused subjects showed the least methylation; it is also notable that emotional abuse showed no effect.

Leaving aside these obvious short-comings, more fundamentally we question the explicit association between methylation and permanent change; how well has this link been established? We will see in chapters seven and eight that methylation is far from immutable or 'fixed for life'; rather, it seems to form part of an adaptive metabolic response to changing circumstances. A recent study, for example, of the effects of acute exercise in healthy sedentary men and women showed reductions in methylation 20 minutes after one bout of exercise; the reductions were specific to genes associated with metabolism, and the various graphs in the paper suggested the reductions could be as much as 50% (Barre et al, 2012). A parallel experiment on mice in the same paper demonstrated similar findings. The authors conclude that 'acute exercise leads to transient changes in DNA methylation in adult skeletal muscle ... provid[ing] further evidence that the epigenetic marks across the genome are subject to more dynamic variations than previously appreciated' (p 408). Another example of the lability of methylation comes from a study of Tai Chi practitioners. The abstract of the study claims it shows 'significant slowing (by 5–70%) of the age-related methylation losses or gains observed in the controls, suggesting that tai chi practice may be associated with measurable beneficial epigenetic changes' (Ren et al, 2012). Incidentally, a study of expert meditators showed rapid changes in histone modification associated with meditative states (Kaliman, 2014).

But we are not experts ourselves, so we leave the final word to those who are. Marchal and MiottoI (2015) in an authoritative review paper entitled 'Emerging concepts in DNA methylation', write as follows:

> DNA methylation has proved to be a dynamic process, requiring continuous regulation and potentially having an important regulatory role for tissue specific differentiation or cellular signalling ... While mostly stable it has been

soon noticed that in certain developmental processes and human diseases DNA methylation can be, globally or locally, erased. (Marchal and Miottol, 2015: 743)

Writing of both methylation and historic modifications, Kevin Struhl, Principal Investigator of the Struhl Laboratory at Harvard University, concludes in a recent opinion piece:

> More generally, epigenetic inheritance is determined primarily by transcriptional circuitry, and not by histone modifications or DNA methylation ... Thus, both DNA methylation and histone modifications are generated by targeted recruitment of enzymatic activities, and these modifications serve a reinforcing, but not instructive, role in maintaining epigenetic states. (Struhl, 2014: 3)

Mark Ptashne in a paper entitled 'Epigenetics: Core misconcept', makes the following instructive comments:

> [It] is said, chemical modifications to DNA (e.g., methylation) and to histones ... drive gene regulation. This obviously cannot be true because the enzymes that impose such modifications lack the essential specificity (p 1) .... in neither case is it correct to refer to nucleosome modifiers as 'epigenetic'—they, like the very many proteins recruited to genes by specific transcription regulators, are parts of a response, not a cause, and there is no convincing evidence they are self-perpetuating. (Ptashne, 2013: 3)

Such remarks suggest that, as our understanding of epigenetics ultimately evolves, the idea that epigenetic 'marks' once inscribed are static, deterministically driving bodily processes and behaviour, may come to seem, at the very least, contestable and simplistic. If the 'epigenome' were not fundamentally adaptive and malleable, one might pertinently ask, what is its point – the ability to adapt a fixed DNA structure to the varying contingencies of the environment is the very essence of epigenetic machinery. But as we shall see, this is not the view that prevails in all circles; many folk fervently believe otherwise.

Epigenetics, stress and the HPA axis

The role of epigenetic processes in the regulation of responses to stress is an important motif in current research relevant to the project of human improvement, and we shall consider this research in some depth in chapter eight. Drawing on a recent thorough review article by Cunliffe (2015), we will now provide an overview of the physiology of the stress response. We have already touched on stress and brain circuitry earlier in this chapter, so it is useful at this point to look more closely at how epigenetic processes come into the picture.

The operation of a neuro-hormonal system known as the HPA axis plays a ubiquitous role in neurobiological narratives of stress and has achieved something of canonical status. The HPA axis is made up of two brain structures (the hypothalamus and the pituitary gland) and the adrenal glands (located above the kidneys). The hormone cortisol, encountered earlier, is integral to its operation. Summarising Cunliffe's account, the argument runs as follows. Stressful stimuli (encompassing social and environmental stressors) cause the hypothalamus to secrete corticotrophin releasing hormone (CRH) and arginine vasopressin (AVP), which in turn stimulate the release of adrenocorticotrophic hormone (ACTH) by the pituitary gland (transcribed by the *POMC* gene). This circulates in the blood to the adrenal glands, where it stimulates the release of cortisol. This acts systemically throughout the body via two receptors, including the GR transcription regulator we met earlier. The effect is to mobilise the organism for acute action.

An important negative feedback circuit is provided by the operation of cortisol on the hypothalamus, where it represses CRH synthesis, and in the pituitary gland by attenuating *POMC* gene expression. This repressive effect is mediated by the GR receptor, to which cortisol binds in the cell, as we have seen. The purpose of this regulatory loop is to ensure that cortisol is only released in the continuing presence of the external threat, and the concomitant secretion of CRH and AVP. Once their secretion stops, cortisol production will also cease. The stress response is obviously adaptive in response to acute stressors: it induces us to avoid and run away from things that are dangerous. This is the flight/fight response, known for over 50 years since the pioneering work of Hans Selye. Although such an immediate response to an acute threat clearly benefits the organism, long-term exposure to stress can have permanently deleterious effects. Chronic exposure to cortisol in the brain is held to be responsible for such consequences.

We will end the chapter with a short digression, summarising the main features of a recent review by Finsterwald and Alberini (2014) which brings current brain research back into the picture, focusing on the role of glucocorticoids in the brain processes subserving learning and memory. The review focuses on one brain structure in particular, the hippocampus, widely seen as playing a crucial role in these cognitive processes, and memory especially. The 'seahorse' features centrally in some of the seminal epigenetic research which we will look at in depth in chapter seven. The review notes that glucocorticoid receptors are ubiquitous in the brain, with high levels in the hippocampus and the amygdala in particular. A large body of research has shown that the release of glucocorticoids via the adrenal glands (induced as we have seen by arousal/stress) activates these receptors in the hippocampus. The effect is adaptive, in that memory and learning are enhanced, contributing to better coping with challenging circumstances, now and in the future. Early animal studies, for instance, showed that removal of the adrenal glands produced memory deficits; more recent studies, involving pharmacological inhibition of glucocorticoid synthesis, have shown similar effects.[22] Stress-induced secretion of glucocorticoids also targets the amygdala, leading to the general view that 'glucocorticoid is critical for memory formation and modulation' and (via the amygdala) that a wide range of cortical areas are involved (Finsterwald and Alberini, 2014: 20).

The review highlights the complexity of the role played by GR in the brain. As well as its action on the nuclear DNA, it has a direct non-genomic effect on synaptic efficiency by enhancing the release of glutamate, the main excitatory neurotransmitter in the brain. The overall effect is to raise the level of excitation in the hippocampus (and amygdala) 'thereby promoting long-term memory' (p 18). GRs also directly activate another biochemical system, the endocannabinoid system, which involves both the hippocampus and amygdala (BLA); the effect again is to enhance the consolidation of emotional memories.

As stress is an important theme in our story, we ask the reader to bear with this digression a little longer. Finsterwald and Alberini draw attention to the well-known Yerkes-Dobson law, formulated a century ago, which depicts the relationship between stress and performance (including memory) as an inverted U. Neither too little or too much stress produces optimal performance; a moderate level is best, that is, a decent dose of stress is good for learning and memory. The review notes that studies involving injections of cortisol in humans, for instance, show peak memory performance at intermediate dosages. Severe or chronic stress in animal models, on the other hand, has been shown to 'provoke deficits in hippocampal-dependent forms of memory' (p 23), including synaptic atrophy.

There are several points to register here, all emphasising the complexity of brain systems, and that simplistic accounts that focus on one aspect (such as methylation levels of a single gene, or the localised depletion of a receptor protein) are impoverished and likely to be misleading. First we note that the primary influence of glucocorticoids in the hippocampus is adaptive, promoting learning and memory in normal conditions of moderate, manageable stress. Second, we again encounter a narrative couched around networks of multiple centres acting in concert. It is also clear that the various nodes in these networks play differing, complementary roles; the effect of severe stress in the amygdala, for instance, is to 'enhance neuronal activity, synaptic transmission, spine formation, and dendritic growth' (p 24).

In terms of the neuroscientific thought style, Finsterwald and Alberini's conclusion is also noteworthy. They consider treatment implications for conditions such as post-traumatic stress disorder (PTSD), proposing[23] a potential role for 'GR inhibitors in combination with trauma reactivation as a potential novel therapeutic approach … against stress-related psychopathologies' (p 24). Pharmacological remedies, we note once more, are seldom far away.

Conclusion

In this chapter, we have provided a critical overview of the 'thought styles' (the nexus of concepts, research priorities, preferred methods, latent assumptions, and so on) which characterise two of the 'new biologies'. These are beginning to exert a potent influence over our sense of identity as human beings, and ideas about the sort of society in which to live our lives. By drawing on examples of some of the original science in one of these fields, neuroscience, we have sought to convey something of the complexity and unsettled nature of the science as it circulates within what Fleck dubbed the esoteric zone, where the original work is done. We have seen both the promise, but also the tyranny of technology as it shapes what can be studied and how we conceptualise the object of study. We have seen how easily tropes can settle, for example, that the brain is like a machine, or that methylation marks a permanent aberration in gene expression.

In particular, we have witnessed how actants such as 'stress' and 'the HPA axis' unite neuroscientific and epigenetic forms of understanding in a powerful actor network. We shall see in the chapters that follow how this actor network is driving policy aspirations towards human perfectibility in a characteristic direction, raising important questions about the desirability of this trajectory. The next chapter will afford examples of neuroscientific research on developmental disorders, together with an example of conventional genetic research (that is, not epigenetic). Chapters four and five review the translation of a particular version of handbook neuroscience into the policy domain, particularly family policy. Later chapters (seven and eight) will provide examples of journal science within the epigenetic domain, examining seminal studies on both animals and humans.

Notes

[1] Searching 'HPA axis', for instance, as we write, produces 173,000 hits on Google Scholar. The majority of the studies thrown up by the search focus on mental health and stress.

[2] As we shall see in chapter six, Heckman draws on a particular version of neuroscience to buttress his macroeconomic arguments for early intervention.

[3] Nor was an obvious shortcoming spotted: the failure to take into account nutritional differences, which are well known to impact on body size in general, and therefore brain volumes.

[4] We also note that the form of the model can itself suggest spurious structural characteristics. The use of the block diagram, for instance, suggests that there are discrete psychological modules which somehow exist physically in space, and can therefore potentially map into a physical object, such as the brain. Of course, this is entirely an artefact of the arbitrary choice of the diagrammatic representation; a prose description of the mind as an information processor would have carried no such connotations. The diagram is purely conceptual: it is not meant to be real. We not really being asked to believe that we have a box in our brain, sorry! mind, for memory.

[5] The ERP, for instance, is a sign, not a code. In other words, at best the ERP can provide a measure of how much 'brain activity' is going on and where. It can tell us nothing about the intrinsic nature of that activity, of the patterns of activity in neural networks at the cellular level. It is rather like summarising the economic activity of an entire population in terms of the GDP; the statistic can be useful but it does not tell us anything about the behaviours of individuals and businesses in the economy that make it work. Brain signs (and macro indicators in general) can certainly be useful; they may serve as useful biomarkers of some mental processes, indeed I once used the ERP, rather a long time ago, to study attentional levels in a study of the ergonomic design of telephone switchboards (Wastell et al, 1982).

[6] More specifically, such scans measure the levels of deoxygenated blood flow, inferred from changes in the magnetic properties of haemoglobin. Less oxygen is held to indicate more glucose metabolism, which is held to indicate more 'firing of nerve cells', which in turn is believed to tell us something critically important about the brain and cognition.

[7] Although we are tempted not to spoil a good story with facts, in the interests of balance we must point out that more recent studies using a similar methodology have not replicated this result, and it has been argued that the images in McCabe and Castel provided additional information beyond the pictorial representation (Farah and Hook, 2013).

[8] Functional brain imaging is capable of more sophisticated representations of brain activity than static maps. As we shall see in the following chapter, they can provide

a dynamic analysis of patterns of distributed activity in different brain areas over time (functional connectivity).

9   In the end, the special issue was not published due to insufficient submissions of the required standard.

10 It is noteworthy that the circuit can by 'incited' at two points: the cerebral cortex and the hypothalamus. It would appear that emotions can be triggered directly by sensory experiences (via the hypothalamus) or through conscious thought (via the hippocampus). We may surmise that these distinct pathways correspond to emotions that arise in direct response to noxious stimuli from the environment (disgusting images, smells; loud noises) and situations where cognition mediates, for example, to appraise a situation as threatening.

11 Again, we note the rhetorical potency of Latin names, and conversely how colloquial language takes the science down a peg or two!

12 Limbic is derived from the Latin term for 'border'; here it designates a 'transitional area between the neocortex and the subcortical structures'; the limbic system includes a number cortical, subcortical and diencephalic components (hippocampal formation, amygdala, septal nuclei, cingulate cortex, entorhinal cortex, perirhinal cortex and parahippocampal cortex), several of which, as we have seen, are thought to play a key role in emotional regulation and motivational processes.

13 Norepinephrine (also known as noradrenaline) is an organic chemical of the family known as the catecholamines, a family which also includes dopamine and adrenaline (epinephrine). It functions in the brain and body as both a hormone and neurotransmitter (a chemical released by nerve cells to facilitate the transmission of nerve signals to other neurones). Its general function is to mobilise the organism for action in situations of stress or danger (the so-called fight-or-flight response). Those parts of the body that release or respond to norepinephrine are referred to as noradrenergic.

14 Quoting from p 1426: 'The N2 component of the scalp recorded ERP has been shown to arise in the anterior cingulate and is related to the resolution of conflict … We found N2 differences between congruent and incongruent trials of the ANT in trained 6-year-olds, that resembled differences found in adults.'

15 Like norepinephrine, dopamine is a catecholamine. In the brain, it functions as a neurotransmitter, playing an important role in the 'pleasure system' which governs motivated behaviour. It also helps regulate movement and emotional responses, and is implicated in various aspects of cognitive function. Low dopamine activity has been linked to addiction, and dopamine deficiency results in Parkinson's disease. More controversially, it has been linked with risk-taking, sensation-seeking propensities.

16 Because so many potential 'activation sites' (voxels) are available in a single scan, the chances of finding hot-spots even when there are none is high. A scan of pure noise (that is, no brain present) will identify peaks, for example, leading Vul et al (2009) to speak of 'voodoo correlations'. Although statistical procedures are available to control for the rate of such 'false positives', the very large number of voxels scanned means that such procedures do not guarantee security. It is likely that the inconsistency of findings across studies in part reflects the inadequacy of such controls. The same point has been made in a recent paper by Eklund et al (2016) regarding the inflation of false-positives in fMRI images.

17 RNA polymerase.

18 In bacteria, for instance, small clusters of genes (called operons) often work in close cooperation. In the bacterium *E. coli*, for instance, the so-called Lac operon

encodes the proteins required to import and digest the milk sugar, lactose (Alberts et al, 2014). Two transcription regulators are involved: a repressor and an activator. When the cells' preferred energy source (glucose) falls, levels of the activator rise, switching on the Lac operon, allowing the cells to use alternative sources of energy including lactose. But this would be fruitless if there were no lactose, and it is the function of the repressor to switch off the genes in these circumstances. Thus the combined operation of the two transcription regulators provides a finely tuned genetic circuit enabling lactose metabolism only when both conditions are met: there is depleted glucose and available lactose.

[19] One of the simplest and most important involves the transcription regulator activating its own gene; this 'positive feedback loop' ensures that the regulator is inherited by both daughter cells, and by all subsequent generations. Alberts et al (2014) comment that this mechanism is 'probably the most prevalent way of ensuring that daughter cells remember what kind of cells they are meant to be'.

[20] More specifically, methylation controls genes as follows: a protein (MeCP2) binds to the methylated CpG node, which in turns attracts other proteins which in concert help to switch the gene off.

[21] Although when cells divide, daughter cells only receive half of the parent's (modified) histone cells, enzymatic action propagates the modifications to new histones, thus fully re-establishing the chromatin structure of the parent cell.

[22] The mechanism for such effects is, in part, genomic, though not wholly so: GR regulates a range of genes involved in 'long-term memory formation' (p 18).

[23] The proposal is based on pharmacological studies of memory *reconsolidation*, the process whereby retrieved memories are rendered into a 'fragile state'.

THREE

Blaming the brain

In the age of the existential vacuum ... pathology results
not only from stress but from release of stress which ends
in emptiness ... Like iron filings in a magnetic field, man's
life is put in order through his orientation towards meaning.
(Frankl, , 1962)

In chapter two, we examined the neuroscientific and (epi)genetic
thought styles, attempting to summarise the current settlement within
the 'thought collective'. In this final chapter of Part I of the book, we
consider how these work their way into a broader style of thinking,
and programme of research, which aims at the reinterpretation of
deviant behaviour as a disorder of the brain. We examine the ways
in which biology has been brought to bear in understanding forms
of behaviour variously known through the ages as madness, mental
illness or developmental disorder. This has culminated in current
preoccupations with finding the genetic markers and neurological
traces for a variety of manifestations of the human condition, seen as
deviant. Here we see how clinical researchers also follow well-trodden
paths. We take a peek into how the primary science of the laboratory,
discussed in the last chapter, makes its way into, in this case, psychiatric
practice via its own form of journal science.

We begin with an overview of the ascendancy of biological psychiatry
as the dominant explanatory narrative in the field of mental 'illness'.
This synopsis will include an extended general survey on the long
history of research into the hereditability of mental disorder, and of
the various methodologies which characterise this tradition. We then
proceed to examine in depth two categories of mental disorder which
are particularly pertinent in the context of child development. We first
look at the state-of-the-art in autism research from a neuroscientific
perspective, applying the Fleckian concepts we examined in chapter
two. We then consider attention deficit hyperactivity disorder (ADHD),
also of relatively recent origin, focusing on genetic research into its
hereditability.

Statistical prelude: genesis of a (pseudo)scientific fact?

Before getting under way, the reader at this point is referred to appendix C. This takes the form of a thought experiment based on a real study (Hikida et al, 2007), the investigation of a gene (the disrupted-In-schizophrenia-1 gene, *DISC1*) which has been 'implicated' in the aetiology of schizophrenia. The main purpose of the appendix is to introduce readers to the basic principles of statistical reasoning involved in the evaluation of research evidence (statistical significance, the null hypothesis, measurement of effect sizes, correlation coefficients, and so on) which play a crucial role in our argumentation throughout the rest of the book. In particular, it is important not to be bamboozled by claims of statistical significance; this merely means that a numerical result is not a chance finding, but what really matters is the size of the effect produced by the experimental manipulation, and other forms of putative causal variables. We shall emphasise this crucial point throughout the book – it is vital, if research is to be applied, that it has a substantial impact beyond what might be needed to test and develop academic theory.

The appendix also provides a pertinent example of the style of laboratory research on genetic mechanisms; it exemplifies the use of animal models to provide analogues of human behaviour, in this case, the 'forced swimming test' in which rodents are forced to swim by immersion in a cylinder of water from which escape is impossible. Suspend your incredulity, yes, this is indeed used as a surrogate for depression in humans! The authors of the original paper conclude: 'DN-DISC1 mice displayed increased immobility in the forced swim test, which is frequently used as an indicator for depression but may parallel anhedonia found in patients with SZ [schizophrenia].'

Intrigued? Scientific fact, or pseudoscience? You are invited to read the appendix, and decide for yourselves on what might seem a somewhat startling anthropomorphic leap.

The inexorable rise of biological psychiatry

The general notion that deviant behaviours have a medico–biological cause has a long lineage. Rimke and Hunt (2002) refer to this phenomenon as the medicalisation of morality, tracing its emergence back to the 'vice society' of early 19th-century Britain. Alarmed at the decline of traditional authority generated by the revolutions at home (the industrial revolution) and abroad (the French), various 'projects of moral regulation' (Rimke and Hunt, 2002: 62) were instituted;

often philanthropic on the surface, at their core was the idea that a moral code could be imposed from above. The critical development was the 'invention' of the idea of 'moral insanity', as a new species of mental disease: 'one in which diagnostic focus was upon the pathology of the individual's moral faculty' (p 70). Crucially, 'persons perceived as deviating from the moral norm thus became the proper subjects of medicine' (p 74). An important corollary of this shift was the focus on hereditary factors, that forms of 'degeneracy' were the 'antisocial upshots of a process of degeneration in their descent'. Rimke and Hunt quote Kitching who wrote in the *British Medical Journal* in 1857: 'It is a long known fact that drunkards, for instance, have idiot children in a far larger proportion than sober people ... Depraved or drunken parents cannot transmit a healthy organization to their descendants' (Rimke and Hunt, 2002: 78).

It is tempting to liken the history of psychiatry to a pendulum swinging between a concern with 'soma' and 'psyche', that is, between biological and psychological models of causation. Pickersgill (2010) questions this, arguing that, for most of psychiatry's history, both explanatory frameworks have coexisted, with biology and psychology together shoring up the professional practice of psychiatry. Psychosocial explanations were particularly persuasive when applied to 'delinquent' children, depicting individuals' circumstances, rather than their bodies, as pathogenic (Pickersgill, 2010: 299).

Over the course of the latter part of the 20th century, a decisive swing to the somatic (biological) pole appears to have taken place. The biological perspective holds that all human behaviour is controlled by 'nothing more than electrical and chemical reactions in the brain' (Raabe, 2013: 12). When exactly the ascendancy of this thought style was achieved is debatable, but the title of an article in 1989 by Samuel Guze (then head of the Department of Psychiatry, Washington University) suggests that its dominance had been established well before the end of the last century. The title of the paper leaves no room for equivocation: 'Biological psychiatry: is there any other kind?'. The following extract captures the paradigm's central claim:

> what is called psychopathology is the manifestation of disordered processes in various brain systems that mediate psychological functions ... The genotype establishes a range of possibilities and limits. Development ... shapes the way these turn out ... *biology clearly offers the only comprehensive scientific basis for psychiatry, just as it does for medicine.* (Guze, 1989: 317–18, emphasis added)

Going back a decade or two, Davies (2013) identifies the publication of a paper by Joseph Schildkraut in 1965, in the *Journal of Psychiatry*, as a decisive gestational moment. Although the idea that fluctuations in mood reflect chemical imbalances in the brain was not novel, Schildkraut's paper ('The catecholamine hypothesis of affective disorders'), proposed a very specific conjecture, that depression reflected a deficiency in the important neurotransmitter, norepinephrine, which we encountered in the previous chapter. Not long after, a second neurotransmitter (serotonin, popularly associated with feelings of wellbeing and happiness) was proposed by another researcher (Coppen, 1967), to be subsequently joined by a third, dopamine (Davies, 2013), which we also encountered in chapter two. The logic has an appealing simplicity: neurotransmitters are involved in the transmission of nervous impulses across the synaptic clefts that separate neurones, and are therefore:

> crucial to how our brains operate. This is why the chemical imbalance theory states that if there's a deficiency in these chemicals, this will impair our brain's function ... the theory is seductively simple, and has remained so for nearly 50 years. (Davies, 2013: 121–2)

Integral to the ascendancy of the biological paradigm is the idea that mental illness has a genetic basis. Around the beginning of the 19th century, the ideas of the celebrity phrenologist, Johann Gaspar Spurzheim, on the heritability of crime, led to lobbying for the regulation of reproduction to prevent the intergenerational spread of criminal tendencies (Greenberg, 2010). The degeneration theories of the late 19th and early 20th centuries followed, taking their inspiration from the eugenics movement in the UK, initiated by Sir Francis Galton under the influence of social Darwinism.

The study of a rural clan, the Jukes, by prison superintendent Richard Dugdale provides a noteworthy landmark (Dugdale, 1877). The Jukes clan, it was claimed, had produced across seven (de)generations 1,200 bastards, beggars, murderers, prostitutes, thieves and syphilitics (Rafter, 1988). The 'fact' that forms of psychopathy 'run in families' by no means proves a genetic aetiology, as environmental factors could just as easily account for the transmission of the dysfunctional patterns of behaviour. Nonetheless, despite its obvious scientific defects, the Jukes study gained widespread acceptance within the academic community for over 50 years (Pam, 1995). The next major report by a eugenics-oriented researcher (Henry Goddard, 1912) concerned Deborah Kallikak, diagnosed by Goddard as 'mentally deficient' when still a child. Tracing her ancestry, Goddard attributed her condition (via recessive genetic transmission) to the liaison between a soldier forebear and a 'feeble minded' barmaid during the American civil war. No strong pattern of intellectual disability was manifest in the subsequent genealogy, and Deborah herself was apparently an accomplished young woman; she had merely scored poorly on an intelligence test (Pam, 1995). Such testing was then in its infancy, but had nonetheless led to the enactment in several states of new laws enabling lifelong detainment of convicted 'feeble minded' persons on eugenic grounds (Rafter, 1997).

In *Blaming the body*, Ross and Pam (1995) chart the historical development of research on the heritability of mental illness and provide a robust critique. Noting that biological psychiatry has 'always striven to find similar genetic mechanisms for functional disorders' (p 10), Pam (1995) goes on to distinguish various forms of so-called 'pedigree studies', that is, the generic idea that family bloodstock determines the quality of offspring. Pam's critique is thorough and cogently argued, and the interested reader is recommended to review his original text; here there is only space to highlight some key insights. Following Dugdale and Goddard, what Pam describes as the 'modern era' is entered, beginning with the seminal work of Franz Kallmann, who took up the eugenic cause, arguing schizophrenia to be an 'inbred and a reproductive threat to society' (Pam, 1995: 14). Despite his widespread approbation as 'the first biological psychiatrist to research schizophrenia in many extensive, systematic and technical advanced pedigree studies' (p 14), others have taken strong exception to Kallmann's work. Lewontin, Rose and Kamin (1984) provide a thorough critique. Pam notes their description of Kallmann's research as 'bloodcurdling pseudoscience' (p 15), highlighting the espousal in his early work of the case for 'the compulsory sterilization of schizophrenics *and* their healthy siblings' (Pam, 1995: 15).

Besides these moral concerns, there are interesting technical questions regarding the interpretation of Kallmann's key statistics, and of other research of that era, which continue to be relevant to the whole field of pedigree research up to the present, as we shall see. Slater (1968) summarises the overall findings of many studies, including Kallmann's. Noting the generally agreed prevalence of schizophrenia in the population as a whole of 1%, the rate of schizophrenia in the children of schizophrenics is 12%. While this is clearly elevated, it is impossible in such data to disambiguate nurture from nature, upbringing from genes; the inevitable bias on the part of clinicians to diagnose schizophrenia when there is precedent in the family history must also significantly skew the statistics. In point of fact, when we look backwards at the percentage of schizophrenics who have a schizophrenic parent, the figure is only 3.8%. In other words, over 96% of schizophrenics do not have any family history. The data clearly show that heredity, at most, plays only a minor part, but this is not the received interpretation (Pam, 1995). The idea that schizophrenia is genetic has become something of a meme; its persistence despite contradictory evidence may suggest the influence of a thought style.

Twin studies have played, and continue to play, a key part in bolstering the thought style. The classic twin paradigm is the comparison between monozygotic (MZ) identical twins versus dizygotic (DZ) nonidentical, controls; the former derive from a single fertilised egg and are therefore genetically identical, the latter from two eggs. At this point, let us introduce some of the key concepts of such 'pedigree research'. In the terminology of Turkheimer (2011), the aim is to partition the variation in some phenotype or trait (such as autism) into three components, attributable to genes (A), to the common/shared environment (C) and to the nonshared environment (E). Similarities in the children may be attributed to either A or C; and any differences to E. The essence of the MZ vs DZ comparison, for twins reared together, is that E is zero (the so-called equal environments assumption). All the environmental influences are thus common to both types of twin. Therefore, the only source of difference is A, the genotype, which is identical for the MZ twins but different for their nonidentical (DZ) counterparts. Any greater similarity must therefore be genetic in origin.

To characterise the degree of heritability of the trait, a statistical measure of 'concordance' is calculated. Although there is some controversy as to the optimal way of calculating this 'risk' (McGue, 1992), in its simplest form, concordance measures the percentage of twins in which both twins are affected, given that at least one twin shows the trait. This is called the pairwise method. Although Kallmann carried out several concordance studies, his claimed pairwise rate of 68% for MZ twins is wildly higher than subsequent studies (Pam, 1995): in a review of eight twin studies in 1992, McGue (1992) reported an average pairwise concordance of 29%[1] for identical twins compared to 6% for nonidentical controls, an elevated risk of 23%.

Although twin studies seem to provide compelling evidence of heritability, they nonetheless are subject to major limitations. First, the 'equal environments assumption' seems highly questionable. As Lester (1989) notes, nonidentical (DZ) twins generally develop in separate placentas and postnatally there is scope for further divergence; being less similar, they are more likely to differ in 'talents, interests, friends, occupations and share far fewer common experiences' (p 37). More fundamental is a limitation built into the design of the twin study. In order to isolate the effect of genes, the twin study necessarily seeks to eliminate any differential environmental influences, or 'confounds' as they are known in scientific argot. But in doing so, it becomes intrinsically impossible to measure the relative strength of the genetic effect compared to the influence of the environment.

Let us take poverty as an example. There is overwhelming evidence that poverty (relative poverty in particular) is strongly associated with the *diagnosis* of schizophrenia: the poorest are roughly four times as likely to be so-diagnosed, a result shown consistently over many countries and decades of research reaching back to the first systematic study in Chicago in 1939 (Read, 2010). But the effect of poverty could not in principle be shown by the classic twin study, simply because the common environment assumption entails that only twins living in the *same circumstances* can be compared; in this example, the same socioeconomic conditions. The comparison between identical twins reared apart would be required (e.g. one in affluent, the other in deprived circumstances) to show the effect of poverty, but the 'reared apart' eventuality occurs so rarely (just 12 cases worldwide in 1982 according to Pam, p 26) that systematic research is highly problematic.

Although such methodological difficulties have led to calls of for the abandonment of twin studies (for example, Burt and Simons, 2014), in the interests of balance we note that they still have their advocates and are certainly highly influential, as we shall see. In the field of criminology, Moffitt and Beckley (2015) have argued that because *discordant* MZ twins (identical twins raised together but exhibiting different behaviours) are 'never perfectly identical in their offending behaviour', this gives criminologists 'a special opportunity to study what reduces behavioural similarity' (p 123). They provide the example of a study which showed that 'within pairs, the twin who received relatively more maternal negativity and less warmth developed the most aggressive behaviors' (p 123). There is an obvious circularity in the logic here to which we will return, as well as a normative stand on parenting, which will also form a recurring motif in later chapters.

The neurobiology of developmental disorders

Having set the scene with this brief overview of biological psychiatry, highlighting the dominance of genetic thinking in particular as well as the foundational idea that physical disorders of brain are responsible for mental afflictions, we now turn our attention to two categories of mental disorder which are particularly pertinent in the context of child development. We first look at the state of the art in autism research from a neuroscientific perspective, followed by analysis of another disorder (attention deficit hyperactivity disorder), also of relatively recent origin, focusing in this case on the genetic line of research and its putative underlying biology.

Exhibit 1: the neurobiology of autism

Diagnosis of autism is controversial. Verhoeff (2014) provides a Fleckian account of its emergence and evolution as a disease concept. Given the influence of Fleck in our general approach, it is appropriate to spend a page or two tracing out the main lineages of Verhoeff's analysis. Central to this is the concept of 'medical thinking' as a distinctive style of thought, a style which Fleck argued emerged in the late 19th century. Fleck's characterisation of medical thinking is summarised by Verhoeff (2014: 41–2) as follows. The first step is to create general disease categories around which 'abnormal morbid phenomena are grouped ... producing laws of a higher order'. These 'ideal types' are 'more beautiful and general than the normal phenomena which suddenly become profoundly intelligible':

> These types, these ideal fictitious pictures, known as morbid units ... are produced by the medical way of thinking ... by far reaching abstraction, by rejection of some observed data ... As soon as medical thinking has found a certain ideal type in an infinite plurality of apparently atypical morbid phenomena it faces a novel problem: how to reduce them to a *common denominator*. (Verhoeff, 2014: 40–1, emphasis added)

Thinking in such terms sees diseases as 'distinct entities', existing independently (transcendentally) outside their unique manifestations in individual patients, and reducible to a common essence. Such a worldview represents a fundamental change from the pre-modern holistic view of disease, dominated since Hippocrates by humoral theory;[2] under this traditional regime, treatment was individual and holistic, based on restoring humoral balance. In psychiatry, Emil Kraepelin is generally regarded as the founding figure of the modern, medicalised approach. At the end of the 19th century, his *Lehrbuch de Psychiatrie* propounded a categorisation (nosology) of 16 distinct categories of mental disorder, defined by patterns of symptoms and specific biological disturbances. As Verhoeff notes, this medical thought style was slow to establish itself; psychiatric thinking in North America was a contested domain for much of the 20th century, dominated for long periods by psychodynamic and humanistic approaches. But the publication in 1980 of version three of the *Diagnostic and Statistical Manual of Mental Disorders* (DSM-3) by the American Psychiatric Association (APA) marked 'a definitive neo-Kraepelinian turn'. Autism, for example, was included as a distinct disease entity in the 'new and soon prevailing nosological taxonomy in psychiatry' (Verhoeff, 2014: 69).

The need for clear categorical demarcation, and the identification of 'common denominators', has been problematic for all psychiatric disorders, but has been particularly troublesome for autism. The search for the common denominator has been in a state of seeming constant flux, initially focusing on existential distress ('extreme self-isolation and obsessive insistence on sameness', Verhoeff, 2014: 70), through problems in symbol handling and language, to deficits in social cognition and language. Debates about the relationship between autism and other disorders (for example, schizoid personality, ADHD) have abounded, and whether other apparently similar disorders (for example, social communication disorder) should be subsumed. The details are not as relevant as the general point that: 'Without the contemporary style of thinking in terms of ontologically distinct diseases, these constant comparisons between disorders and the difficulties in demarcating boundaries would be unthinkable or meaningless' (Verhoeff, 2014: 71).

Reflecting the ascendancy of biology in psychiatry, current medical thinking about mental disorder reflects the 'neuromolecular style of thought' (p 72), which we looked at in some depth in the previous chapter. Quoting Rose and Abi-Rached (2013), this mode of thought may be summarized as follows:

> All mental processes reside in the brain, and each mental process will reflect ... brain events. Thus any mental state or process (normal or abnormal) will have a relation ... with a potentially observable material process in the organic functioning of the neuro-molecular processes in the brain. (Rose and Abi-Rached, 2013: 43)

Reflecting this, the initial aim of the most recent incarnation of DSM (DSM-5) was notably audacious: quoting a former director (Steven Hyman) of the National Institute for Mental Health (NIMH), it was nothing less than to 'translate basic and clinical neuroscience ... into a classification of psychiatric disorders' (p 72). Verhoeff (p 73) then cites the current director of NIMH making the bold prediction that 'reclassifying disorders based on brain function could yield a system of diagnosis based biomarkers ... which would very likely revolutionize prevention and treatment' (p 73). For autism, faced with the challenge of defining its essential nature in the face of its protean character, the hope and expectations that neuroscience will solve diagnostic and therapeutic problems have been understandably high.

With the revival of Kraepelinism, and the entrance of neuromolecular thinking, 'autism has become a yet-to-be-identified biological thing' (Verhoeff, 2014: 73.) For mental disorder in general, such 'biologisation' has turned out to be somewhat premature. The challenges for autism are particularly stiff, with its myriad diagnostic features: 'If you've seen one child with autism, you've seen one child with autism; autism's like a snowflake', in the words of one leading autism researcher (Verhoeff, p 74). Such heterogeneity poses a formidable challenge to maintain the integrity of autism as a 'steady diagnostic category' (p 74). Verhoeff contends that the official shift in DSM-5 from autism to 'autism spectrum disorder' marks an important change in thinking:

> Reframing autism as a spectrum disorder converts problematic and ubiquitous heterogeneity ... into an intrinsic feature of the disorder. This reframing ensures the existence of an autism category: it postpones the problem of validity; and creates new opportunities for neuroscientific research directed at fundamental and specific brain-based disease mechanisms. (p 74)

Appendix D sets out the definition of autism spectrum disorder (as it is now called) in DSM-5, in more or less complete form. The reader is urged to consult this before proceeding. The failure to couch its definition in biological terms is self-evident: the criteria for its diagnosis remain primarily behavioural and psychological; the reader will also note its diagnostic complexity and plasticity.

In the remainder of this section, we provide an overview the last ten years or so of neuroscience research on autism, much of it involving brain images.[3] We begin our analysis with a recent review article (Maximo et al, 2014) which commences as follows:

> Today, ASD is regarded as a pediatric health issue of growing urgency given that 1 in 88 children are being identified with this disorder ... While there has not been a definitively

accepted etiology for ASD in the scientific community, research has become increasingly focused on understanding the neurobiological mechanisms underlying this disorder. (Maximo et al, 2014: 1)

The review traces the idea of a 'potential biological origin' for autism to a paper by Kanmer in 1943, progressing through the pioneering work of Damasio and Maurer (1978) who noted correspondences between autistic symptoms and behaviours associated with frontal lobe damage. Early work using brain images is usefully reviewed by Yurgelun-Todd et al. Their review begins by noting the inadequacy of behavioural criteria for 'distinguishing the vast combinations of symptoms and symptomology seen in these children' (Yurgelun-Todd et al, 2006: 185). The authors go on to note that morphometric imaging studies (which focus on shapes/volumes of brain structures) have 'produced inconsistent and contradictory results in the identification of regional brain anomalies' (p 186). The review looks forward to the promise of functional MRI scanning, citing two studies showing decreased activation in the fusiform gyrus (FFA) and amygdala (and other areas) in tasks involving the processing of facial information. We have, of course, encountered these structures and fMRI imaging in the previous chapter.

How has the 'knowledge base' moved on since Yurgelun-Todd et al? In 2014, Maximo et al observe: 'Given its complex nature and the heterogeneity in symptoms, attempts to explain autism as a focal brain region abnormality have repeatedly fallen short' (Maximo et al, 2014: 2). In the face of this 'void', they state that investigations of the brain 'at the network level' affords 'a promising new avenue in characterising the neurobiology of complex syndromes like autism' (p 2). As we saw in the previous chapter, central to the network metaphor is the idea that anatomically distinct areas of the brain are specialised for different functions (functional specialisation) and that they work in a coordinated fashion to accomplish tasks (functional integration). To measure brain activity in such putative networks, the most commonly used technique is that of 'functional connectivity'. This simply measures the degree to which activity in different brain regions correlates synchronously ('moves in step')[4] during the performance of cognitive tasks, or indeed during the resting state.

Overall, studies of autistic subjects have shown a 'preponderance of underconnectivity', that is, less synchronous activity in inferred brain networks. The number of brain centres that have been identified in different studies is prodigious,[5] as is the number of potential networks.[6]

Maximo et al conclude that, while these studies all report functional underconnectivity in ASD, 'the findings vary across a wide variety of pairs of regions and across a large range of tasks, making it difficult to isolate a specific pattern of disturbance' (p 5). The authors also note that a minority of studies have shown 'overconnectivity', but explain away such 'overabundant' connectivity as localised to 'non-essential regions, allowing for low-level cross talk resulting in increased noise in the system' (p 5). Heads I win, tails you lose, the sceptical reader could be forgiven for thinking; every result can be made to fit, however anomalous. Taken together, 'these findings point to ASD as a disorder of [long distance] aberrant cortical connectivity involving multiple brain networks' (p 8). The paper goes on to consider variations between studies in term of tasks, methods and data analysis; they comment on the dearth of longitudinal studies of developmental trajectories in autism, on the need for anatomical studies of neuronal connectivity, and for studies which look at brain dynamics over long periods, as 'functional connections are in constant flux'.

Genes eventually make their appearance. The complexity of the genetic landscape is emphasised: 'the most frequently occurring genes appear in at most 2% of cases ... This implies that ASD is heterogenetic, with the located genes reflecting various mechanisms' (Maximo et al 2014: 11). The paper notes that, given its phenotypic heterogeneity, 'it is unlikely that the behavioral aspect of ASD can be equated to a single pathological entity on the neurobiological level' (p 11). The review concludes by noting the potential of neuroimaging as a diagnostic tool, providing 'a promising starting point for brain-based classification and identification of neurodevelopmental disorders' (p 15). The potential of novel brain-based treatments is also noted, specifically, repetitive transcranial magnetic stimulation (rTMS), a noninvasive technique for manipulating cortical activity involving the use of scalp electrodes.

While it is not our main aim to critique primary research, we have misgivings regarding the last two claims.[7] Regarding rTMS, we note that while the relevant study did show changes in EEG indicators and alleviation of symptoms, rTMS has been suggested for the treatment of just about every mental disorder known to humankind. George et al (2009) conclude that TMS 'as a treatment for most psychiatric disorders remains exciting but controversial' (p 15). With befitting modesty, although a little at odds with their general spirit of optimism, Maximo et al conclude their review as follows:

> Attempts to establish alterations in connectivity as potential
> neural signature of autism, and to target faulty neural

circuitry through intervention are significant from clinical and public health perspectives. Nevertheless, lots need to be done in fine-tuning the methods *before even considering to adapt neurological findings to clinical world*. (Maximo et al, 2014: 16)

Exhibit 2: attention deficit disorder

Alongside disorders on the 'autistic spectrum', the recent burgeoning of the diagnostic category attention deficit hyperactivity disorder (ADHD) has invigorated biological child psychiatry, another reflection of the pendulum's dramatic swing to the somatic pole of the nature–nurture axis. These disorders, which construct the pathology as somehow intrinsic to the child, have drawn the attention of social scientists interested in the 'medicalisation' of the human condition (Conrad, 2007). Debate has been, and continues to be, intense about the use of psychotropic medication in young children, and indeed whether ADHD exists at all. Like autism, it is contested as a disease category. Sociological accounts have shown that, when diagnosis becomes possible, ideas about the behaviours it seeks to explain change, and the problem is removed from the moral domain. As Cooper (2014) notes:

> Prior to the omnipresence of ADHD diagnoses, one could imagine many different explanations for the activity of disruptive children. Maybe the teachers are boring? Maybe young children are naturally ill suited to spending days cooped up studying maths? Maybe the problem is simple naughtiness? Maybe contemporary parenting styles are somehow inadequate? Diagnosis with ADHD acts to push these competing explanations on one side ... Instead the cause of the disruption is located inside the children's brains. (Cooper, 2014: 4)

Again, the brain science has been thoroughly conscripted in support of the expansion and refinement of the diagnostic category, and the attempt to understand its aetiology in terms of the ever-elusive (biological) common denominator. Technological advances have fuelled the neuro-enchantment, and a recent clinical textbook (Shaw, 2012) reviews 14 neuro-imaging studies of the brains of children diagnosed with ADHD. Just as we saw for ASD, anomalies in a wide variety of brain regions and neural correlates are described, including increased grey matter (tissue comprising nerve cell bodies), decreased cortical folding, grey matter deficits in left fronto-parietal regions, grey matter deficits in right superior frontal gyrus, and on and on (Shaw, 2012: 56–7).

As with autism, alongside fishing for structural anomalies in the brains of children there has run a search for the genetic basis for the condition (Dillon and Craven, 2014), together with an expansion of the definition of ADHD in DSM-5 to make it more likely that adults can receive a diagnosis (Barkley, 2010; Cooper, 2014). Heated debates about its existence as a disease category have drawn on its longstanding recognition as a disorder; there are claims that it made its debut appearance in 19th-century children's literature (Thome and Jacobs, 2004) and in Goethe's *Faust* (Bonazza et al, 2011). We make no adjudication here on the status or causation of ADHD; our point is that viewing it as a neuro/genetic disorder fundamentally changes the manner in which we think about, and explain, human life, as well the ways research is funded and priorities are set. When we look for things hard enough, we tend to find something, but whether the finding matters is another question. Speaking of the search for genetic determinants of ADHD, Dillon and Craven note:

> They may be of the same small effect size as other genes that may influence common behaviours such as one's propensity to play sports, political alliance, and fashion sense—traits that ordinarily are not referred to as genetic in nature. (Dillon and Craven, 2014: 25)

At this point, we dissect a recent landmark study to give a proper sense of the current state of the journal science. The paper (Williams et al, 2012) is by a large team with around 50 authors, in itself reflecting a remarkable turn in the way medical science is now carried out, as a prodigious industrial-scale exercise. It reports the efforts of the team to find an association between DNA abnormalities and ADHD. The idea that common disease-causing alleles (gene variants) will be found in all human populations which manifest a given disease is known as the common disease–common variant (CD-CV) 'hypothesis'. The paper opens with the paradoxical failure (paradoxical for the authors) of previous studies, focusing on single target genes, to find an association of common genetic variants with the ADHD phenotype. This is despite the latter's high prevalence (3%–5% of children) and its apparent high heritability (from twin and adoption studies) of 76%. It is noteworthy that there is no critical interrogation of the claim of heritability, yet there are certainly questions to be asked. A 2005 review paper is invoked

(Faraone et al, 2005); the most recent paper in this review reports a questionnaire study of parents rating their own children's attentional behaviour, on a simple rating scale. This is hardly a scientific exercise, based on robust clinical assessment. The paper suffers from all the methodological problems intrinsic to twin studies, exacerbated by the reliance on crude subjective ratings. Moreover, less than 3% of the children in the study had an ADHD diagnosis.[8] One would have to question seriously whether this study should have been included by Faraone, and more fundamentally why such pedigree research is not more critically interrogated by those who axiomatically rely on it.

But far from being a failure, the inability to find the genetic culprit is said to 'fit well with the view of ADHD as a polygenetic, multifactorial disorder, to which many common variants … of small effect contribute' (Williams et al, 2012: 196). The authors go on propound their interest in the role of 'rare genetic variants with moderate to large effect size' (p 196) rather than common variants; it is asserted that rare variants have been implicated in other psychiatric disorders, such as schizophrenia and autism. Such chromosomal anomalies typically denote aberrations, called copy number variants (CNVs), corresponding to relatively large regions of the chromosome where DNA sections have been deleted or duplicated.[9]

The authors briefly note the failure of the first genome-wide analysis[10] (GWA) of CNVs to find a higher rate in ADHD patients; instead, they give (speculative) prominence to the 'fact' that 'a number of the rare CNVs identified in ADHD patients spanned some intriguing candidate genes … at loci that had been previously implicated in other disorders such as autism, schizophrenia and Tourette's syndrome' (Williams et al, 2012: 196). Another genome-wide study is then described as having found 'an overall increased burden of large, rare CNVs in the ADHD patients, which were also significant enriched at loci that had been previously implicated in autism and schizophrenia' (p 196). 'Implicated' is, or course, something of a ubiquitous 'weasel word', typically indicating the absence of robust evidence, while suggesting there really is something going on after all! The concluding comment of this somewhat cursory 'literature review' conveys a strong sense of the somewhat desperate nature of the search: 'The most recent study investigated 248 children with ADHD and their parents and observed *de novo* CNVs in 1.7% of the children and inherited CNVs in genes previously linked to ADHD or other neurodevelopmental disorders in 8%.'

More research is clearly needed! The study itself involved the genome-wide analysis of 896 children diagnosed with ADHD, compared with 2,455 'unrelated comparison subjects'. As such this is the largest study carried out to date. Of the 732 ADHD cases that passed technical quality control for the DNA analysis, 81% had 'combined-type' ADHD, 14% 'primarily inattentive' and 5% 'hyperactive impulsive' diagnoses. A total of 1,562 CNVs that were both rare and long were identified: 462 of these were in the ADHD cases and 1,102 in the controls. There was a general tendency for more rare variants in the ADHD cases (15% more), and particularly so for longer variants (28% higher). We then come to the crux of the paper, whether anomalies at specific genetic loci can identified that are associated with the disorder. We quote the result from the paper:

> The 1,562 CNVs included in this study segregated into 912 independent loci ... Genome-wide locus-specific analysis identified one region [on chromosome 15] that was nominally associated with ADHD (p = 0.012), although this finding did not survive correction for genome-wide testing (p = 0.79).

Although statistically nonsignificant, further 'post hoc' analyses were nonetheless carried out. These pinpointed the source of the 'effect': 8 individuals out of the 732 ADHD cases (1.1%) showed duplications in a specific locus of chromosome 15 (location 15q13.3), compared to 6 in the comparison group of 2,010 subjects (0.3%). Of course, this means that 98.9% of the ADHD group were rather similar to the 99.7% of the control group in not showing the genetic anomaly. To corroborate this result, data from four other studies were combined with the primary study. In the combined sample, 1.25% of ADHD cases (37 out of 2,966) showed the anomaly, compared to 0.61% (64 out of 10,556) in the comparison group. The results section concludes by noting that 3% of ADHD cases 'overlapped with one of the 32 loci previously implicated in autism' (p. 198), and that 5.4% of ADHD cases had some overlap with 8 loci previously 'implicated' in schizophrenia compared with 3.6% of controls.

The paper's Discussion makes a number of salient points. First, it is noted that despite an earlier study finding duplications on chromosome 16, this study found no such effects. No explanation for this discrepancy is offered. Following recapitulation of the anomaly at 15q13.3, the paper moves into full-blown speculative mode, noting first that 'rare CNVs in this locus (deletions and duplications) have previously been implicated in several psychiatric disorders (e.g., autism, schizophrenia, intellectual disability)' (Williams et al, 2012: 200). Striking an optimistic note, it claims that this region contains 'a plausible candidate gene for ADHD, *CHRNA7*'. This gene 'encodes the a7 subunit of the neuronal nicotinic acetylcholine receptor [which] … participates in an ADHD-relevant pathway by mediating dopamine release' (p 200). Ignore the technical jargon, there we have it, our old friend dopamine, the scarlet pimpernel himself! The paper continues:

> Dopamine dysregulation is strongly implicated in ADHD … Two candidate gene studies of microsatellite markers and a SNP in and near this gene in ADHD have been negative. However, a recent study implicates the receptor in the response to stress and shows that maternal genotype has a strong effect on offspring phenotype. This might suggest that this gene is a particularly interesting candidate for parent-of-origin and gene-environment. (Williams et al, 2012: 200)

Confused? The sense of 'clutching for straws' is unmistakable: small effects here and there in small numbers of sufferers; spurious links with supposedly different disorders … but lots of clever-sounding 'science'. The genetic anomaly really is there; it just keeps hiding, as elusive as Macavity the cat, that Napoleon of crime! In the 17th century, Newton developed theories of both gravitation and optics on his own; Einstein in his *annus mirabilis* accounted for the photoelectric effect and theorised special relativity; 50 years later, it took two to unravel the secrets of DNA. Now it takes a team of 50 to tell us, being polite, not very much so far. Although we have struck a sceptical tone in recounting this 'strange tale', our purpose is not to attack the credentials of this study, but rather to show how tenacious is the hold of the neuromolecular thought style.

> Macavity's a Mystery Cat: he's called the Hidden Paw –
> For he's the master criminal who can defy the Law.
> He's the bafflement of Scotland Yard, the Flying Squad's despair:
> For when they reach the scene of crime – Macavity's not there!
>   T.S. Eliot, *Old Possum's Book of Practical Cats*

Biological psychiatry: critical reflections

Despite the high hopes for the biological paradigm in psychiatry, its promise has been largely unfulfilled as our two exhibits attest. Reflecting on the search for structural anomalies of the brain in autism, Verhoeff (2014) laments the general lack of consistent results: structurally, enlargements of total brain volume, increased white to grey matter (that is, nerve pathways versus cell bodies), enlarged amygdala, cerebellum and frontal lobes have all been reported; functionally, a plethora of nodes and networks have been implicated. But scant evidence of a consistent pattern has been forthcoming.

Research on the genetics of autism, driven as we saw for ADHD by its apparently high heritability, has fared little better, despite the truly industrial scale of the research, second only to investigation of schizophrenia in terms of the number of hits on Google Scholar.[11] With this level of industry (to say nothing of its inherent expense) we should surely expect significant progress. As with other disorders, studies have looked both for localised abnormalities in candidate genes, thought likely to be implicated on some a priori basis, as well as genome-wide association studies. But no consistent route from gene to disorder has been found: 'the number of genes associated with autism may be a couple of hundred or more; they are probably not specific for autism and the most common mutations are found in less than 1 percent of children' (Verhoeff, 2014: 73).

Since the inception of the human genome project, the hunt has been on to identify genes for all the major psychiatric disorders, such as schizophrenia, bipolar disorder, ADHD, autism and so on. A decade later: 'a generation of genetic researchers have tried, yet have failed, to identify the genes that they believe underlie the major genetic disorders' (Joseph, 2012: 65–6). Nevertheless, as we have seen, the hunt doggedly goes on; the disappointments have inspired even greater efforts, as negative results are reframed and explained away. To fulfil this role, a key concept has emerged, featuring in the title of 2009 article in *Nature*: 'Finding the missing heritability' (Manolio et al, 2009). Missing heritability, rather than nonexistent heritability, is the explanation. Why is this so? Because 'a substantial proportion of individual differences in disease susceptibility is known to be due genetic factors' (p 748). In other words, because we already know that genes are the cause. This is despite the inherent flaws of twin studies which provide the foundational evidence, which typically go uninterrogated, as we saw in the Williams study. Pedigree studies provide the taken-for-granted axiomatic basis of the genetic project, thereby creating a self-sealing, incorrigible, circular argument (Joseph, 2012). As Latham and Wilson drolly put it: 'Since heritability studies suggest the genes for disease must exist, they must be hiding under some as-yet-unturned genetic rock' (Latham and Wilson, 2010, para 25).

Why not, ask Latham and Wilson, take the null results at face value: 'the dearth of disease-causing genes is a scientific discovery of tremendous significance'. Denial of this result risks missing a finding of momentous proportions, but this would mean admitting entire careers had been spent working in what Ioannidis (2005) has dubbed a 'null field'. So the search goes on, with newer technologies, new statistical techniques, new genetic 'prey', be it rare variants or epigenetic marks (chapter seven). Joseph comments in a similar vein on the 'failure' of the genetic quest, arguing that this should really be a cause for rejoicing:

> it is unfortunate for people making their living conducting gene searches and for people whose careers are based on promoting genetic theories of psychiatric disorders. But for humanity in general, the failure to find genes is a welcome discovery and even a cause for celebration. If genetic factors play little or no role in the development of psychiatric disorders then we can turn our full attention to the environmental conditions that cause them. (Joseph, 2012: 78)

Taken together, this inconsistent, shifting collage of results leads Verhoeff (2014) to agree with the conclusion of Rose and Abi-Rached (2013) regarding the neuropsychiatric project in general: 'each of the pathways that neuropsychiatry has attempted to trace through the brain seems to run, not to the bright uplands of clarity, but into the murky, damp, misty, and mysterious swamps of uncertainty' (Rose and Abi-Rached, 2013: 138). *Ignis fatuus*, no less. For Miller, the idea that 'Mental illnesses are real, diagnosable, treatable brain disorders' (Miller, 2010: 717) rests on a basic logical flaw, which includes the seductive idea that biology in some way constitutes a more fundamental level of explanation. Writing with respect to schizophrenia, he argues that brain dysfunction can never provide an adequate account of mental disorders:

> This is not possible, given that we conceptualize the clinical phenomena in terms of psychological constructs. We conceive and define it [schizophrenia] as a psychological disorder involving delusions, hallucinations, disorganized speech ... These features are all psychological constructs—

> not merely symptoms/indicators of schizophrenia but
> central to the concept. (Miller, 2010: 717–18)

Such observations apply just as pertinently to autism (and ADHD), where the diagnostic criteria of DSM-5 have a strongly behavioural tone. We are back to the mereological fallacy we introduced in chapter one, and the sign/code debate of chapter two, exemplified by the football heat map. It is the psychological and behavioural constructs that are primary; the physiological relata are only known as a consequence of the psychological manifestations. Making the case for a purely behavioural approach to the understanding and treatment of autism, eschewing physiology in particular, Reese (1996: 62) argued that 'the concepts in an explanation must be at the same level as the phenomena to be explained and must be in the same [ontological] domain' (Reese, 1996: 62). This does obtain for pure genetics research, where both the code (gene) and the coded (protein) reside in the same microbiological domain. But mental disorders are not the same things as proteins! In a similar vein, Ghezzi et al (2014) invoke Skinner (1950): 'An explanation for a given phenomenon is useless if it "appeals to events taking place somewhere else, at some other level of observation, described in different terms and measured, if at all, in different dimensions".'

They also go to make the case for a purely behavioural approach for the treatment of developmental disorders. Wielding Occam's razor, mental and physiological states may be excluded from this on the grounds that the former are 'unobservable and unverifiable' (Ghezzi et al, 2014: 114) and the latter are at the wrong level of explanation. Referring to the treatment and education of young children with autism, they conclude that:

> The resounding success that applied behaviour analysis
> has had ... shows that knowing about a child's physiology
> does not improve the ability to know how to predict and
> control the child's behaviour ... It is far more effective and
> expedient to work at a purely behavioural level, that is at
> the level of interacting in and with the physical and social
> environment ... there is no compelling reason to reduce
> behaviour to the actions of a deficient or mismatching
> nervous system. (Ghezzi et al, 2014: 113–14)

It seems that reports of the death of behaviourism have been somewhat exaggerated!

In our opening overview, we briefly alluded to the catecholamine theory of depression as the poster child of biological psychiatry. At this juncture, it would seem pertinent to see how the theory has fared over the half century since its inception. Put bluntly, is the theory correct? Norepinephrine, serotonin and dopamine all belong to the class of neurotransmitters known as monoamines. The reader will appreciate from the following extract that the chemical imbalance theory was far from a 'done deal' over 40 years after its inception. In an authoritative review, citing nearly 150 references, Ruhe et al sum up as follows:

> We conclude that ... monoamine depletion does not directly decrease mood. Although previously the monoamine systems were considered to be responsible for the development of MDD [major depressive disorder], the available evidence to date does not support a direct causal relationship with MDD. There is no simple direct correlation of 5-HT [serotonin] or NE [norepinephrine] levels in the brain and mood. (Ruhe et al, 2007: 354)

Davies' (2013) position is blunt: 'After nearly 50 years of investigation into the chemical imbalance theory, there is not yet one piece of convincing evidence that the theory is correct' (p 129).

Andrew Scull in his recently published history of mental disorder from the time of the Greeks to the present day (*Madness in civilisation*, 2015) is more scathing. Reflecting on the biologisation of mental disorder over recent decades, he reflects:

> Patients and their families learned to attribute mental illness to faulty brain biochemistry, defects of dopamine or a shortage of serotonin. It was biobabble as deeply misleading as the psychobabble it replaced. In reality the origins of major forms of madness remain almost as mysterious as ever. (pp 400–1)

He avers that no cure for mental disorder is afforded by pharmacological treatments, which in many cases yield little or no systematic therapeutic relief, and any palliative benefits may be more than offset by side effects (such as the tardive dyskinesia produced by the first generation 'anti-psychotics'). That controversy continues to reign in the psychiatric community regarding diagnostic definitions, and as categories of mental illness expand to bring more and more of the merely unusual into the psychiatric ambit (hoarding behaviour, to pick an egregious example from DSM-5), provides further evidence of cracks and flaws in the current paradigm. Here, it is well beyond our competence to judge on what are somewhat complex and contested matters, and no doubt there will be many who fervently believe in the biological story. But our business is not to pronounce, but to draw the attention of lay audiences to controversy, and to destabilise settled views. In this spirit, we think it fitting to cite Scull's conclusion, which should at the very least prompt an appropriately critical attitude:

> Will madness … be reducible at last to biology and nothing but biology? There one must have serious doubts. The social and cultural dimensions of mental disorders, so indispensable a part of the story of madness in civilization over the centuries, are unlikely to melt away … [Madness] remains a fundamental puzzle inescapably part and parcel of civilization itself. (Scull, 2015: 411)

But even were such a reduction achievable, there are other more fundamental consequences: 'return to reductionism would be disastrous for the cognitive and behavioral sciences, requiring the dismantling of most existing achievements and placing intolerable restrictions on further work' (Miller, 2010: 721).

Conclusion

In conclusion, we have clearly come a long but circuitous way from the kind of psychiatry characterised by Frankl in the chapter's epigraph, which viewed much of mental disorder as 'problems in living', that is, as existential.[12] There have been dissenting voices since the first inception of the biological thought style. Guze's proselytising, with which we opened this disquisition, was followed by an editorial rebuke from Charlton, the editor of the journal (*Psychological Medicine*) in which Guze's article had appeared (Charlton, 1990). More recent dissenters include Cooper (2014) and Raabe (2013) as well as those commentators (Miller, 2010; Scull, 2015) mentioned above, as well as many more. Despite the cracks, paradigms are however difficult to dislodge once they have taken hold (Kuhn, 1962). In this account, we have foregrounded the work of two groups of actors, researchers[13] and psychiatrists, in developing and sustaining this settlement. But the network of actors goes much wider than this, of which we will say more in the final chapter. It embraces patient advocacy groups, pharmaceutical companies, insurance companies, governments, health and welfare bureaucracies, funding bodies, health services professionals and social workers. There are enormous vested interests in the status quo; this paradigm is not readily for shifting.

Although our position is sceptical, we are nonetheless nonpartisan. Our interest is purely sociological, drawing attention to the cultural hegemony of a paradigm and the totalising tendencies of its thought style. We do not, for example, align ourselves with the anti-psychiatry movement, of Szasz, Laing and others, though we applaud their heterodoxy; we need more of it and there is much we can learn from those prepared to court unpopularity and challenge the status quo. Szasz speaks menacingly of the therapeutic State, replacing the theological State (the alliance of the church and State): 'today "we know" that all mental illnesses are brain diseases. The therapeutic state – the alliance of medicine and the state – has decreed it so (Szasz, 2008: 89). Both of us read Szasz's *The Myth of Mental Illness* (1974) as undergraduates and returned to his writings in the preparation for this book. The idea that mental illness is a myth (in the conventional sense) may seem unpalatable, although in the sense used by Barthes the trope validly draws attention to its conversion from a socially constructed category of behaviour (a cultural product) into an objective entity inhering in nature. Szasz makes an unassailable point in drawing attention to the fundamental 'category error' in the very idea of mental illness as a brain disorder: 'the claim that mental illnesses are brain diseases is profoundly self-contradictory: a disease of the brain is a brain disease, not a mental disease' (Szasz, 1974: 3). In short, the mind is not the brain.

In Part II of the book, we turn away from journal science and into the worlds of policy and practice. We will first examine the impact of the style of thinking we have witnessed in the area of child welfare, in the UK in particular (chapters four and five) before moving on to consider the deeper ramifications of the natural alignment between the medical thought style and the increasing influence of macroeconomic thinking, which has given rise to the phenomenon of 'prevention science'.

Notes

[1] Individual-level risks come out at a higher level: for McGue's preferred 'proband' method the figures are 40% (MZ) compared to 10% (DZ), giving an elevated risk of 30% at the individual level, that is, the risk that if one member of the twin has the trait, his/her co-twin will also be affected.

[2] Humoral theory holds that the human body is filled with four basic substances: black and yellow bile, phlegm and blood. When these are in balance, a person is healthy; diseases are attributed to an excess or deficit of the humours. Humoral theory formed part of the system of medicine expounded by the Greco-Roman

physician, Galen. It dominated western medicine right up to the work of Harvey on the circulation of the blood, and continued to inform medical practice beyond this. Treatment was individual and holistic, based on restoring humoral balance; this holistic approach is captured by the title of one of Galen's best-known treatises, *That the best physician is also a philosopher.*

[3]   It is important to note that earlier phases of autism research operated in terms of a definition of the condition which, although descriptively similar, has evolved in important aspects, for example, the inclusion of Asperger's syndrome within the autistic spectrum. Such shifts have clear implications for the comparability of research studies over time, as definitions have evolved and continue to do so.

[4]   The degree of functional 'connectedness' of two regions is assessed by examining fluctuations in activation at the level of individual voxels over the duration of the task. If the activity of two voxels goes up and down at the same time, then they would be adjudged connected. Voxel-level correlations are then aggregated to provide an index of the degree of functional connection between the higher-level 'centres' in which they are located.

[5]   Including medial prefrontal cortex, temporoparietal junction, superior temporal sulcus, fusiform gyrus, amygdala, insula, anterior cingulate, primary and supplementary motor areas, anterior cerebellum, thalamus, posterior cingulate, cuneus and caudate nucleus (Maximo et al, 2014).

[6]   The following are enumerated: fronto-parietal network, the frontal-fusiform network, the frontal inhibition network and the inferior parietal lobe, visual cortex and frontal, anterior cerebellum and thalamus, thalamo-cortical, prefrontal-premotor-somatosensory, the fusiform-amygdala, the posterior cingulate and the cuneus, superior frontal-caudate (Maximo et al, 2014).

[7]   Cheng et al (2015) describe a classifier based on a whole-brain analysis of resting-state functional connectivity. Over 500 images of ASD and normal individuals were compared and brain regions identified with either weaker or stronger connectivity. Interestingly, of the 20 regions described, slightly more were stronger (11) than weaker (9). Correlations with symptom severity were also somewhat weak. Using a machine learning algorithm, a classifier was developed which apparently classified cases as ASD with around 80% accuracy. Although some validation was undertaken, this fell short of the acid test of how well the classifier would perform with new cases; more importantly, the 'reasoning' of such classifiers is opaque and therefore unaccountable.

[8]   The figure for heritability of 76% is taken from Faraone et al (2005) which provides an early review of genetic research on ADHD. The paper opens with a short, three-paragraph review of 20 twin studies; the figure of 76% is based on a crude average across these studies. The most recent of these is by Rietveld et al (2003) and the estimate of heritability derived from this study (visual inspection of figure 1 in their paper) appears to be close to 80%. But the paper is far from the classic twin study. It investigates attentional problems and overactive behaviours in children at various age points, using a simple questionnaire sent to a large sample of parents of twins in Holland. The key results are the correlations between parental *ratings* of behavioural problems in MZ versus DZ twins. At 3 years, the correlation for MZ and DZ twins respectively was 0.63 and 0.08, and at 12 years 0.73 and 0.28. Of note is the authors' estimate that only a small percentage of the children in the sample would have met DSM threshold ADHD, between 2-3% of the 3-year-olds and 1.3% of the 12-year-olds.

[9]   For example, the chromosome that normally has sections in order as A-B-C-D might instead have sections A-B-C-C-D.

[10] Analysis of the whole genome, rather than targeted areas of theoretically relevant genes.

[11] The rise in the number of papers since 1990 is staggering, from 42 (1990–95) to 1,070 (2000–05) rising further to 3,210 (2010–15).

[12] Frankl did not see biology as irrelevant, indeed, as professor of neurology he was an advocate of ECT and drug treatment. He was anti-reductionist, though in those days Freudianism was the dragon to be slain.

[13] We are tempted to make a mischievous, though nonetheless serious, point. Following the line of argumentation in an entertaining paper by Wiener (1995) entitled 'The genetics of preposterous conditions', research on the biological origins of mental disorder tends to foreground one group of actors, namely, patients who are seen as abnormal. There is another key group of course, the researchers themselves doing the studying, but neither their brain chemistry nor genetic profiles are up for scrutiny. This asymmetry seems rather unfair. Subjecting to examination the biological signatures of typically well-off, ambitious, middle-class professionals might well yield a distinctive neuromolecular profile! Sociologically, such a study would be fascinating, but we suspect the funding needed would not be forthcoming.

Part II
Fixing real people

FOUR

The precarious infant brain

Healed the abyss of torpid instinct and trifling flux,
Laundered it, lighted it, made it lovable with Cathedrals
   and theories
      W.H. Auden, *The Age of Anxiety*

In this first chapter of Part II, we switch register and examine the way
biological thinking is merging and melding with the project of human
improvement. Here, we review recent policy, tracing the ways in which
neuroscience, in particular, has been invoked to relocate an older moral
project on the high hard ground of scientific rationality. The previous
chapter reviewed the fields of biological psychiatry and examined the
potential impact of a neuro-developmental thought style. We argued
that, for all its sound and fury, surprisingly few killer insights have been
produced. In this chapter, we explore the emergence of a preventive
mindset in social policy: if only we could get things right in the first
few years of life, madness, badness and all manner of vexing social
problems, including poverty, would be effectively nipped in the bud. In
chapter one, we referred to Valentine, Valentine et al's (1975) critique
of the theory of sociogenic brain damage. Despite such critique, the
idea of impairment to the infant brain has proved appealing and very
hard-wearing to politicians, policy makers, academics and reformers
of both conservative and liberal mindsets, as it promises to explain
intergenerational social disadvantage. It has been a potent myth.

   The Valentines' trenchant objections to the thesis of sociogenic
brain damage, and its associated theology, took place at a time when
neuroscientific understandings of the impacts of environment on
brain development were alluringly novel. Since the 1970s, there has
been an explosion of brain science and, as we have noted, it is now
exerting a strong influence on mainstream social policy. Significant
use of neuroscientific evidence is being made to warrant claims about
the irreversible vulnerabilities of early childhood and the proper
responses of the State. There is a particular emphasis on the promotion
of 'targeted early intervention' to enhance the lives of disadvantaged
children. Sociogenic brain damage is back in the technicolour,
bewitching detail of fMRI imagery. The 'damaged' infant brain, or
rather the promise of social improvement implied by the optimisation

of its development, is popular across the political gamut. It is seen as 'progressive', appealing to all parties seeking to occupy the moral righteousness of the political centre ground. Optimising the brain's development can solve the problem of unequal life chances; it can render social justice at a stroke.

There is much to commend a 'progressive' agenda of help for the most deprived of children and offering this at the earliest juncture. It is neither the desire to help vulnerable children, nor to use the best scientific knowledge available, that we contest here. Rather, in this chapter, we endeavour to demystify the 'myth of the optimised brain' by examining some key neuroscientific claims in use in contemporary policy, and examine how these translate and transform journal science to support prior ideological positions. When we examine their use in policy, neuroscientific explanations appear to be operating as powerful trump cards, but when the rhetorical veneer is scratched away, more contentious terrain is revealed. Neuroscientific claims do not provide a scientifically neutral evidence base: like other forms of expert knowledge, they have been conscripted and translated, flocculating with existing political, policy and professional forms of thought. One effect of such myth making has been to strip away *moral* debate and delimit the number of policy and professional responses to a range of human and family frailties.

Telling persuasive policy stories

> 'Evidence' for policy making is not sitting in journals ready to be harvested by assiduous systematic reviewers. Rather, it is dynamically created through the human interaction around the policy making table ... achieved mostly through dialogue, argument, influence and conflict and retrospectively made sense of through the telling of stories. (Greenhalgh and Russell, 2006: 36)

As Greenhalgh and Russell note, 'evidence' is not straightforwardly 'out there', just waiting to be discovered. Rather, knowledge in the policy world is fashioned (in all senses) through serendipity, lobbying, the contingent actions and conversations of a great many actors, all operating with their own rationalities and motives. In an ethnographic study of the use of evidence in UK policy making, Stevens (2011) describes how civil servants are faced with an oversaturation of evidence, very little of which provides direct answers to the policy question before them. Their sense of personal efficacy, and hope of career preferment, is advanced when the government of the day accepts their proposals as policy. A good deal of the civil servants' day is spent in discussion and argument with others within the State apparatus. Crafting persuasive stories is central. Stevens tells of the process whereby a document he had drafted, on an area of considerable academic uncertainty, was subject to many weeks of revision. All the caveats, and references to areas of unsettled knowledge, were gradually edited out. When the document was finally passed to another department, heated concerns were raised that it conflicted with a previously published document. In the final version, the headline estimate of a previously published report was used, obviating the need for supporting data. Any surviving caveats were relegated to an appendix.

> Uncertainty was seen … as the enemy of policy-making …
> My discussion of caveats … was characterised by our team
> leader … as 'verging in the philosophical'. He evidently saw
> them as an obstacle to the practical issue of what action to
> take, right here, right now. (Stevens, 2011: 243)

More specifically, the use of neuroscience in policy has been explored by Broer and Pickersgill (2015), who interviewed policy makers in Scotland. They show how opinion formers use science to give 'epistemic authority' to policies which they feel are politically and morally right:

> Well you know, if you tell a society that the way in which
> they nurture children changes the way their brains develop,
> and you show them pictures that corroborate that, it's
> pretty compelling. No one wants to damage a child's
> brain, or to deny a child the opportunity to develop their
> brain properly. It's emotive, and it's powerful. (Broer and
> Pickersgill, 2015: 55)

While some of their respondents were cautious about applications of neuroscience, others engaged self-consciously in 'pragmatic reductionism' (p 59) to render the science into simplified form, 'packaged' to persuade. One of their respondents explains:

> "What we do is condense all the findings and say these are
> the kind of key findings, right. What we then don't do, is
> go, but this person thinks it's ridiculous because it doesn't
> show x, y or z … this has only been done with middle class

parents or these people think it's not valid because it wasn't done with a controlled group etc. … because otherwise we would just confuse people." (p 61)

Translations have had to take place to render the science lucid and apodictic. Facts have been written and assembled on the social stage. Thus, the version of science pervading the policy domain is very much the handbook account. In Fleck's terms, this is the world of the vade mecum. There is evidence that many scientists are rather unhappy about the hype that attends the circulation of their work in these arenas, and somewhat disparaging about colleagues who court the headlines (Pickersgill, 2016), but temperate and equivocal voices, it seems, are not the loudest.

Bringing home the brains

The aspirations of the current UK policy settlement would seem to be summed up by the catchphrase: 'Build a better Briton, for a better Britain'. The maxim comes from the 2015 report of the UK's All Party Parliamentary Group for Conception to Age 2: the First 1001 Days, which was entitled *Building Great Britons*. Its core message, infused with moral panic, could have been penned at any point in the last hundred years or so:

> Society prospers, and is an enriching environment in which to live, according to the nature of its citizens. The more citizens are physically and mentally healthy, well educated, empathic, prosocial, hard-working and contributing to the costs of society, the better society will flourish. As there is a rise in the proportion of citizens who are damaged, physically or mentally ill, poor at relationships, antisocial, violent or criminal in their behaviour, and placing a drain on society's resources, so the quality of society worsens. In the UK today there are too many citizens in the latter category. (pp 13–14)

So what should be done about these lamentable, feckless folk? The report goes on: 'We do not blame – they are to a large extent the product of their childhoods as, in turn, were their parents and grandparents'. Starkly, the report continues: 'We do propose that decisive action be taken to ensure the proportion of good citizens rises sharply in the future'. The infant brain makes an early appearance in the report, with an emphasis on (sociogenic) 'damage' and irreversibility:

> Just as a positive environment can support optimal development for babies, so too can a negative environment disrupt development, with potentially lifelong damaging effects on the developing brain which can predispose to mental health problems, risk-taking behaviour, depression, anxiety and even violence throughout the lifespan. (p 8)

This is only one example in a gamut of policy aimed at early intervention and the amelioration of social disadvantage and its damaging sequelae.

The invocation of brain science in the contemporary UK policy context can be traced to the United States, and the so-called 'decade of the brain' launched by George Bush in 1990; its aim was to enhance citizens' knowledge of the benefits to be derived from brain research.

> I, George Bush, President of the United States of America, do hereby proclaim the decade beginning January 1, 1990, as the Decade of the Brain. I call upon all public officials and the people of the United States to observe that decade with appropriate programs, ceremonies, and activities.[1]

A broad range of interventions, largely clinically oriented, across the life course emerged, such as the aspiration to use neuroscientific evidence to inform new treatments for Alzheimer's disease. There was also a particular focus on the impact of the uterine environment and parenting on infant development, with the hope of intervening early and thereby preventing later costs to the individual and society. The reduction of misery, in itself, is an uncontroversial aspiration; no one can be against it! We shall see in chapter six how it has spawned an entire new interdisciplinary field, that of prevention science, the many facets of which we discuss later. An example of the influence of neuroscience, shifting the gaze from the social world into the intracranial spaces, is provided by projects such as the Prevention Action project, entitled 'Putting Brain Science Back on Streets of Los Angeles'[2] (cited in Rose, 2010: 193).

Rose (2010) traces the arrival of brain science on this side of the pond to an agenda passionately promoted by Iain Duncan Smith, a former leader of the Conservative Party, and his ally across the House, Labour MP Graham Allen. They teamed up in 2008 to produce a report entitled *Early intervention: Good parents, great kids, better citizens* (Allen and Duncan Smith, 2009). The general line of argumentation was developed in two subsequent reports (Allen, 2011a, 2011b, discussed in detail below). Brains feature prominently in the first of these reports: 'The structure of the developing infant brain is a crucial factor in the creation (or not) of violent tendencies' (Allen and Duncan Smith, 2009: 57). Thus, criminality is depicted as hard-wired in the brain. With celerity, this leads to the conclusion that pre-emptive intervention is a self-evident moral imperative for any right-minded person in a civilised society. Vigorous supportive campaigning from child welfare activists ensued, with one high-profile charity, Kids Company (since discredited by financial scandal), launching a campaign to raise money for brain imaging research to look into the 'damaged' brains of the 'damaged' children with whom the charity worked (Rose, 2010). As Rose notes, and as we have argued, these propositions are fundamentally the same as those articulated by reformers from the late 19th century onwards.

In 2010, another Labour MP, Frank Field, pitched up. Again, the lofty aspiration was to end poverty and disadvantage, with the infant brain as a primary change agent. The allusion to stunted brains in the text below relates to the work of Bruce Perry, to which we shall return in due course for it is a ubiquitous point of reference in the 'handbook science' of policy:

> The development of a baby's brain is affected by the attachment to their parents and analysis of neglected children's brains has shown that their brain growth is significantly reduced. Where babies are often left to cry, their cortisol levels are increased and this can lead to a permanent increase in stress hormones later in life, which can impact on mental health. Supporting parents during this difficult transition period is crucial to improving outcomes for young children. (Field, 2010: 43)

This campaigning ultimately resulted in the establishment of the Early Intervention Foundation in 2013, a recommendation of the two 'Allen Reports' mentioned earlier. It is to these reports that we now turn for critical analysis, interrogating in particular the translation work that has been necessary in 'settling' the current vocabulary and thought style of the neuro-reformers.

Graham Allen: settling neurosocial policy

> ... babies are born with 25 per cent of their brains developed,
> and there is then a rapid period of development so that by
> the age of 3 their brains are 80 per cent developed. In that
> period, neglect, the wrong type of parenting and other
> adverse experiences can have a profound effect on how
> children are emotionally 'wired'. (Allen, 2011a: xiii)

In Allen's interim report (2011a), published in January 2011, the brain
is mentioned nearly 60 times, and the front cover carries dramatic
images, which have become ubiquitous in child welfare texts, of an
infant brain damaged by neglect (figure 3). Allen's second report,
published in the summer of 2011, retains the brain image on the
cover, now joined by symbolic bars of gold to mark the economic
sense behind 'early intervention'; one gold bar magically becomes nine
in terms of 'costs to the taxpayer', emphasising the dramatic returns
from investment in the early years (Allen, 2011b). Saliently, the brain
is not mentioned in the second report; the case having been made, it
is now simply a question of taking action and implementing policy
measures. The document goes on to argue for various preferred ways
through which Allen believes the social ills of disadvantaged families
may be remedied. Advocated are a range of 'evidence based', time
limited, targeted interventions into 'parenting', delivered on the basis
of 'payment by results'; these are also the instruments commended by
Field in his report of 2010.

The imagery on the front cover of the reports is stirring stuff. Could
a more powerful case be imagined for early intervention than the
dramatic comparison of these two brains? However, all is not quite
as it seems. We shall inspect the narrative of the report, beginning
in chapter 1, where the neuroscientific case for early intervention
starts to take shape. Quoting from paragraph 17 (p 6), the crux of the
argument runs as follows:

> The early years are *far and away* the greatest period of
> growth in the human brain. It has been estimated that the
> connections or synapses in a baby's brain grow 20-fold, from
> having perhaps 10 trillion at birth to 200 trillion at age 3.
> For a baby, this is an explosive process of learning from the
> environment. The early years are a very sensitive period
> when it is much easier to help the developing social and
> emotional structure of the infant brain, and after which *the*

basic architecture is formed for life. However, it is not impossible for the brain to develop later, but it becomes significantly harder, particularly in terms of emotional capabilities, which *are largely set in the first 18 months of life.* (emphasis added)

Figure 3: The front cover of the Allen Report, January 2011

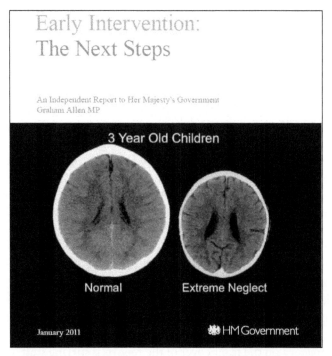

Here Allen draws on what Bruer (1999) has called the 'myth of the first three years'. The idea that the first three years determine the rest of the child's life provides the 'core story of development' forming the basis for much of the moral case for early intervention. Having noted the 'now or never' urgency it lends to the cause, we move on to appraise in critical depth the specific evidence as assembled by Allen.

The myth of the first three years

[Propaganda works by] giving modern man all-embracing, simple explanations without which he could not live. Man is doubly reassured by propaganda: first, because it tells him all the reasons behind the developments which unfold, and second because it provides a solution for all the problems which arise, which otherwise would seem insoluble. (Ellul, 1965: 147)

Myth, as we have argued, ingeniously moves from 'ought' to 'is', stealthily performing its cultural work of naturalising the status quo (Wastell, 2007). In the words of Fitzpatrick (1992): 'Myth thus ventures forth to create the real, to endow it with forms and norms … a sustained creative force extending itself to and ordering a temporal world' (pp 42–3). We have already discussed how potent the idea of a 'normal human' has been in ratifying policy shifts from 'is' to 'ought'. Indeed, we would go further: the idea of precarious normality fundamentally redefines what 'is'. The swing from 'treatment' to 'prevention' means we must infer the latent presence of madness and badness within the brain, and move swiftly to restore normality.

In the 'decade of the brain', to which we referred above, the idea that the first three years of a child's life are critical took a strong hold in the US. Much of the emergent social policy was evangelically driven, with campaign groups in the vanguard (Rose, 2010), but key policy documents, such as 'Neurons to Neighbourhoods' (Shonkoff and Phillips, 2000) display a degree of nuance and scientific sophistication somewhat missing from their subsequent UK equivalents. In a well-researched critique, Bruer traces these developments, examining how they were propelled by policy research, and shaped by the early intervention campaign groups, such as the Ounce of Prevention Fund. In the field of education policy, developments included initiatives such as *Early Head Start* (the precursor of the UK's Sure Start programme) which extended the scope of the extant Head Start scheme to cover the years 0 to 3. Bruer charts a slew of these and other federal and state level 'early intervention' programmes in education, welfare and healthcare, highlighting their neurodevelopmental foundations: 'The findings of the new brain science have become accepted facts, no longer in need of explanation or justification, to support childcare initiatives' (Bruer, 1999: 61).

Three neuroscience strands run through the policy discourse and the surrounding public debate. First, that the early years represent a period of 'biological exuberance' in the development of brain connectivity, characterised by an explosive growth in the number of synapses. Second, that this constitutes a once-and-for-all 'critical period' for brain development. Third, that enriched, more stimulating environments will augment brain development, boosting brain power. Woven together, these strands created a potent neurobiological meme: 'The first three years provide policymakers, caregivers and parents a unique, biologically delimited window of opportunity, during which the right experiences and early childhood programs can help children build better brains' (Bruer, 1999: 12).

The discourse of the campaign groups took a predictable line. For example, Rob Reiner, leader of the 'I am your child' campaign, is quoted by Bruer as proclaiming, at an influential White House Seminar in 1996, that: 'if we want to have a real significant impact, not only on children's success in school and later on in life ... We are going to have to address the first three years of life. *All roads lead to Rome'* (Bruer, 1999: 8). And later, a rather more chilling proclamation by Bruce Perry, the source of the imagery of damaged brains: 'We need to change the malignant and destructive view that children are the property of their biological parent ... Children belong to the community, they are entrusted to parents' (Perry, 1997: 146). This is truly utopian, indeed Platonic, in its belief in the State as child rearer.

Bruer argues that the hold of the myth is powerful because it promises to solve so many social problems:

> A myth grows and attracts adherents when it appears to provide emotionally evocative insights into a complex human problem. This why many people – the childcare and early education research community, scientists, policy advocates, and parents – want to believe the Myth of the first three years. (Bruer, 1999 64)

But the myth nevertheless *is* a myth, based on simplified and misinterpreted science, which Bruer witheringly deconstructs. We recapitulate here the essence of his critique.

First, the synaptic strand. What does the scientific record actually say? Certainly, the picture is not a simple one. Counting synapses is a technically tricky and very expensive business, involving the laborious analysis of tissue specimens from the brains of dead animals. Sectional samples are extracted, embedded in wax, sliced, stained, and magnified many thousand times. Synapses themselves are hard to descry to the untrained eye: the images are indistinct and blurry. It is not surprising that there are very few such studies, and these involve mainly cats and monkeys, looking at limited parts of the brain: the visual cortex in earlier work, but the frontal cortex in more recent studies. The seminal work of Huttenlocher (1979) provides the main source of evidence for humans. In two decades of research on autopsy material, the synapses in three regions of 50 brains were meticulously counted; 24 of these brains were from children under age 3, but only 4 cases were in the range 4 to 11 years. This in itself shows the extreme limitations of the evidence base. And what does all this 'neural accounting' reveal? For monkeys and humans, initial 'synaptic exuberance' in the early years is only part of the story. There is a second stage in which the number of synapses reaches a plateau, and then a third stage of synaptic pruning in which densities decline to adult levels. The time course varies by brain area. For humans, peak density in the auditory cortex occurs around 3 months, but for the frontal cortex the peak is at 3.5 years. Synapse elimination on the other hand is complete for the auditory cortex by age 12, but continues until mid-adolescence for the frontal area.

Given the nature and paucity of the evidence base, the idea that there is a proven connection between 'brain power' and synaptic profusion is self-evidently wrong. Einstein's brain itself shows this, the real one that is, not its mythical version. One does not need to read the original articles to know that no attempt was made to measure the intellect of the 24 dead children or the parenting skills of their mothers, and to relate this to their synaptic tallies. Huttenlocher does report one case of a 'mentally defective' child, but this child apparently had abnormally high synaptic density (Huttenlocher, 1979: 85)![3] Whatever else, it is clear that more synapses do not mean greater intellectual prowess in any simple way, except in the realm of myth. The evidence, if anything, points to a clear dissociation between the two phenomena: whereas synapse density follows an inverted U curve, learning and intellectual development do not, instead following a steadily rising curve which then flattens out. Indeed, just at the point in adolescence when humans begin to learn and master more and more complex bodies of knowledge, their synapses are undergoing mass elimination.

Having disposed of the first strand of the myth, it should be no surprise that the other elements do not stand much 'stress testing' either. First, the idea that there are 'critical periods'. Here the iconic neuroscience is that of the Nobel Prize winners, Hubel and Wiesel, on the visual cortex of cats, which showed that kittens deprived of visual input in one eye remained permanently blind in that eye.

> The blind kittens generate a powerful mental image –
> blind little kittens pathetically groping for a ball of yarn …
> conjuring up [parents'] worst fears about severely disabled,
> developmentally impaired children … The new brain
> science does 'ratchet up the guilt'. (Bruer, 1999: 102–3)

But again, the story is not so simple, as Bruer goes on to elaborate. In simple terms, what seems to be happening in the cats' brains is not so much the loss of neural capability for the blinded eye, but rather the annexing of this capacity by the functioning eye. When both eyes are closed at birth, experiments on monkeys have shown limited permanent damage caused by deprivation: 'Hubel, Wiesel and LeVay did those experiments. And much to their surprise the monkeys that had both of their eyes closed for the first six months had normal vision at maturity' (Bruer, 1999: 119). So, what the neuroscience actually shows is not some fixed and vulnerable architecture; quite the opposite, the brain is actually seen to be highly plastic and adaptable. A recent review article, for instance, opens as follows: 'Neural plasticity is conceived as the ability of the brain to reorganize neural pathways that are based on new experiences *encountered throughout the course of life span development*' (Cicchetti, 2015: 319, emphasis added). A recent study by Zhou et al (2011), for instance, shows that rats, deprived of acoustic stimulation during rearing, show a full restoration of cortical function and structure when exposed to noise during adulthood. In the face of such counter-evidence, critical periods have been recast as *sensitive periods* to reflect the fact that they are not so critical after all: 'sensitive periods are conceived to be periods when experience exerts a strong effect on the brain and behavior ... that are adaptive for the individual' (Cicchetti, 2015: 319). Moreover, as research burgeons, what seems to grow is not certainty but uncertainty:

> Presently it is not known whether the difficulties displayed by individuals who have experienced significant adversity are irreversible or whether there are particular sensitive periods when it is more likely that neural and behavioral plasticity will occur. Moreover, it is not known whether some neural or behavioral systems may be more plastic than other neural or behavioral systems. (Cicchetti, 2015: 319)

Bruer goes on at length to demonstrate the plasticity of the brain, drawing on the educational literature, on language learning in particular. Critical periods are the exception, not the rule. Although there is evidence that mastering grammar is age dependent, even here the decline with age is only a gradual decline, not a 'window slamming shut' (Bruer, 1999: 133). To the extent that there is a critical period, this reaches well into puberty. For vocabulary there is no evidence for any critical period. Nor for other cognitive skills: literacy can be taught effectively at any stage in life, for instance. The capacity of the human for lifelong learning is so self-evidently the case, one may rhetorically ask why the idea of critical periods, and the 'now or never' imperative, have taken such a tenacious hold on the imagination. Perhaps this says more about the moral convictions of those who espouse such dogma than empirical reality.

Attachment theory is often recruited in connection with critical periods. Bruer notes correctly that there is no link between these literatures, and that brain science and research on attachment coexist largely independently, though they are now beginning to converge, as we shall see in due course. The evidence, at the time of Bruer's book, failed to demonstrate any causal connection between secure attachment and specific parental behaviours, or that attachment patterns, once formed, are stable and set forever. Reliable predictions can be made only in situations where child-rearing conditions have remained the same: 'When parenting, childcare or family conditions change ... early experiences do not predict later behaviour. What matters is early experience plus whatever happens afterwards' (Bruer, 1999: 58). Quoting from a major review at the time: 'sometimes early attachment relationships remain consistent over time and sometimes they change. This variability makes it impossible to identify a normative level of consistency in the security of attachment' (Thompson, 2000: 146).

We note that this nuanced position is the one held by many attachment researchers today. For instance, a recent study by Levendosky et al (2011) compared attachment patterns at ages 1 and 4, and the impact of domestic violence (DV) and income on such trajectories. The study concluded:

> Overall, attachment was unstable for 56% of the sample ... Trajectories of DV and income both predicted attachment patterns. Positive outcomes (secure-secure and insecure-secure) were related to initially low levels of DV that stayed constant or became lower as well as initially high or low levels of income that increased over time. (Levendosky et al, 2011: 408)

The third, neurobiological filament of the myth is succinctly encapsulated in the following quote from 'Starting Smart: how early experiences affect brain development', another key pamphlet of the 'decade of the brain' cited by Bruer: 'Early experiences can have a dramatic effect on this brain wiring process, causing the final number of synapses in the brain to increase or decrease by as much as 25 percent' (Bruer, p 144).

Again Bruer begins his deconstruction with the canonical work supporting this assertion. Research on sensory deprivation in animals (for example, Harlow's monkeys) could be seen as indicating the importance of early experience, and the detrimental effect of its lack, but as Bruer points out, the conditions endured by laboratory animals in deprivation experiments are extreme. He likens such conditions to the destruction of normal development with a sledgehammer. Bruer dwells at length on the seminal work of Greenough and colleagues, beginning in the 1970s, on the impact of environmental conditions on rat brain development. These experiments studied the effect of three types of environment: the rat in a small cage by itself (isolated), in a larger cage with several others (social), and in a larger enclosure with obstacles, toys and so on (complex). Examining the brains of rats raised for 30 days post-weaning in these environments, the researchers found roughly 20 to 25% more synapses per neurone in the visual cortex of the 'complex rats', than in either of the other groups, and that these rats also ran mazes faster, and so on.

Examining the results in depth again reveals a more complex picture. For instance, while there were more synapses for the 'complex rats', the difference was much less for nonsensory areas of the brain, the frontal lobes in particular, which, as we have seen, are associated with the higher cognitive functions. Second, the weanlings were 50 days old after their period of deprivation, that is, sexually mature, into advanced childhood in human terms. Third, the conditions experienced by the rats are extreme; compared to their life in the wild, even the most stimulating condition is hardly natural. For Bruer, equating Palo Alto with 'complex' and the South Bronx with 'isolated' is nothing less than absurd. Fourth, as we have seen, inferring anything positive or negative from synaptic density is tendentious at best. Fifth, generalising from rodents to humans itself is a rather large step. We also note that further experiments showed increases in dendritic density as a result of 'enriched experience' at any age: adult rats raised in 'deprived' conditions, and then placed in a complex environment at 120 days, had the comparable synaptic density to the weanlings of the earlier studies. The window is far from slammed shut.

Assembling evidence on the social stage: the mystery of curious choices

Despite its importance and relevance, the reader will probably not be surprised to learn that the Allen Reports pay no attention to Bruer's thorough and respected critique; indeed, it is not mentioned at all! This neglect exemplifies the policy-making behaviours we discussed at the start of this chapter: the imperative is to persuade, not to present faithfully the state of the scientific field. The report is a particularly striking example of the rhetorical use of journal science; it does not, as we shall see, really matter what the research papers say, so long as the brain is drafted in to give the veneer of scientific objectivity. Chapter 2 (p 12), entitled 'Using our brains', is devoted to the detailed elaboration of the neuroscientific evidence. Its epigraph is noteworthy: 'A lack of appropriate experiences can lead to alterations in genetic plans. Moreover, although the brain retains the capacity to adapt and change throughout life, this capacity decreases with age[3].'

The superscript '3' at the close of the quote is noteworthy. The use of such numbered citations is an interesting device. They implicitly construct the report as academic and evidence based. But when the endnote referred to is consulted, and we wonder how many readers actually looked it up, a rather telling picture emerges of the report's real relationship with the original science. The endnote invokes three journal articles; the titles of these are as follows: 'Adaptive auditory plasticity in developing and adult animals'; 'Cortical plasticity: from synapses to maps'; 'Experience-dependent plasticity in the adult visual cortex'. Given the burgeoning bulk of neuroscience research stretching over several decades, with much of it bearing directly on Allen's claim, this is a puzzling selection. Why these three papers with so many from which to choose? Even the titles suggest an uneasy fit with the report's thesis, all mentioning 'plasticity', and two in the context of the adult brain. In fact, the titles accurately reflect what the three papers actually depict: a plastic, adaptable nervous system, not a brain 'formed for life'. This is what the neuroscience, when looked at dispassionately, tends to show, as we have seen.

Into the neuroscience warp is soon woven the weft of attachment theory. The importance of secure attachment is invoked (p 13):

> Children develop in an environment of relationships that usually begin within their family. From early infancy, they naturally reach out to create bonds, and they develop best when caring adults respond in warm, stimulating and consistent ways. This secure attachment with those close to them leads to the development of empathy, trust and well-being.

Predictive claims are quickly made regarding long-term effects of such early attachment patterns, especially the beneficial effects of secure attachment and the detrimental impact of the failure to cement such bonds (p 15).

Recent research also shows insecure attachment is linked to a higher risk for a number of health conditions, including strokes, heart attacks and high blood pressure, and suffering pain, for example from headaches and arthritis.

Huntsinger and Luecken showed that people with secure attachment show more healthy behaviours such as taking exercise, not smoking, not using substances and alcohol, and driving at ordinary speed.

The impression is again created of lasting damage and disadvantage caused by early deficits. It is instructive to examine how certainty and uncertainty are *linguistically* marked here. The use of 'shows' and 'showed' leaves one in no doubt about the factual, indisputable nature of the claims. Certainty does not exist out there waiting to be discovered; it is brought into being through the strategic use of language to create such a sense of 'evidentiality' (Chafe, 1986).

Once more it is important to read the journal science. Two studies are cited (McWilliams and Bailey, 2010; Huntsinger and Luecken, 2004) as the basis for the claims in the quotes. However, these are not studies of children, but of adults; in the first case, a sample of the US adult population, and in the second of 793 psychology students at Arizona State University (age range 18–35). Both studies use 'attachment style' as a way of conceptualising the adult personality; they do not directly address how children were actually parented. They both employ self-report questionnaires to assign respondents to one of several personality categories, one of which is indeed entitled 'secure attachment'. Inspecting the second study in a little more detail, the various elements mentioned (exercise, smoking and so on) refer to answers to another questionnaire measuring health behaviours. The study does not discuss the lasting damage of insecure attachment in infants, the study simply shows that students with 'secure style of interaction with loved ones' also report themselves as engaging in generally 'healthier health behavior' (Huntsinger and Luecken, 2004: 523). Aside from numerous methodological weaknesses (low response rate, the limitations of self-report measures, the unrepresentative nature of the sampled group), it is quite clear that this study neither shows, nor purports to show, any link with early childhood experiences.

In subsequent paragraphs, damaged emotionality and damaged brains are united; the finger wags, it is deficient parenting, more specifically the spectre of the inadequate mother, that is to blame:

Parents who are neglectful or who are drunk, drugged or violent, will have impaired capacity to provide this social and emotional stability, and will create the likelihood that adverse experiences might have a negative impact on their children's development as they mature. Although poor parenting practices can cause damage to children of all ages, the worst and deepest damage is done to children when their brains are being formed during their earliest months and years. The most serious damage takes place before birth and during the first 18 months of life. (Allen, 2011a: 15)

The only evidence brought forward by Allen for these broad and portentous claims is the prenatal use of alcohol: 'fetal alcohol spectrum disorder' is invoked, denounced as 'the leading known cause of intellectual disability in the Western world'. But that's it, morbidly extreme drinking is the culprit: no one would doubt this is injurious (not only to the child), but no other evidence is adduced. The implicit logic here is noteworthy. It amounts to 'extrapolation' from a clinical extreme to the normal range, a generalisation designed to serve a moral cause. This is a fallacious form of logic, relying on highly contestable assumptions, that we shall meet again in the ensuing pages.

Now let us look into the provenance of the images on the Allen Report's front cover (figure 3). The report attributes them to the Child Trauma Academy (www.childtrauma.org), a campaigning 'child advocacy' organisation run by the aforementioned Bruce Perry. A reference is given to an article by Perry (2002) published in *Brain and Mind, a Transdisciplinary Journal of Neuroscience and Neurophilosophy*. This slightly cranky subtitle implies that this is not a front-ranking scientific journal. The critical section of the paper (Perry, 2002: 92) is less than a page long, with but the sketchiest of methodological and clinical detail. Only one or two general statements are made regarding the garnering of the evidence, such as 'History was obtained from multiple sources (investigating CPS workers, family, and police)'. Two main groups of cases are compared in the reported research, children suffering from 'global neglect', defined as a history of sensory deprivation in more than one domain (for example, minimal exposure to language, touch and social interactions), and those suffering 'chaotic neglect' which we presume to reflect the more normal circumstances of families in adversity.

Measuring head size as a proxy for brain size, Perry's main result is that the head sizes of the globally neglected children were extremely abnormal, all below the 5th percentile, whereas those suffering from chaotic neglect were within the normal range.

> Furthermore in cases where MRI or CT scans were available, neuroradiologists interpreted 11 of 17 scans as abnormal from the children with global neglect (64.7%) and only 3 of 26 scans as abnormal from the children with chaotic neglect (11.5%). The majority of the readings were 'enlarged ventricles' or 'cortical atrophy'.

The cover image of Allen's report derives from Perry's paper. No details are provided of the two brains. Without details of the case history for the shrunken brain, such an image is impossible to interpret; perhaps the child was the subject of massive birth trauma, or some congenital condition. We simply do not know, and nowhere are we told. The picture somehow suggests that the neglected brain would have been more like the normal one if there had been no neglect, but why is this comparison valid? These are just two arbitrarily selected images, chosen to make an argument. The perceptive reader will also note that the category of 'chaotic neglect' is likely to have much in common with the sort of routine circumstances of concern to child welfare professionals. It would seem that the brains of such children are typically indistinguishable from normal.

Despite such obvious flaws, a book focused on translating neuroscience for social workers, entitled *Neuroscience and social work practice* (Farmer, 2009), shows just how convincing these images can be, particularly for those who already believe. Figure 5.2 in Farmer contains this same picture, and two others reproduced from Perry's website. There is no critical comment: the figure legend merely contains the phrase 'severe sensory deprivation in early childhood'. Each brain image is paired with a *different* 'normal brain', although the basis for the pairing is again not explained. The three normal brains are themselves all rather different; one, indeed, is more or less the same size as one of the neglected brains. We are also not told why these normal children have been subjected to a scan. There are numerous other instances of the Perry images, and the paper from which they derive, being recruited by the child welfare campaigners. We remarked in the introduction to this chapter that Perry's work is the only citation in Frank Field's report to support his (sociogenic) 'brain damage' argument. The images also make their appearance in a document designed to inform professional decision making by the family judiciary in cases involving children at risk, which we discuss in some length in the next chapter.

These are not the only brain images to have been used in this way. Bruer (1999) mentions another pair of PET scans which appeared in a special issue of *Newsweek* in 1997. Again, the normal brain is juxtaposed with a 'neglected one'. The images created a predictable stir, and were picked up by campaigning organisations who used them prominently in their literature. Bruer tracked down the scans to Dr Chugani at Wayne State University. It transpired that the neglected brains were those of Romanian orphans. Apparently, Chugani presented his PET images at a scientific meeting in 1999.

> He told the meeting that subsequent statistical analysis of his data revealed no significant differences between the brains of the neglected children and the brains of his 'normal' comparison group. He had no plans to write up the data for publication in a scientific journal. It is a non-result. (Bruer, 1999: 204)

Returning to the Allen Report, the following quotes succinctly exemplify more of the author's neuroscientific worldview and its depiction of the vicissitudes of the precarious infant brain. We also witness the same approach to evidence to which we have become wearily accustomed:

> Different parts of the brain ... develop in different sensitive windows of time. The estimated prime window for emotional development is up to 18 months, by which time the foundation of this has been shaped by the way in which the prime carer interacts with the child ... Infants of severely depressed mothers show reduced left lobe activity (associated with being happy, joyful and interested) and increased right lobe activity (associated with negative feelings). These emotional deficits are harder to overcome once the sensitive window has passed. (Allen, 2011a: 16)

> If the predominant early experience is fear and stress, the neurochemical responses to those experiences become the primary architects of the brain. Trauma elevates stress hormones, such as cortisol. One result is significantly fewer synapses (or connections). Specialists viewing CAT scans of the key emotional areas in the brains of abused or neglected

children have likened the experience to looking at a black hole. In extreme cases the brains of abused children are significantly smaller than the norm, and the limbic system (which governs the emotions) may be 20–30 per cent smaller and contain fewer synapses. (p 16)

Let us dig into the (frontal) lobe evidence invoked in the first paragraph. The work cited is a paper by Dawson et al (1994), which reviews psychophysiological studies (using scalp-recorded brain activity, the EEG, which we covered in chapter two) of emotional disturbances in the children of depressed mothers. Dawson's experimental evidence actually goes in the opposite direction to that claimed in the Allen Report. Referring to a study on the reactions of children when mothers left the room, an intervention 'designed to elicit distress', the EEG response is described as follows: 'The infants of symptomatic mothers exhibited an unexpected pattern of greater left than right activation during the maternal separation condition' (Dawson et al, 1994: 772). More 'positive' emotion, it would seem.

Conclusion

In this chapter, we have described the assembly of evidence for policy purposes using exemplars primarily from UK policy. We have shown how two pervasive traductions of the journal science characterise the modus operandi of the Allen Report in particular. First, the instability and uncertainty of the knowledge base are not disclosed. The 'evidential coding' in the report's language leads the reader to believe the opposite, that all is now known with perfect certainty. Second, from the vast neuroscientific literature, papers are repeatedly selected that Allen claims support his policy position, even though they typically do not. The insights from the studies of the policy-making process, referred to at the start of the chapter, perhaps make these choices less perplexing. Finding evidence for policy can be something of a fishing expedition. Persuasiveness, not accuracy, is the primary criterion at work. The evidence has been interpreted as consistent with a particular form of received wisdom, and hence little argumentation is required to make it work rhetorically.

In sum, the Allen Report would not appear to be a particularly distinguished exemplar of the public use of science. Rather, science has been selectively used to grant epistemic authority to the cause of early intervention. 'Pragmatic reductionism' has taken place to make this message powerful (Broer and Pickersgill, 2015), supported by a strong belief that the moral message was bigger than the science. We have shown that contemporary settlements about parenting, and its role in the prevention of social ills, have a long history; the eager enrolment of 'biotechnoscience' by contemporary votaries has made the current foray of old moralities into policy somewhat charmed. Graham Allen's review has selected and interpreted a range of papers from the realm of journal science to support an argument for resources to intervene early in the lives of disadvantaged children. In the contemporary climate of retrenched services and resources, the report has been remarkably successful in promoting this agenda.

We will return to realm of 'prevention by early intervention' in chapter six, for it is not altogether an uncontroversial good. Nevertheless the 'pragmatic reductionism' of policy makers has worked. Across a range of policy, social disadvantage is recast as a biological effect, curable by professional interventions at the level of individuals. Such narratives are equally potent when they shift from campaigns to secure resources for disadvantaged groups to the aspiration to guide professional judgement in individual cases. As we shall see in the next chapter, there is seemingly no stopping the therapeutic State.

Notes

[1] Proclamation 6158 of 17 July 1990.

[2] http://preventionaction.org/node/320

[3] Brains of patients with the genetic condition known as Fragile X syndrome, who often have intellectual disabilities, are also characterised by high synaptic densities.

FIVE

The cat is out of the bag: from early intervention to child protection

In the last chapter, we argued that there is a consensus across the left and right of the political spectrum that 'early intervention' is imperative to safeguard children's health and development. In this context, the neuroscientific arguments, however transformed and traduced, may be seen as part of a progressive, ethical project to make the world a better place. The very same arguments, however, can be marshalled in support of the more coercive activities of the State (Featherstone et al, 2014b). For instance, alongside the attention to primary prevention, the UK has a policy allowing the permanent removal and placement for adoption of children without parental consent, pejoratively dubbed by its critics 'forced adoption'. Early intervention and nonconsensual adoption may seem polar ends of a spectrum of State intervention in family life, but they are often closely related in terms of their legitimating narratives.

UK Prime Minister David Cameron, on 11 January 2016 in a speech on 'life chances', exemplifies the prevailing policy thought style:

> Thanks to the advent of functional MRI scanners, neuroscientists and biologists say they have learnt more about how the brain works in the last 10 years than in the rest of human history. And one critical finding is that the vast majority of the synapses ... develop in the first 2 years. Destinies can be altered for good or ill in this window of opportunity ... we know the severe developmental damage that can be done ... when babies are emotionally neglected, abused or if they witness domestic violence. As Dr Jack Shonkoff's research at Harvard University has shown, children who suffer what he calls 'toxic stress' in those early years are potentially set up for a life of struggle, risky behaviour, poor social outcomes, all driven by abnormally high levels of the stress hormone, cortisol.

And: 'We also know — it's common sense — how a safe, stimulating, loving family environment can make such a positive difference. ... So mums and dads literally build babies' brains. We serve, they respond.'[1]

The tennis trope is an interesting one: we note in passing that it owes its provenance to the proselytising work of Shonkoff alluded to in the first extract. We will be encountering Shonkoff's Harvard Center [on the Developing Child] and the influence of its core story of development in due course, but for now we note the shift in register from improving life chances to the language of abuse.

In 2015, UK adoption policy received criticism from the Council of Europe. The UK is not unique in allowing nonconsensual adoptions. These are also possible in other European jurisdictions; for comparative purposes, in Germany in 2010, 250 children were placed for adoption without consent, whereas in the UK in 2013, the equivalent figure was 3,020 children (Fenton Glynn, 2015: 9). The UK has been specifically criticised by the Council for its removal of children from women who have been subject to domestic abuse, or who are suffering from depression; in short, those mothers who may be potential beneficiaries of 'early intervention' strategies. These trends continued to accelerate, as Fenton Glynn (2015) notes:

> In the year ending 31 March 2014, 5,050 children were adopted from public care, an increase of 26% from 2013, and of 58% from 2010. Adoptions are now at their highest point since the start of complete collection of data. (p 20)

There has been a particularly steep rise in removals of infants at birth (Broadhurst et al, 2015a). The President of the Family Division of the UK civil courts, Judge James Munby, notes the recent shift in the profile of children placed for adoption: 'the typical adoption today is of a child who has been made the subject of a care order … and where parental consent has been dispensed with'.[2] Moreover, the Children and Families Act 2014 limits the duration of care proceedings (proceedings to remove a child deemed to be at risk from their family) in England and Wales to 26 weeks in all but 'exceptional cases'. Achieving this in congested family courts, blighted by long delays due to multiple expert witnesses, was bound to be complex and contentious, with concerns for family rights (particularly in a climate of reduced funding for legal aid) vying with discourses of child-centredness (both articulated in the name of social justice) over the imposition of tight time scales. January 2016 saw the announcement of further reforms to adoption law to achieve an increase in numbers. It is not clear what might be the optimum number, but it is most definitely 'more than now'.

The action plan for the implementation of the family justice reforms was the establishment of a 'knowledge hub', and the production of a set of knowledge reviews to guide judicial decision making. One such review was entitled *Decision-making within a child's timeframe: an overview of current research evidence for family justice professionals concerning child development and the impact of maltreatment* (hereafter abbreviated to *A child's timeframe*) by Rebecca Brown and Harriet Ward of the University of Loughborough. The review made extensive use of neuroscientific claims and furnishes the main exhibit of this chapter. The report was commissioned by the Department for Education and the Family Justice Council. It explicitly stated its purpose as ensuring 'consistent training ... for family justice professionals'. It contains a number of strands, and neuroscience figures strongly in its core argument: namely, that 'time frames for intervening ... are out of kilter with those of the child' (Brown and Ward, 2013: 8).

A family lawyer, Eddie Lloyd Jones, noted in the journal *Family Law*, shortly after the publication of *A child's timeframe*:

> An email circulated by a designated family judge ... left no one in any doubt as to the status of this document. All needed to be familiar with its contents upon which courts were likely to place 'considerable reliance'. The report ... is used in judicial training and one participant has already observed that it is treated as 'completely authoritative'. (Lloyd Jones, 2013: 1053)

At this point, we take an autobiographical turn, as we were involved in a debate with the report's authors shortly after its publication. The somewhat testy nature of the exchange and the controversy that followed are worthy of examination in their own right, attesting to the fact that debates about parenting, childhood vulnerability and the State's role arouse the passions. Here we focus an analytic lens on the argumentation within the review, on our counter argument, and the case mobilised as a rejoinder that followed from the report's authors. Our summary of the debate provides evidence of the difficulties besetting the search for solid ground on which to base complex professional judgements about children deemed to be at risk, and illustrates the imprint of the neurobiological thought style.

Anatomy of a debate: autobiographical interlude

Early in 2013, the authors were contacted by a number of family lawyers who had received the compulsory training to which Lloyd Jones refers. We had recently published a paper analysing the neuroscientific claims in the Allen Reports (Wastell and White, 2012) and the lawyers were seeking an opinion on the status of the evidence in *A child's timeframe*. There was considerable disquiet about the implications for decision making in the family courts in child protection cases. This was in the context of concerns about rising numbers of care proceedings (see for example Cafcass, 2015) and a government agenda promoting nonconsensual adoption. There was a concern from some lawyers that the report would lead to the increased removal of infants on the *precautionary principle*, in order to prevent brain damage allegedly consequent upon neglect.

In response, we produced a critique of the neuroscientific strand of *A child's timeframe*; it was made available to the judiciary and was published online (White and Wastell, 2013) so that it could be read and cited by lawyers if they so wished. Since then, there has also been critical commentary on other aspects of *A child's timeframe*, on both methodological and ideological grounds (Bywaters, 2015). This underscores the fact that 'evidence' is being mobilised by all sides of this debate to support preferred moral positions on the relative merits of child-centred versus whole-family paradigms, and on the case for, and nature of, State intervention in family life. The evidence manifestly does not speak for itself: it must be spoken for and there are number of ways in which it can be rendered, with each party believing themselves to be on the side of rightness and goodness.

Our argumentative strategy was to draw on the voice of journal science, and set it against the handbook version of neuroscience which we contended had informed *A child's timeframe*, leading it to present the knowledge base as fixed and settled. *A child's timeframe* discusses a range of academic literature, some of it straightforward, uncontroversial and helpful apropos child maltreatment and the causes of delay in the courts. Brown and Ward stated that the evidence in the main body of their report was drawn 'from papers which reported on, or which provided a methodologically sound review of primary research' (p 9), complemented by recent government funded reports and material which can be 'easily accessed by family justice professionals'. The source of much of the 'primary research' was material produced by the Center for the Developing Child at Harvard University.

Our principal argument was that these decisions regarding inclusion and exclusion had had a profound effect on the integrity of the neuroscientific strand of the report. *A child's timeframe*, we contended, had relied heavily on synthesised secondary sources and non-peer-reviewed textbooks. The Harvard Center in particular is not a site of primary research, but specialises in such secondary syntheses. Thus we argued that the report provided an excessively simplified guide to a complex field of work, where knowledge was far from settled, and certainly not 'policy ready'. In fact, Brown and Ward did begin in just this place, citing thorough reviews of the emergent knowledge on the neuroscience of parenting by Belsky and De Haan (2011), and another by McCrory et al (2012). Slightly expanding the actual quotation used by Brown and Ward, Belsky and De Haan argue that, although the brain 'packs a punch' for policy makers, 'the study of parenting and brain development is not even yet in its infancy; it would be more appropriate to conclude that it is still in the embryonic stage' (Belsky and De Haan, 2011: 409–10).

After beginning their review with fitting caution, the knowledge base is thereafter treated by Brown and Ward as though it delivered certainty about the damage caused to the brain by neglectful parenting. This, as we have seen, is a strong motif in the popular imagination, with considerable political traction.[3] The simplification of the neuroscientific claims in *A child's timeframe* made our counter argument relatively straightforward to construct from within the neuroscientific discourse itself. We have seen already in this book that much of the primary work is on animals and, even here, findings have often proved difficult to replicate. This is willingly acknowledged by the primary scientists. The work on humans has largely come from extreme clinical populations, most notably children raised in orphanages in Romania, Russia and sometimes China (supplemented by a small number of postmortem studies, and cohort studies, of abused children or adults with psychiatric or psychological symptomatology).

These latter studies yield important understandings of the effect of extreme institutional abuse, and thankfully much promising evidence of plasticity and resilience (Wastell and White, 2012). However, we argued, they cannot be used as though they have predictive validity for anything other than a tiny and extreme minority of the UK population of poorly parented children. Nevertheless, this is precisely how these studies were being used by certain child welfare campaigners from North America. This was also reflected in their use by Brown and Ward, suggesting that they were heavily in the thrall of such campaigners. To support our argument, that the case was overstated, we used a number of examples from Brown and Ward's report to illustrate a somewhat superficial approach to the presentation of the current science. For example, a graph reproduced with the permission of the Harvard Center appeared to show 'sensitive periods' for the development of a range of abilities. However, not only did the graph fail to have a 'y' (vertical) axis (defining the trait in question), it also appeared to show that a child's critical period for language acquisition is about 7 months of age. The figure suggests that the window is all but slammed shut by the age of 1 year when the child may, of course, have lots of receptive language, but is unlikely actually to be able to speak. Higher cognitive functions are shown as peaking at the age of 2. What is key is that this graph is not scientific evidence; rather, it is a visual aid, packaged to persuade through the verisimilitude of science.

Thus packaged, the arguments are powerful, and have infiltrated the worldview of senior practitioners. For example, asked to comment in a BBC interview in early 2012[4] on the recent unprecedented increase of child removals, the (then) President of the Association of Directors of Children's Services observed that this was, in part, due to "a better understanding of the corrosive and damaging impact of neglect on children's development … it is about understanding the effect of neglectful parenting due to drug and alcohol problems and the physical damage to brain development it can do with very young children" (Wastell and White, 2012: 410).

To understand how the complex and often contradictory evidence from neuroscience had come to be assembled with such confidence in *A child's timeframe* we must look at the conditions of its production. As Ward and Brown note in their response to our critique, their original report had been:

> overseen by a steering group, and was then peer-reviewed by three independent academics, all of professorial status and each with expertise in a relevant field (early years, law and neuroscience). The report benefitted from their suggestions for change and improvement. Neither the referees nor the steering group criticised our approach, which they regarded as both balanced and consistent with current evidence. (Ward and Brown, 2013: 1181–2)

They overtly state (p 1182) that they were 'not commissioned to present "contradictory" or "controversial" evidence, rather to produce the best possible account of the accepted consensus currently within the field'. Furthermore, they clarify that they were asked to produce a simplified guide to the knowledge base, and indeed had been asked by the steering group to simplify the arguments in a previous draft still further. There had been, therefore, a specific instruction in the brief to engage in 'pragmatic reductionism' for the purposes of clarity. They end their response with a suggestion that our critique would undermine the case for more timely intervention to protect children from the effects of abuse and result in further harm to their wellbeing. This is a potent rejoinder, for sure, but one which could curtail important debate.

Science meets practice: precaution vs proportion and the public politics of evidence

A child's timeframe had thus been commissioned explicitly to simplify and demystify journal science. In this it had succeeded, and in speaking through the voice of journal science, our critique was perhaps no more than an irritating, glancing blow. None of the specific arguments we had made about the impossibility of predicting the degree or likelihood of damage in asymptomatic infants were addressed in Brown and Ward's rejoinder. It was not necessary to address such concerns, since the neuroscience assembled in their review seemed to show what everybody already knew, sitting so commonsensically alongside other aspects of the developmentalist narrative which ran through their work. Neuroscience so-packaged thus buttressed an older argument about the role of the State in family life, old wine in new bottles. But the seductive new 'certainties' deflect moral and ethical questions from their proper context, and render sensible debate a somewhat risky business. That was our underlying concern.

The parameters of the real debate about neuroscience and child welfare are more effectively framed as those of 'precaution' versus 'proportion' (White et al, 2015). These are two contrasting moral positions which can support reasoned formulations about safety and risk. They coexist as potential mandates for a diverse range of possible decisions in individual cases, where the presentation is open to interpretation. The central moral tension remains between, on the one hand, the rights of the many to freedom from scrutiny and intrusive intervention into the intimate spaces of family life; and on the other, the rights of the relatively few vulnerable individuals who come to serious harm at the hands of their carers. The precautionary principle is constantly in a discursive and moral dance with proportionality, with the judiciary often holding the balance.

> Society must be willing to tolerate ... diverse standards of parenting ... [and] children will inevitably have both very different experiences of parenting and very unequal consequences flowing from it ... These are the consequences of our fallible humanity and it is not the provenance of the State to spare children all the consequences of defective parenting.[5]

The allure of neuroscience, particularly in its handbook form, is that it seems to provide a decisive means to resolve these difficult matters. It proves precaution is right; once the damage to the child becomes visible, it is too late. So act now, or never! The enrolment of neuroscientific knowledge in the cause of precaution has been facilitated by a particularly effective process of translation from its esoteric origins, carried out by the Harvard Center alluded to previously. In their rejoinder, Ward and Brown sedulously defended the work of the Center:

> The Center on the Developing Child was established by academics who are experts in the field of neuroscience. The purpose of the site is to ensure that the findings of a deeply complex science are disseminated clearly and appropriately to practitioners and policy makers. The scientists involved are at the top of their field and their research is published in the most prestigious journals. To describe this site as 'selective', 'campaigning', 'a priori' and 'lurid' is a travesty; no doubt Harvard will be dealing appropriately with these allegations. (Ward and Brown, 2013: 1183)

However, on tracing the history of the Harvard Center, it becomes apparent that their work of 'clear dissemination' is actually a skilful and coordinated act of persuasion, involving collaboration with FrameWorks Institute, a communications company. In a peer-reviewed paper, one of the founders of the Harvard Center explains:

> Science has an important role to play in advising policymakers on crafting effective responses to social problems that affect the development of children. This article describes lessons learned from a multiyear, working collaboration among neuroscientists, developmental psychologists, paediatricians, economists, and communications researchers who are engaged in the iterative construction of a core story of development, using simplifying models (i.e., metaphors) such as 'brain architecture,' 'toxic stress,' and 'serve and return' to explain complex scientific concepts to non-scientists. (Shonkoff and Bales, 2011: 17)

Of course, this packaged story has consequences. For example, toxic stress is arguably a tautological concept. If stress has been damaging, it is by definition toxic, but this gives us no indication of necessary dose.

That the brains of children reared in extreme institutional conditions should show structural damage is not surprising, but we cannot infer that a lesser dose indicates a proportionate amount of damage. It may very well mean no damage at all. There is no basis for supposing a linear extrapolation, a fallacy we pointed out in the last chapter.

The aspirations of this extended, cross-disciplinary project were thus to produce a faithful translation of the science, aiming to create a public sense of shared responsibility for children and for strategic investment in their future. The tone of the Harvard Center's mission is communitarian, not totalitarian. Nevertheless, the production of a 'core story' required the development of a new metaphorical vocabulary. The processes by which this was achieved were complex, drawing on anthropology, cognitive science and linguistics to map 'conceptual models' in public use, synthesising these with expert knowledge to develop 'powerful frame cues' (Shonkoff and Bales, 2011: 20) in the form of metaphors and values. Expert knowledge was thus recast through folk understandings, to show people what they think they already know: of course, domestic abuse is a bad thing, it damages children's brains.[6]

But nothing in the realm of language can ever be a dispassionate view from nowhere; it is always argumentative, and there is always a counter position to which it is addressing itself. The act of translation by the FrameWorks collaboration, in the US context, involved challenging a dominant cultural notion that childhood adversity was something to be overcome by rugged individualism and self-reliance (Bales, 2004). This, by necessity, had to involve stoking up the 'damage' and 'toxicity' of suboptimal childhoods. The stage was thus set for the 'core story' to inform policy, not least at the more coercive end of the State apparatus.

It is worth examining debates in the national press in the UK at the time, as these are illustrative of the thought styles of both the sceptics and the neuroenthusiasts. Journalist Zoe Williams in *The Guardian* (26 April 2014) set the cat among the kittens, arguing:

> Neuroscience is huge in early years policy. This week, in what's been characterised as the largest shake-up of family law in a generation, the 26-week time limit for adoption proceedings has come into force, much of it justified by the now-or-never urgency of this set of beliefs, that the first three years (or sometimes first 18 months) hardwire a baby's brain, either give it or deny it the capacity for a full life. This is the engine of what is known as the First Three Years movement, which has transfixed politicians from across the

spectrum. Allen and Duncan Smith's report opened with an illustration of the 'normal child's' large brain and the shrivelled, walnut brain of the neglected child.

A number of academics, Val Gillies (Goldsmiths College, University of London), Jan Macvarish (the University of Kent) and ourselves, were cited by Williams. The piece ends:

> White concludes: 'There is an argument for removing children, a precautionary principle argument. You can say, "Right, let's remove all children who are in suboptimal parenting situations." Regimes have done that, over the years. But we're not having those debates. What we're having is this misuse of the neuroscientific evidence, to suggest that it's very dangerous for children to be left in certain situations. I'm not talking about leaving them in situations where they're at risk of injury or sexual abuse, more: "Your mum's in a bit of a mess, she's drinking a bit and not interacting with you optimally and she's also poor, which is why she's not been able to keep the state out of it." It's only when the children who've been removed grow up, and ask, "But did anybody try to help my mum?" That's what you would ask, isn't it?'[7]

Such arguments are the 'other side' of the case for acting with alacrity to remove children at potential risk. A series of responses in the form of letters was published in *The Guardian* on 29 April 2014, under the headline 'Early years interventions and social justice'.[8] We cannot cover all of the responses here, but the reader is encouraged to look them over on the newspaper's website. Some are directly supportive of Williams' piece; others endorse the arguments about the dangers of overstatement. One, from Harriet Ward (co-author of the Brown and Ward report), recognised the possibility that neuroscience may be conscripted into a form of practice that denigrates the poor and vulnerable, while at the same time arguing (again) that Zoe Williams, and the other contributors, were risking dangerously derailing the cause of early intervention.

We will juxtapose two of the other letters here to underscore how thesis and antithesis confront each other in an apparently unnavigable moral maze. The first, from a well-known academic and a respected clinician,[9] was stridently critical of Williams:

Zoe Williams' article suggesting that the neuroscience about the importance of the first three years doesn't stand up to scrutiny is as flawed as the arguments of the small group of proponents on whose writings it is based. What this group of critics have in common is a highly rhetorical use of the evidence to oppose state intervention to support early parenting.

This is a particularly unhelpful development for two reasons. First, these critics are misrepresenting the evidence to sabotage the work of academics [Brown and Ward] whose rigorous and appropriate use of the neuroscientific evidence will ensure that the 45% of child protection cases who are under four years are protected in a more timely manner than has been the case to date. These changes were urgently needed, and they simply confirm what the wider evidence tells us about the developmental impact of seriously suboptimal parenting.

Second, the evidence about the sensitivity of the brain during the first three years to early environmental input is now beyond dispute, making this the period sine qua non, in terms of investing limited resources to optimise outcomes, particularly for the disadvantaged children exposed to multiple risks.

The time has come for the neuroscientists to start challenging this misrepresentation of their work.

A neuroscientist[10] did indeed speak up in another letter:

Zoe Williams is rightly critical of the scary image of the shrivelled brain reproduced from the cover of MP Graham Allen's report to the government on the importance of the first three years of a child's life, for it makes a travesty of what neuroscience can and cannot say about early child development. The image derives from a short unrefereed report at a US neuroscience meeting, without information as to its provenance other than that it is from a three year old abused child. That children's brains and their synaptic connections develop rapidly in early years is well established. That young children benefit from a stable, loving and secure environment is … common sense. But there really is no good evidence that these two statements are related. That is indeed a bridge too far.

A further *Guardian* piece by Patrick Butler describes a visit to the UK by Bruce Perry, responsible for the iconic brain images we met in the last chapter. During this visit, Perry met privately with many senior members of the UK Cabinet. Butler points to the florid argumentation used by Perry in his addresses to a policy audience at an inaugural event organised by the Early Intervention Foundation:

> In around 100 years' time, multi-generational 'problem' families will constitute a quarter of the population, sucking in billions of 'our' tax dollars and placing 'an ungodly burden' on our children and grandchildren, says US psychiatrist Dr Bruce Perry. His grim prediction came at the end of a recent presentation in London designed to persuade policymakers to intervene early in problem families. Reach their children early, through parenting classes and other 'individualised intervention plans', before their brains are irrevocably hardwired – and you not merely rescue the child from disaster but you, the taxpayer, will save billions in social security payments. 'It's a big economic bang for your buck.' (Butler, 2014)

Butler goes on to describe Perry's style as involving the stitching together of data, shocking anecdotes and emotive imagery. Apparently Perry warned the, no doubt very receptive, audience, that in the absence of investment in early intervention, society will reach a 'tipping point', after which it will 'become impossible to break the cycle by which hopeless parents spawn unloved children prone to educational failure, obesity, mental illness and criminality, before those children themselves become hopeless parents, accelerating societal and financial meltdown' (Butler, 2014).

In the same *Guardian* article, Eamon McCrory (a respected neuroscientist whose work we touched on earlier in this chapter and who was part of the team in the *Irish Times* article mentioned in chapter two (at p 33)) also disputed the 'irreversible damage' thesis. Perry himself, it seems, recognised the dangers of the irreversibility argument: backstage, he apparently confided in Butler that: 'People will say: "My god, look at the brain! Why should we invest in criminal interventions, such as offender rehabilitation, because the brain is cooked by the time you are three" … that's not exactly the take-home message here' (cited in Butler, 2014). This is precisely the problem with the core developmental neuroscience story; it has the unintended effect of permanently condemning the 'damaged'. They are, or are forever at risk of being, irretrievably 'mad or bad' and thus in need of fixing, or worse.

Language matters profoundly, as one of us (with colleagues) has argued elsewhere:

> A language of support opens up possibilities in terms of thinking about what is going on for all of us and what we need at differing times and keys into an international family support literature containing very valuable insights on what people value, when and how … Support allows for a recognition of the chronicity of need, it is not intrinsically tied to individualised change – 'responsibilization' or to a tyrannical and unforgiving notion of time ... Such a project cannot be chopped up into short-term, time limited, discrete 'interventions' delivered by disembodied experts. (Featherstone et al, 2014b: 1744-5)

Perry's intentions, like those of the Harvard Center, may be good; they are utopian, they are about fixing people. Noble causes make good excuses for a little exaggeration, the end justifies the means, and a little exaggeration goes a long way. But good intentions can be the road to hell.

Conclusion

The real problem with the policy leap from the extreme to the normal range, from orphanage to housing estate, is that we do not have any reliable understanding of the 'dose' of neglect required to produce a given degree of 'damage'. More fundamentally, what do brains actually add to the argument? Why do they pack such a punch? Either we can see the damage behaviourally or physically, and thus do not need the brain to make our moral arguments, or we cannot. If we cannot see the damage, current knowledge does not provide the grounds for conjuring it into being. Conversely, if the brain were normal, does this mean the child should stay in adverse circumstances? We may have very good reasons to feel an infant should not stay with their family, such as the risk of physical harm, or because they are having a really miserable life, but we must make those arguments on the basis of manifest evidence. Is the idea of a miserable life in need of a brain image to make us take it seriously?

There are currently no diagnostic tests which could be used reliably and ethically to check on a child's neurobiological apparatus, and what if there were? What if one routinely tested a child's salivary cortisol levels (thought to be a biomarker for stress)? Of course, if the professional opinion were in favour of State intervention (even removal) and the cortisol levels were raised, this would provide a degree of helpful, augmentative evidence. However, as we shall see in later chapters, the relationship between biomarkers, such as cortisol level, and lasting brain damage is unproven. More fundamentally, it is surely the stress which is bad, not the raised cortisol. Furthermore, should not the whole moral basis be questioned of taking any action, without making an assessment of family circumstances, levels of support, capacity to change and so forth? It is more thorny still to consider what we would do if the cortisol levels were normal. Does that mean that all is well, whatever we may see to the contrary? Were the child manifesting external signs of abuse or neglect, one would simply act on these grounds alone; in which case, why was the cortisol test necessary? Moreover, what to do if the child were developing normally in spite of adverse circumstances? The cortisol test, standing as proxy for biomarkers in general, does not simplify; it seems to add to the moral maze.

Centres of expertise, such as the Harvard Center, operate at the interface between the esoteric world of science and the sublunary realm of policy and practice; but it is important to keep in mind that the real expertise of such centres is communication and persuasion, not the science itself. Science-in-policy functions as a form of public reasoning, described by discursive psychologist, Charles Antaki, thus:

> .... everyday reasoning – at least, reasoning out loud – is often justificatory and always partial. ... ordinary reasoning can be much more a case of authorizing what one is saying than genuinely reaching an answer unknown at the start of the journey. (Antaki, 1994: 182)

Even when such centres appear to acknowledge uncertainties in the primary science, this itself can be a clever trope, to give greater rhetorical force to the a priori viewpoint or opinion, which is already solid and not really up for negotiation. That this rhetorical project has worked at the policy level in the UK is undeniable, indeed it has been spectacularly successful in persuading senior politicians, practitioners and civil servants. Although its scientific credentials may be questionable

(Wastell and White, 2012), the Allen Report, for instance, ultimately led to the establishment of the Early Intervention Foundation, which is likely to exert considerable influence on UK policy and practice. This charity describes its purpose as follows:

> We *assess* the evidence of what works in early intervention for impact and relative cost, *advise* local authorities, charities and investors on the implementation of early intervention on the ground, and *advocate* for investment in *effective* early intervention to local and national policy makers. (emphasis in original, http://www.eif.org.uk/)

This remit is broader than brains, making significant use of economic arguments (which we critically address in chapter six) but the neuro thought style remains highly influential and prominent, as the following section of a commissioned report (*The best start at home*) illustrates. We note the appearance of epigenetic claims alongside the neuroscientific ones; of the former, more in chapters seven and eight.

> Prolonged exposure to stressful experiences can result in elevation of cortisol levels, which can alter the function of a number of neural systems, suppress the immune response, and change the architecture of regions in the brain (e.g. the Hippocampus) that are essential for learning and memory (Qiu et al, 2013). Cortisol can also influence epigenetic processes, in which specific genes are turned 'on' and others 'off' at particular times and locations in the brain. Sensitive and responsive caregiving from a parent or a child-care provider (i.e. when it is provided in out-of-home settings) can serve as a powerful buffer against stress hormone exposure. (Dartington Social Research Unit, 2015: 15)

The first piece of evidence cited (Qiu et al) is one arbitrarily selected piece from a voluminous body of research on the hippocampus, in train for decades. As with all journal science, there is some settled knowledge, much controversy, and much more to be done: in fact, the field grows from year to year with no sign of any abatement, as we saw in chapter two. The second citation refers to a paper authored by the Harvard Center on the Developing Child, which we have noted is a key player in the neuro actor network. *The best start at home* also notably asserts on page 12 that Graham Allen has 'made the scientific and economic case for early intervention to prevent longer-term social and health difficulties for children and families and reduce expenditure on late intervention'. The unequivocal language is markworthy: the case, it seems, has indubitably been made.

We are witnessing the rise and rise of a new phenomenon, 'prevention science'. This is the topic of our next chapter. Its technical argot and bold ambitions seem to dominate even the most apparently benign shifts in the policy and practice discourses. For example, commendable work showing the impact on women of the removal by the State of successive children (Broadhurst et al, 2015a, 2015b) shows signs of being translated into a new category 'repeat removals', with offers of help conditional upon 'consenting' to long-acting reversible contraception. Prevention science is steadily gaining momentum and influence. It builds upon the models and logics of epidemiology, but blends these with claims to predictive validity through careful targeting. Human agency is moralised: 'individuals are not just influenced by environmental toxins but importantly interact with the environment based on their motivations, intentions and self-efficacy' (Sloboda and Petras, 2014: 252). Parental lifestyle and choice make their appearance as relevant variables in developmental risk. Prevention science is steering the trajectory of current policy increasingly towards 'policing' of women's pregnant bodies on the one hand, 'positioning poor mothers as architects of their children's deprivation' (Edwards et al, 2015), and intensified State surveillance over family life on the other (Lowe et al, 2015). Debate is therefore timely and to this we turn next.

Notes

[1]   https://www.gov.uk/government/speeches/prime-ministers-speech-on-life-chances

[2]   *Re N (Children) (Adoption: Jurisdiction)* [2015] EWCA Civ 1112, para. 16.

[3]   Similar arguments have been mobilised in the case for a 'Cinderella law' to criminalise emotional neglect, which came to fruition in the UK's Serious Crime Act, 2015.

[4]   Radio 4, *Today* programme, 9 February 2012.

[5]   Hedley, J cited in *Re B (A Child)* [2013] UKSC 33.

[6]   An argument has recently been advanced by authors from FrameWorks and the campaigning charity NSPCC in the UK context (Kendall-Taylor et al, 2014), urging that communications should focus on the core story of development and not on improving health or helping vulnerable children, neither of which play well with the public apparently. We should note that FrameWorks are also working on producing metaphors, like genetic memory, to translate the complexities of epigenetics for consumption by the American public (Frameworks Institute, 2010).

[7]   http://www.theguardian.com/education/2014/apr/26/misused-neuroscience-defining-child-protection-policy

8   http://www.theguardian.com/society/2014/apr/29/early-years-interventions-social-justice
9   From Dr Jane Barlow, Professor of Public Health in the Early Years, University of Warwick; President, Association of Infant Mental Health; and Dr Sue Gerhardt, author of *Why love matters: How affection shapes a baby's brain*.
10   Steven Rose, Emeritus Professor of Neuroscience, The Open University.

SIX

Perfecting people: the inexorable rise of prevention science

> A new type of law came into being, analogous to the laws of nature, but pertaining to people. These new laws were expressed in terms of probability. They carried with them the connotations of normalcy and deviations from the norm. The cardinal concept of the psychology of the Enlightenment had been, simply, human nature. By the end of the nineteenth century, it was being replaced by something different: normal people. (Hacking, 1990: 1)

In the previous chapters we have outlined how biological sciences have historically offered, and continue to promise, new means by which the State can attempt to render the behaviours and frailties of its citizens tractable. As Hacking indicates above, this transformation also needed statistics and maths. It needed quantity. In 1815, Paris had more suicide than London – a phenomenon thus in need of an explanation. A preoccupation with moral degeneracy had led to the collection of thousands of statistics on suicide in France which spawned Durkheim's painstaking sociology on the matter. Statistics need categories: one cannot measure something without a name. Social engineering is made possible by counting the bits of society we don't want or which offend our sensibilities, and imagining technologies for their amelioration. Hacking (1990) describes how two uses of the concept of 'normal' emerge from the 19th century onwards.

> The normal stands indifferently for what is typical, the unenthusiastic objective average, but it also stands for what has been, good health, and for what shall be, our chosen destiny. This is why the benign and sterile sounding word 'normal' has become one of the most powerful ideological tools of the twentieth century. (Hacking, 1990: 169)

'Normal' is a crucial concept in shifting the emphasis from 'is' to 'ought': utopian projects need both kinds of normal, in particular to effect the augmentative shift from the typical to the perfectible ideal.

As we anticipated in the previous chapter, the late 20th and early 21st centuries have seen the rise of 'prevention science'. Uniting both versions of 'normal' within the grand project of human improvement, the paradigm seeks to ensure people achieve normalcy by intervening to stop damage in its tracks, and also to ensure optimal human flourishing. Prevention science could build better people. An early paper sets out the goals as follows:

> The goal of prevention science is to prevent or moderate major human dysfunctions. An important corollary of this goal is to eliminate or mitigate the causes of disorder. Preventive efforts occur, by definition, before illness is fully manifested, so prevention research is focused primarily on the systematic study of potential precursors of dysfunction or health, called risk factors, or protective factors respectively. (Coie et al, 1993: 1013)

The five keystones of prevention science are *risk,* with its associated probabilistic reasoning, the notion that *variance* is a form of 'illness', a preoccupation with identifying *underlying causes,* ensuring efficacy and *cost-effectiveness* of interventions with rigorous methods and *translation* of the scientific findings for an audience of policy actors. 'Whatever national program for prevention research is developed, it must ultimately be translated into practical applications that will "sell" in schools, hospitals, playgrounds, homes, clinics, industries, and community agencies nationwide' (Coie et al, 1993: 1020).

Human development features strongly in the preventive narrative. Early intervention usually means early childhood intervention based on indicators of risk. Thus 'targeting' is another distinctive hallmark of the paradigm. Prevention science is not concerned with mass immunisation, or fluoridation of the water supply. It is behavioural 'dysfunctions' and 'diseases' it seeks to nip before they bud. Troublesome 'non-malleable' problems, such as socioeconomic disadvantage, must be recast as something different entirely.

> Variables that are hypothesized to be relatively non-malleable but that have major significance for the development of psychopathology, such as heredity, social class, or gender, should be translated into constructs that are susceptible to influence by interventions. (Coie et al, 1993: 1020)

Prevention science incorporates the familiar tenets of developmentalism, merging these with economic concepts (macroeconomic modelling, behavioural economics) and a particular version of evidence-based research focused on the generation of 'effect sizes' to establish economic benefits, or not, as the case may be. Prevention science has set itself some ambitious goals and, after some 25 years, we might arguably be expecting to see the amelioration of a considerable degree of human dysfunction. Prevention is supposed to prevent things. If it works, we may surely expect it to put itself out of business within a generation or two. As we shall see, the rather modest effects of many programmes are not dampening the enthusiasm; if anything they are escalating the commitment to find the magic bullet.

In the policy domain, we have already discussed the establishment of the Early Intervention Foundation in England. Another particularly potent exemplar can be found in recent policy in Scotland. In 2014, the Scottish Government passed the Children and Young People (Scotland) Act (CYPA) 2014. This designates a 'named person', typically a professional from health or education services, to oversee the family and mitigate risks to the child. The legislation, which was due to come into effect in 2016, covers children from the day they are born up until the age of 18. Guidance on the implementation of the legislation, issued in 2015, states that the 'named person' could be involved with families before birth: '… we now know that there is a strong link between antenatal anxiety and maternal depression, and poor outcomes for children including development, parental bonding and behavioural problems' (Scottish Government, 2015).

The 'named person' is charged with ensuring the wellbeing of the child or young person and 'sharing information' about them as they see fit. As noted by some critics, this reconfigures the relationship between the family and the State in profound ways: 'The idea that "services" and not parents and families guarantee children's wellbeing and that services must monitor parents, and intervene "as they see fit" has become almost unquestioningly accepted' (Mellon, 2015: 71).

On 28 July 2016, the UK Supreme Court deemed aspects of the named person legislation relating to information sharing to be beyond the legislative competence of the Scottish Parliament, so as we write, the scheme is stalled. This has not curbed the enthusiasm of its supporters, however, who have vowed to make the necessary changes to ensure the scheme's enactment.

At this point we will focus on the specific economic and scientific arguments which are at play in the context of policy, using the UK as our main example. We take the following features of prevention science in turn and examine the presuppositions and myths that support them. First, we explore the economic modelling which has legitimated the targeting of particular forms of intervention. As it is central to the economic logic, we then revisit developmentalism and the idea that early years are foundational in the development of normalcy and deviance. The preferred method of ameliorating risk is through targeted programmes which in turn must be subject to robust evaluation. Public accountability for spending on prevention, particularly in the US context where universal provision is scarce, relies on certain mandated forms of evaluation and evidence: the State (and other benefactors) will only pay for 'what works', and only some methods will provide the 'effect sizes' the economists need to make their models add up. We then explore the assumptions and the impact of the experimental paradigm in this context, and the circularity it creates in the reasoning processes of prevention science. We conclude our discussion in this chapter with an introduction to the next phase of the prevention project – looking under the skin and into the womb for biological markers of risk. New forms of targeting are on their way and they are big biotechnical business.

The macroeconomics of early intervention

Policy in the USA since the late 1990s, and increasingly in the UK, has relied heavily on economic models of investment in human capital, underpinned by the following underlying assumptions and metaphors: that the first three years of a child's life are crucial to further development; that these three years are characterised by a precariousness to environmental stressors (such as suboptimal parenting); and that 'learning begets learning' (Howard-Jones et al, 2012). These guiding assumptions, with their a priori moral authority, are also informing investments in the monitoring of child development across the globe supported by the World Bank (for example, Denboba et al, 2014).[1] Given the focus on children, these policy developments appeal to both left and right, as the entitlements of the very young are not sullied by any moral stain their parents may carry:

> The idea of giving people equal opportunity early in life, whatever their socioeconomic background, is embraced across the political spectrum as a matter of fairness for the left and as a matter of personal effort for the right. (Paes de Barros et al, 2009: 18)

The work of the Nobel Prize winning economist, James Heckman, has been very influential. The confluence of mathematical modelling, child development and brain science forms the hallmark of his work. In a widely cited, seminal paper, Cunha, Heckman and Schennach (2010) introduce the core ideas of their modelling: they describe how their 'multistage technology' maps developmental stages in the child's life cycle, and estimates 'substitution parameters that determine the importance of early parental investment for subsequent lifetime achievement' (p 884). The mathematical modelling is complex and its claims to economic validity carry much weight. The work is attractive to policy makers as it promises a rigorous scientific basis to guide public investment. The published paper (Cunha et al, 2010) is 50 pages long (with a further 50 pages of supplementary information) and is dense with mathematical equations and esoteric economic terminology. We have attempted to summarise the work in appendix E, though as the reader will appreciate this was a challenge. This appendix also sets out our critique. We see significant limitations in the work, despite its mathematical sophistication. Here we will attempt to provide a non-mathematical synopsis and to summarise our primary concerns.

In essence, Cunha et al provide a development model of human skill formation with two distinct elements, cognitive skill and noncognitive (social) skill. Two developmental stages are distinguished (0 to 6 years, and 7 to 14), broken down into two-year periods. The level (stock) of cognitive or noncognitive skill in any period is held to depend on the 'stock of skill' in the previous period, the level of 'parental investment' in the current period, and parental skill (cognitive and noncognitive). To this basic model, Cunha et al add another ingredient, designated 'elasticity of substitution'; this is defined, somewhat obscurely for the non-economic reader, as 'a measure of how easy it is to compensate for low levels of cognitive and non-cognitive stocks inherited from the previous period with current levels of parental investment' (p 887).

In order to evaluate the model, a substantial empirical study is reported using data from the Center for Human Resource Research at Ohio State University. The data derive from the National Longitudinal Survey of Youth initiated by the Center in 1979. In 2004, 7,538 of the original participants were interviewed, and of these Cunha et al analysed data for 2,207 first-born white children. The survey includes a broad range of seemingly well-established instruments for measuring the cognitive ability, temperament, motor and social development and so on of children as well as their home environment. Further details are provided in appendix E. Here we note the method used to measure *parental investment*, which involved a subset of items from the HOME questionnaire developed by Bradley and Caldwell (1984). Examples include: the number of push/pull play toys possessed by the child, the number of books the child has, and how often the child is taken to museums or musical concerts. The reader will get the gist.

In summarising the results of their work, we have focused on cognitive skill as scholastic performance would seem the primary interest. The results of their modelling are presented in terms of the model's mathematical parameters, and effect sizes are not consistently reported, which makes interpretation difficult. We have done our best to present an accurate summary of their findings, and have added our improvised estimates of effect sizes. Overwhelmingly, the most powerful predictor of 'current period' cognitive skill for both development stages is cognitive skill in the previous period, and this very effect is much stronger for the second development stage (age 7–14) than the first stage (0–6). Noncognitive skills in the previous period show no predictive effects. Parental investments in the current period appear to assist the child in stage 1, but not during stage 2. Parental social skill benefits the child during stage 1, but not stage 2; whereas for parental cognitive skill, the reverse is found – greater benefits are found once the child is fully established in school. There also appears to be a very small effect of 'elasticity of substitution'; Cunha claim that this is present only for the pre-school stage, although our analysis suggests that it only applies once the child is at school, when it is reduced. Whatever is the case, once the variability of their estimates is taken into account, it would seem that the effect is rather small, certainly compared to the influence of some of the other factors.

Broadly, the pattern of results in our analysis seems to make intuitive sense. By far the best predictor of cognitive performance is cognitive performance in the prior period (designated 'self-productivity') and particularly so once the child has gone to school, as would be expected. Parental investment in stage 1, with the child primarily at home, is more effective than in stage 2; again, according with common sense. Once the child is in full-time schooling, the parent's cognitive skill seems to matter more, whereas their noncognitive skills are less influential. Again, this seems intuitive as they are now in a better position to help with schoolwork. But this is not how Cunha et al sum up the implications of their work. The centre of attention is 'elasticity of substitution':

> The elasticity of substitution for cognition is smaller in second stage production. It is more difficult to compensate for the effects of adverse environments on cognitive endowments at later ages than it is at earlier ages. This

... helps to explain the evidence on ineffective cognitive remediation strategies for disadvantaged adolescents.

Further aspects of the paper are of interest; for example, a planning simulation is posited which assumes a fixed investment budget and '*that the state has full control over family investment decisions*'. The simulation purports to show that 'Eighty percent more investment is required for children with the most disadvantaged personal endowments' and that 'the optimal policy is to invest relatively more in the disadvantaged compared to the advantaged in the early years'. Leaving noncognitive skills out of the model, on the other hand, leads to the opposite conclusion that 'it is optimal to perpetuate initial inequality and not to invest relatively more in disadvantaged young children' (Cunha et al, 2010: 927).

In appendix E, we make a number of criticisms of Cunha et al's work, which can be summarised as follows. First, the model fails to test any alternative 'models of growth', other than a 'concave curve' which appears intrinsically biased in favour of early development. The model also omits any consideration of socioeconomic status, reflecting a sceptical position articulated explicitly in other writings, as we see below. When Cunha et al talk of 'disadvantage', this does not designate poverty, just a decrement in either cognitive or noncognitive skill. Equally, investment does not mean State investment, it means parental investment, as measured by the HOME inventory, that is, time spent with children, the provision of toys, music lessons and so on. Regarding such investments, the simulation appears to assume that such investments are portable and can be redistributed, somehow taken away from families with bright children and given to families with underachieving children. No wonder the policy maker has full control! We also note that their modelling, and the manner in which it has been operationalised, embodies a normative model of how parenting should be done, of people who want to do the best for their kids to propel them into middle-class careers. But not every mother or family necessarily wants this, which of course is the real crux of the whole argument:

> Sizeable differences in achievement by parental income are already evident by very young ages ... This raises the possibility that a generation's fate may be sealed by the time it enters school. Economic and social policy requires convincing answers to the vexing question: Why do poor children perform so poorly? (Caucutt et al, 2015: 1–2)

A better understanding of parental decision making is clearly part of this. A recent paper by Attanasio (2015), which draws on Cunha et al's model, shows a rather more sophisticated understanding of some of the complexities which are involved:

> Parental decisions are complex and several factors ... interact to determine them. Parents will invest in children by dedicating time to them and buying toys and books depending on the costs of these investments, how effective they think these activities are ... They will also consider the trade-offs between spending time with children, work and leisure. ... Finally, parents often have to make decisions to allocate scarce resources among several children, who differ in their age, gender, perceived ability and so on. (Attanasio, 2015: 956)

Finally in appendix E, we express our concerns over the deployment of complex maths and esoteric terminology. As with brain images, there is an obvious concern that policy makers (and practitioners) are seduced by the arcane vocabulary and mathematical squiggles, that their critical faculty is bamboozled and they do not raise key questions. The issues examined in the study can readily be explored using much simpler and accessible techniques in bespoke, carefully designed experiments, not piggybacked expediently onto a dataset untailored to test the model. The appendix gives an example: in a simple questionnaire study, Bradley and Caldwell (1984) report correlations between various aspects of the early home environment and subsequent academic performance at first grade, 6 years later. No mystery or mystification here.

More fundamentally, Cunha et al's study raises epistemological concerns arising from the 'level of analysis'. Abstract concepts such as elasticity of substitution, and even parental investment, require more direct access to the real world for their proper analysis and understanding. How exactly do 'parental investments' help, and so on? An adequate explication of the effect of parental support on socio-emotional and cognitive development, and how the dynamics of these factors play out in the family milieu (prior to and throughout the course of schooling), cannot be answered by a mathematical equation; ascent to the particulars of the real world is needed. But no such access is available to demystify the economic abstractions. Macroeconomic models are fundamentally reductionist, providing an impoverished account of the world, an account couched at a single level of description, lacking explanatory power.

Considering more of Heckman's research, as noted above, poverty is not part of the 'equation' as the following extract from a widely cited earlier paper shows:

> The widely discussed correlation between parental income in the child's college-going years and child college participation arises only because it is lifetime resources that affect college readiness and college-going … Job training programs targeted at the disadvantaged do not produce high rates of return and fail to lift participants out of poverty … these programs are largely ineffective and cannot remedy the skill deficits accumulated over a lifetime of neglect. (Heckman and Masterov, 2007: 475)

Instead of poverty, Heckman prefers to invoke biology: 'a particular variant of the monoamine oxidase A gene, which has been associated with antisocial behaviour and higher crime rates is triggered by growing up in a harsh or abusive environment' (Heckman, 2013: 16).

Of course, this thought style takes us in a predictable policy direction. Adverse child environments are typically associated by Heckman (and co-workers) with unwed, single parent, teenage or uneducated mothers. Heckman and Masterov (2007) note that the reality of lone parenting is associated with 'many pathologies' (p 463). The solution is for mothers to try harder: 'Controlling for maternal ability, never-wed mothers who provide above average cognitive stimulation to their children can largely offset the circumstance of single parenthood in terms of their child's cognitive outcomes' (p 466).

There are similar moral judgements on race and poverty. It is asserted that gaps in the college-going rates of different racial and ethnic groups, 'nominally due to gaps in parental family income', are actually due to child college readiness and this, of course, is a consequence of poor environments – which again means poor parenting.

> It is especially problematic that poor environments are more common in the minority populations on which America must depend for the growth in its labor force. Unless these environments are improved, one cannot rely on a growth in the skills of these groups to propel growth in workforce quality at the rate we have experienced in the past. (p 466)

Where does this take us in policy terms? As we shall show in due course, it seems to lead to a preoccupation with targeted parenting programmes. Heckman and Masterov note that early investment will not produce 'effective people' unless followed by later investment:

> We are also not offering any claims that the early years are the sole determinants of later success, or that persons who are raised in disadvantaged families should be absolved of any guilt when they participate in crime. We are simply arguing that early environments play a large role in shaping later outcomes and that their importance is neglected in current policy. (p 488)

But given a climate of finite funding, and the natural sentimentality associated with the welfare of small children, investment through the life course seems something of a vain hope. Heckman's economic argument for early intervention, expressed impressively as 'return on investment in human capital', is synthesised in figure 4, taken from Cunha et al (2006) (cited in Howard-Jones et al, 2012).

Figure 4: Heckman's economic model showing the rate of return for investment declining sharply with age (adapted and simplified from the original figure).

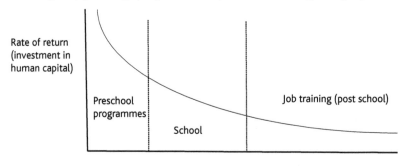

It is important to note that this figure is a graphical representation of the economic model itself, not a two-dimensional plot depicting real empirical data (Howard-Jones et al, 2012). Yet it is routinely treated by policy communities as though it were populated with data proving the validity of the model. It is not – it is merely a graphic. The evidence adduced by Heckman (and his colleagues) in support of their modelling is, in fact, quite limited (see Heckman, 2013). Apart from the evidence we have already looked at for the Cunha et al work, the support invoked is based primarily on three US studies, the

Abecedarian, Perry and Chicago projects, which provided home-based educational interventions to young infants. These all yielded promising short-terms results in terms of children's cognitive and noncognitive development, but were small scale and often evaluated by people very committed to the projects themselves. They also relied on notions of critical periods and the importance of the first three years, leading to a 'cliff edge' at the end of the intervention periods, so it is unsurprising that results could be difficult to replicate at 24 month and 36 month follow-up periods. Bruer (1999) provides a seminal critique of these interventions and their underlying assumptions and limited long-term, or even medium-term, benefits.

Heckman also cites the Family Nurse Partnership as an example of an efficacious intervention. However, when the evidence for sustainable benefits is examined, the results are equivocal. In a follow-up study when children reached the age of 12, David Olds, the originator of the programme, reports enhanced partner relationships and 'mastery', and less 'role impairment', but no effects on mother's marriage, relationship with the biological father, intimate partner violence, alcohol and other drug use, arrests, incarceration, psychological distress or reports of foster care placements (Olds et al, 2010). These disappointing results may well be an unintended consequence of concentrating resources on the first three years and then slamming the service door. Heckman also draws heavily on popularised versions of neuroscience, especially the work of Bruce Perry whose brain images have played a dubious role in determining policy on both sides of the Atlantic, as we saw in chapter 4.

Preferred responses: parenting and programmes

The preoccupation with the preventive potency of the early years has led to the proliferation of particular types of intervention. A recent study of the evidence for these programmes undertaken for the UK Early Intervention Foundation (Dartington Social Research Unit et al, 2015) reviews over 100 schemes, 32 in depth. These are variously aimed at improving attachment and maternal sensitivity, social and emotional skills, behaviour, language and communication. The review, though 'rapid', is commendably comprehensive, covering both programmes and evaluations in some detail. The overview report concludes: 'We recommend that Early Help services delivered through children's centres and other sites draw more heavily on programmes and practice with a strong evidence base and that there is an improved focus on monitoring outcomes' (p 13).

This is not a particularly surprising recommendation given the proliferation of 'early (childhood) interventions' all with prima facie uncontroversial aims of improving things which are good for children. The paradigm has an incorrigible logic. Programmes must be aimed at producing the optimal conditions for children to flourish, they must be evidence-based and they must have been assessed to find out what works, for whom, under what circumstances. These self-evidently worthy goals nevertheless prove rather elusive. Taking the Family Nurse Partnership (FNP) as an example, we have just witnessed that its long-term benefits seem to be somewhat flimsy.

As an aside, it is instructive to examine how the evidence base for FNP is presented by those in the proselytising camp, as opposed to our admittedly more contrarian position. Dartington's 'Investing in Children' website proclaims a range of 'outcomes affected' by FNP:[2] healthy birth, no chronic ill-health, not abused or neglected, school ready, and so on. In terms of the stated 'impact of intervention', two statistics stand out: on 'child abuse and neglect' an impact of 0.88 is claimed, and for crime, the impact is 0.70. Both impacts are negative, that is, the likelihood of such ills is reduced. The site asserts statistical significance in both cases, but does not explain what these numbers mean. In itself, this is somewhat remiss, especially for a site so wedded to evidence; given the apparent contradiction with Old's recent research, we felt the need to inquire further.

A link to the source of the evidence was provided, which turned out to be a report by the Washington State Institute for Public Policy, entitled '*Return on investment: evidence-based options to improve state-wide outcomes* (Lee et al, 2012)'. The statistics appear to have been extracted from the column of a table showing a meta-analysis of results, across a number of studies, of the efficacy of FNP.[3] Significantly, the relevant column is headed: 'Unadjusted effect sizes'. Adjacent to this column is another column headed 'Adjusted effect sizes'; the corresponding statistics in this column are -0.22 and -0.17. These adjusted effects are somewhat smaller and, with the standard errors provided, appear in both cases to fall short of statistical significance. We were intrigued by this discrepancy; what in particular was meant by the appellation 'adjusted'. The technical annex[4] to the Washington institute's report[5] described the adjustment process as follows:

> An explicit adjustment factor (discount rate) is assigned to the results of individual effect sizes based on the Institute's judgment concerning research quality (study design), research involvement in program design and

implementation, 'laboratory' setting, and weak outcome measure. (p 17)

The 'Well-done random assignment study' is given a weight of 1; at the other end of the scale are studies without control groups, included short case reports, which are excluded. In short, the adjustment reflects the degree to which the various studies contributing to the 'evidence-base' depart from the gold standard of the randomised controlled trial (see next section). When this robust criterion is taken into account, the evidence-based benefits of FNP appear to disappear. It is perplexing when organisations devoted to the evidence-based approach appear not to favour the most rigorous sources of evidence.

Returning to our main thread, 20 years into the prevention science paradigm there is little firm ground for people commissioning services to stand on. It is clear, however, that whatever the commissioners decide to commission, they will be expected to spend money on outcome-focused evaluations of the programmes they have bought, regardless of what claims already exist about their evidence-based credentials. One has to ponder the effect of commercial and career sensitivities on the reporting of the evidence in such reviews. Many of the programmes proclaiming the best evidence base are franchised; this must exert its own effect on those who seek to make comparisons, tending to induce a cautious approach to guard against accusations of commercial bias. After a 'rapid', but still painstaking, review of the state of the research base, it is nonetheless striking that we are left with but a few jejune recommendations, such as that those programmes which improve outcomes for both parents and children are preferable to those that only improve one or other. The Dartington review concludes with the following caveats:

> An assessment against standards of evidence of the quality and weight of evidence of impact for interventions cited in this review is ongoing as part of the work of the EIF Evidence Panel, so it is not possible in this report to give interventions a firm rating. Instead, a simple distinction has been made between interventions with comparison group study evidence of impact and those with formative evidence of impact from pre-post studies or other non-comparison group methods. (Dartington Social Research Unit et al, 2015: 107)

At the time of writing, the Evidence Panel has not adjudicated, but we might anticipate they will be faced with similar uncertainties. The programmes work sometimes for some people in some contexts, but always need further evaluation. A rich seam of work is here to be mined for the evaluators. We can also foresee methodological stipulations which prescribe increasingly rigorous experimental designs in the evaluation of programmes. Evaluations have a long history of equivocation, forever impelling the search for more sophisticated methodological sensitivity, rigour and purity, qualities which often pull in opposing directions.

The fetish of technique: the randomised controlled trial

The randomised controlled trial (RCT), the sine qua non of evidence-based medicine, holds a special place in the liturgies of prevention science. It may be argued that the historical conditions which facilitated the ascent of the evidence-based movement were not so much the desire to correct error, but an attempt to control resources (Saarni and Gylling, 2004). *Plus ça change*. Evidence-based practice/policy (EBP) intrinsically provides a rationale to accomplish a shift from implicit to explicit rationing: under conditions where costs have to be contained, mechanisms must be found for limiting the freedom of clinicians to prescribe and treat, and commissioners to commission.

As the gold standard of EBP, we now consider the RCT in critical depth. RCTs randomly allocate patients between a group who will receive the treatment under investigation, and a control group who will receive a placebo (or no treatment) and/or an existing conventional treatment. Ideally, neither the clinician nor the patient should know who is receiving the treatment (that is, the trial should be 'double-blind'). Meta-analyses and systematic reviews of RCTs are at the very pinnacle of the hierarchy of evidence. A range of specialist centres such as the Cochrane Centre in Oxford (named after Professor A.L. Cochrane who, during the early 1970s, argued for and eventually popularised the randomised controlled trial) have been established to scrutinise research findings for evidence of bias or other flaws in design, in the context of medical interventions (typically surgical or pharmaceutical). In the broad-ranging, often interpersonal, interventions associated with prevention science, RCTs are rather more difficult to apply, but that has not halted the pressure for more of them. As Graham Allen argues in his report, with reference to a typical intervention (Nottingham Life Skills), he makes the case for the establishment of the Early Intervention Foundation, mentioned earlier:

> Like many UK Early Intervention programmes, Nottingham Life Skills has been evaluated many times, always with promising results, but it will need to use a method, such as randomised controlled trial, to meet the standards of evidence used in my review, devised by internationally renowned practitioners. ... This evaluation would produce the specific estimate of impact on children's social and emotional health ... *What the Nottingham Life Skills programme currently lacks, in common with many other excellent UK-designed Early Intervention programmes, is an 'effect size', which the economists can plug into their models used in advising investors about where to get the best return of their scarce resources.* (Allen, 2011a: 77, emphasis added)

Nottingham Life Skills is aimed at strengthening the social and emotional capabilities of Nottingham teenagers. Graham Allen really likes it, but the programme has a long climb ahead if it is to receive his endorsement for public funding. It seems we can no longer support programmes because they are morally right, we must instead invest in a randomised controlled trial, and nothing less. Let us examine the thought style here and its effects. There are some problems with reducing the processes of State intervention to the question 'what works?'. The assumptions of EBP, and the reign of the RCT, have become inextricably tied up with the legitimation of prevention science and the allocation of resources. This has consequences, and we can learn a little about the challenges of this approach by examining debates in the US about the use of RCTs in psychotherapy.

Since the time of Breuer and Freud, psychotherapy has been formulated in one form or another as the 'talking cure', and this assumption has long underpinned the research programme for psychotherapy:

> The patient communicates something; the therapist communicates something in response ... What the therapist communicates is very likely multidimensional ... and may be different at different phases of the interaction for different kinds of patients. Similarly, what the patient communicates and/or experiences differently is likely multidimensional ... and may be different at distinct phases of the interaction. The enormous task of psychotherapy theory and research is that of filling in the variables of this paradigm. (Kiesler, 1966: 130)

Evaluation of such interventions through medical-style methods such as the RCT has become known as the 'drug metaphor' (Stiles and Shapiro, 1989), as it clearly makes explicit analogies between psychotherapy and psychopharmacological research. That is, the paradigm views psychotherapy as comprising 'active ingredients' (for example, interpretations, confrontation, reflection and so on), which are supplied (like a drug) by the therapist to the client, along with a variety of 'fillers' and scene-setting features. At the most simplistic level, if a component is 'active' then 'high levels' within therapy should predict more positive outcomes. If this is not the case then the 'ingredient' is assumed to be 'inert'. The drug metaphor in psychotherapy research precedes the evidence-based practice movement by some three decades, and owes some of its dominance to the medical lineage of psychotherapy. However, its significance has been amplified by the rationing demands of insurance-based health care, and increasingly those of publicly funded interventions in the UK.

There is a robust critique of the paradigm from within psychotherapy research itself. In particular, the drug metaphor has been criticised on the following grounds. It assumes that *process* and *outcome* are readily distinguishable from each other, that is, that client outcomes are a direct linear product of the therapeutic process. In pharmaceutical trials, drugs can be manipulated independently of the patient's condition, but in psychotherapy, process components may reflect changes or 'outcomes' which have already occurred, or are the result of some life event not directly related to the therapy.

The drug metaphor also makes assumptions about 'dosage'. That is, that 'active' ingredients of specific therapies remain constant, regardless of who is practising the therapy and their relationship with the patient, an assumption that Stiles and Shapiro deem 'absurd' (1989: 527). Despite the very real differences which exist between various kinds of therapy in relation to theoretical orientation, techniques and interviewing practices, the outcomes for patients appear to be very similar and independent of the particular therapy deployed. This 'equivalence paradox' (Stiles et al, 1986) again calls into question the notion of linear change based on a number of variables which can somehow be isolated from the therapeutic relationship. Finally, the drug metaphor ignores the effects of the communicative practices of the client (Stiles and Shapiro, 1989). Clients are not inert: they make contingent choices about what they introduce as a topic for discussion, what they conceal and what they reveal. As Owen (1999) notes:

> Rather than all therapeutic input lying under the control of the therapist, it is also the case that clients and their abilities play a part in regulating therapy and in becoming 'active ingredients' in making their own changes. (Owen, 1999: 205)

These arguments clearly apply to any intervention which has multiple actors and an interactional, interpersonal focus. Nevertheless, RCTs have some strong advocates from within the social care profession, and the arguments in their favour merit our examination here. Forrester (2012), for example, explains the value of control groups:

> Randomly allocating families to [a family centre] and to 'normal service' and then following-up their welfare would provide a much stronger measure of the impact of the Centre – because other explanations would be excluded. ... if there were positive differences we could be fairly confident in concluding that they were a result of the Family Centre's work. (Forrester, 2012: 443)

Forrester is right to assert that social work, in the UK in particular, has been slow to adapt the RCT for its own purposes. There are some settings where randomisation would be helpful in disambiguating some of the differences between approaches. However, adaptation is essential if RCTs are to be applied in social care settings. For example, it is difficult to conceive of a double-blind RCT in social work: people obviously know whether or not they are attending a family centre, and indeed whether they are working in one. Furthermore, there is always a problem with context dependency; it may work here but will it work there (Cartwright and Munro, 2010)?

Notwithstanding these concerns, applying techniques from RCTs, like random allocation, may bear fruit in providing evidence which packs a political punch, which is Graham Allen's point earlier. This is why prevention science is so keen on their application. For example, these methods have the potential to evaluate practitioner-led initiatives. Task-centred casework, for instance, followed this very trajectory and provides an instructive example of the biases this inevitably creates (Reid and Shyne, 1969).

> The first RCT of social work examined intensive long-term social work for teenage boys 'at risk' of delinquency and followed them up for some years. The boys and the

workers talked very positively about the service, but on the key measures relating to crime, employment, and other outcomes there was either no difference or the children receiving the intervention did worse. (Forrester, 2012: 443)

So, the promises and the pitfalls of RCTs in socially based interventions are made manifest. What counts as an outcome? Who decides what a 'key measure' is? At what point in time do we measure 'change'? How long do families get 'on the programme', before their 'outcomes' are measured? Tunstill and Blewett (2015) dub this 'outcomes theology', noting its distorting effect on policy and practice. Thus, as Pearce et al note:

> To be sure, randomised trials can offer a counter-weight to unwarranted certainty or decision-making that rests on a narrow set of assumptions drawn from previous experience or personal bias. But judgments must still be made about the nature of the question a trial is meant to address (could it be asking the 'wrong' question?) and about the role of potential bias in interpreting the evidence generated (what assumptions have been made and could they be contested?). This is the paradox of randomised trial evidence: it opens up expert judgment to scrutiny, but this scrutiny in turn requires further expertise. (Pearce et al, 2015: 6)

The current moral settlements on what should be done with 'troubled families' or with 'children at risk' turn these highly political questions into seemingly self-evident social goods. But these are contestable, political and moral matters, whichever methodological approach is taken, and RCTs do not neutralise the choices.

Let us illustrate our point briefly, taking the example of family group conferences (FGCs). Originating in New Zealand, and originally used to allow social work professionals to work in a way consistent with Maori values and culture, a family group conference is a family-led process whereby extended family members, and their networks, meet to plan and make decisions for a child who is deemed to be at risk. Meetings are facilitated by an independent family group conference coordinator to prepare for the meeting. Typically, in the first part of the meeting professionals lay out their concerns about risks and discuss what support could be made available. The second part of the meeting allows 'private family time', in which family members meet to make a plan for the child. Provided the plan is safe, the family is supported to bring it to fruition. There have been, to date, around 100 studies of FGCs (Fisher and Marsh, 2015; Connolly et al, 2009). Fisher and Marsh describe some of the difficulties with the creation of a cumulative body of evidence to support the implementation of FGCs: for example, focusing on the decision-making process in the absence of an analysis of system responses and support. The debates show little sign of abating and, outside New Zealand, FGCs have had patchy implementation, tending to be located in 'projects' and 'initiatives'.

What happens, then, if we stop treating FGCs as interventions in need of evaluation to judge their efficacy and cost-effectiveness? What happens if we treat them instead as the democratic right of citizens – which is indeed the case in New Zealand? Whatever pressing dilemmas and questions may still remain in individual cases, we are at least liberated from the cycle of evaluation. Imagine if the idea of a fair trial, so fundamental to our system of justice, were subject to outcome measures? Only if it can be proven that having a fair trial improves outcomes can you have one, otherwise we just bang you up, or let you go. And which outcomes? Fewer crimes? More satisfied victims? And knowing the impact is surely only a part of the story. We have known for decades that handwashing reduces infection, but we know very little about why people don't wash their hands (Petticrew and Roberts, 2003).

Having somewhere to go, and someone to talk to, are ubiquitous features of most interventions. So, why is it that researchers persist in paring down interventions, so bound up in the communicative practices of people, so self-evidently laden with contingent social meanings and matters of relationship and trust, to a set of 'ingredients', easily separable from their medium of transmission? Under the current policy regime, demonstrating effectiveness has become the essential mantra to securing and sustaining funding, and funding is increasingly targeted. Targeting has become a branch of prevention science of waxing ambition, in which biological markers are beginning to play an increasing role.

Implementation science: targeting and intervention efficacy

The troublesome problems of replicability and robustness of results in a good deal of outcome research have exercised the advocates of prevention science. But such vicissitudes are not seen to be a fundamental problem by proponents; absence of evidence does not mean evidence of absence. Acknowledging the variability in outcome measures for young children experiencing preventive interventions, Barlow and Axford argue:

> Problems in demonstrating benefits are not evidence, as some have argued ... of the weakness of the research about the importance of early parenting. Rather, they reflect a continuing lack of the type of nuanced information about what works, for whom, under what circumstances ... that is necessary to ensure that services are effective in meeting the needs of parents experiencing significant adversity. The lack of success in changing outcomes also highlights the need for better use of the rapidly developing 'implementation science' that enables both practitioners and policy makers to deliver services with integrity, and in ways that match parents' needs and their readiness for change. (Barlow and Axford, 2014)

Implementation science thus rushes to the aid of prevention to offer a possible 'cure' for the problems of generalisability. It seeks to address why the effects of 'evidence based' programmes sometimes wane over time and may have unintended effects when applied in a new setting. It also promises to provide economies of scale by combining compatible interventions in particular sites for targeted populations. Implementation science shares the same vocabulary as prevention science, and hence perpetuates its vexing paradoxes. Like prevention science, it is also taking a biological turn. In a special edition of *Frontiers in Psychology* entitled 'Refining prevention: genetic and epigenetic contributions', the editors set out their case:

> The recent expansion of genetic research to include a focus on epigenetic change provides considerable promise for the development of indicated prevention and individually tailored prevention efforts. ... through this special section, we provide a foundation for a new era of prevention research in which the principles of prevention science are combined with genomic science ... we bring together authors to deal with genetic and epigenetically driven processes relevant to depression, substance abuse, and sexual risk taking ... to inform the development of a new generation of prevention programs that go beyond universal programs and sensitively target key processes while providing greater precision

regarding prediction of population-level impact. (Beach and Sales, 2016: 2–3)

The papers in the special edition explore genetic targeting across a range of substance use and psychosocial problems, including cigarette smoking, the impact of divorce on depression in young adults, and the benefit of 'protective parenting' on inflammatory responses in adolescence. There is nothing modest about these aspirations, and we can get a glimpse of the direction of travel by examining the arguments associated with this genetic turn in further detail. In a special edition of the journal *Development and Psychopathology* addressing 'what works for whom', Belsky and Van Ijzendoorn (2015) discuss the importance of focusing on the 'genetic makeup' of those receiving interventions as potential determinants or moderators of their efficacy. We have already mentioned the built-in costs of the prevention science paradigm, but for Belsky and Van Ijzendoorn this may be resolved by considering variation in susceptibility to an intervention. This, they argue, may provide the arguments necessary to persuade policy makers that they really are getting more bounce for the ounce: more effective genetic and epigenetic targeting is the way forward.

To illustrate the argument, we will look at one of the studies in that special issue in more depth and examine some typical results. The study is by Cleveland et al (2015), and it is instructive to note that there are 10 authors on the team, showing how labour intensive (and costly) this type of research typically is, which in itself should give us pause. The subject of the intervention is alcohol misuse in early adolescence. The study laments that interventions have had variable outcomes, and the authors speculate that variations in parental involvement may be the factor underlying this variability, with 'greater intervention effects' for 'families with more positive and supportive parenting practices' (Cleveland et al, 2015: 51). The authors also conjecture that genetic influences may play a part and accordingly the study 'focused on how both maternal factors and specific genetic influences may jointly impact intervention effects' (p 52).

The 'primary genetic target' is the *DRD4* gene, a variant of which (the 7+ variant) has been 'linked to attention deficit disorder ... and novelty seeking'[6] (p 53). The study itself formed part of the PROSPER project, a 'community-based research project ... for delivering evidence-based preventive interventions through a university, school and Cooperative Extension collaboration'. In brief, 28 school districts were divided into 14 control and intervention conditions; in the latter, the partnership model was used to deliver an 'evidence-based universal family-focused program', the Strengthening Families program in the 7th grade. Maternal involvement was assessed prior to the intervention (6th grade) using a set of four simple questions put to the children in the study. For example, 'youths' were asked how often they and their mother participated in activities together (such as homework). Impact on alcohol use was assessed three years later in 9th grade, again using a self-report measure: youths answered a simple in-home questionnaire comprising three yes/no questions (for example, the somewhat risibly worded 'Have you ever been drunk from drinking alcohol?'), producing a scale running from 0 to 3.

The analysis focused on the 545 families (60% of the whole cohort) for whom genetic data was available. The results showed a small but significant overall effect for maternal involvement on reported drinking behaviour, but only at the least demanding (5%) level of statistical significance. No direct effects of the gene variant were found, and indeed the intervention itself (while lowering reported alcohol use) also failed to produce a statistically significant outcome. No interactions between pairs of factors were found – for instance, the effectiveness of the intervention did not depend on either the degree of maternal involvement or the presence of the *DRD4* gene variant. A significant three-way interaction was, however, found, suggesting that the three factors interacted in a complex way to influence reported drinking behaviour. This appeared to show that the intervention was more effective when accompanied by maternal involvement for the children with the *DRD4* variant. The level of significance was again low at 5%.

But, as we argue in appendix C, statistical significance is not what counts. Significance means simply that we can determine the likelihood that whatever effects have been found are not simply due to chance fluctuations, unlikely to be replicated in another study with a different sample of individuals. What matters, once significance has been established, is the size of the effect; this is especially so in a practical context where the search is for effective remedial interventions, rather than theory testing and development. Various methods exist for quantifying the magnitude of some effect, as we explain in depth in appendix C, which we strongly urge the reader to consult. Of these, Cohen's d is the most widely used. In essence, this takes into account the degree of underlying variability in the data, as well as headline differences in, for example, the means of the various groups being compared. Conventional 'effect size' categories for Cohen's d are as follows: d less than 0.1 (no effect), d between 0.1 and 0.4 (small effect), d between 0.4 and 0.7 (intermediate effect), d greater than 0.7 (large effect). The d value for the interaction, for example, is reported as

0.41, making it a borderline small/intermediate effect. Exploring the interaction further, Cleveland et al pinpoint the locus of the effect. It appears that the combination of high maternal involvement and the family intervention were effective in lowering self-reported drinking from just over 1.3 to around 0.7 on the three-point scale. Cohen's d for this effect was 0.57, putting it comfortably into the intermediate category.

At face value, this would seem a result worthy of minor celebration. Belsky and Van Ijzendoorn's editorial laments that, to the frustrations of their votaries, the average effects of preventive programmes on development are very modest: 'Barely larger than Cohen's criterion for a weak effect (d = .20)' (p 1). But Cleveland et al strike a more cautious note, making claims that are notably modest:

> In terms of complexity, the current work represents an early stage of research into gene–environment transactions. Much more progress in this line of work is needed before it can translate to practice ... The more immediate implication of finding clear intervention benefits for a genetic subgroup across most levels of maternal involvement is that it underscores the downside of rushing to endorse the conclusion that an intervention does not work. (p 64)

And even if genetic targeting were helpful, it raises profound moral issues. Belsky and Van Ijzendoorn themselves are not unmindful of the ethical quagmire their genetic advocacy may create in terms of stigma, inequality in access to services and associated discrimination; for example, only children rescued from the worst effects of Romanian orphanages who carried '5-HTTLPR short alleles' showed a reduction in 'indiscriminate friendliness', a result of high-quality foster care. Does this mean that children without the allele should be afforded worse-quality care?

In terms of thought style, Cleveland et al's study provides a useful exhibit, raising profound issues which, for us, go to the heart of the matter. While the identification of a favourable genetic subgroup may seem to be a great breakthrough, in itself it explains nothing at all. An inauspicious configuration of DNA bases explicates no more than an inauspicious configuration of stars; on its own, it is no more than a correlation, a sign, and to think otherwise is pure magic. Scientific explanations require a cogently worked-out mechanism leading from cause to effect. Genes on their own cannot explain why the intervention worked for one subgroup of mothers for one subgroup of children; they lead only to an aporia, an impasse: as we remarked in chapter three, explanations are useless which appeal 'to events taking place somewhere else, at some other level of observation'. The explanation must be sought at the level of the behaviour to be explained. To know why the intervention seemingly worked for this combination of mothers and children, we need direct insights into the lives, behaviours and dynamics of those family configurations. In other words, if the genetic narrative is to carry weight, we need to ascend from the genetic level to the domain of behaviour.

Of course, genetics does have something to say at this level. From the introduction to the paper, we learn that the *DRD4* gene is associated with an amorphous gallimaufry of exotic behaviours, mainly negative, though some positive in the right context: *ADHD*, novelty-seeking, oppositional defiant disorder, externalising behaviour problems, environmental openness, altruism, social bonding, and so on. Certainly, a promiscuous little gene to give rise to such abundance, and there are candidate behaviours here which could help explain the present findings. Cleveland et al appear to opt for a greater susceptibility to training as the key in their introduction. This would seem a rather tendentious, circular choice, and as their study makes no attempt to measure such a sensibility, it is a choice that must remain in the domain of pure speculation. Family behaviour actually features very little in their paper: after the speculations of the Introduction, the remainder is couched almost exclusively in the genetic realm in terms of 'explaining' their findings, pseudo-explanations which explain nothing.

Yet cogent explanations are available, providing we stay in the world of the behavioural. Although a well-defined behavioural phenotype for *DRD4* is hard to nail down, enough is said to suggest that children with this variant will show challenging behaviours and be difficult to parent. At the behavioural level, we may plausibly speculate that the programme provides welcome support to those mothers struggling with difficult children, and given that both sides benefit, the children are led to report higher levels of 'maternal behaviour' and better behaviour themselves (although neither of these outcomes is objectively shown by the study). And there you have it, a potentially adequate causal explanation albeit a speculative one.

The lesson is clear. We are not arguing that this explanation is correct, merely making the point that the behavioural domain of explanation is the appropriate one, and that the genetic one is not; it is hopelessly reductive, lacks 'requisite variety',[7] and is at the wrong level. The genetic thought style on its own adds nothing other than a veneer of pseudoscience. Here it also responsibilises mothers, lionises the targeted intervention, and gives no agency to children. Worse than this, we must interrogate its direction of travel: genetic explanations bespeak genetic remedies, where else can they go? It is telling, for instance, that the only form of targeting of interest in such studies is genetic: why not targeting based on behavioural criteria? Ontologically, it would surely be more sensible to look at behavioural markers, which might well prove more effective. At least it would be better to base the choice of criteria on empirical grounds rather than ideological preconceptions.

We could go on and make further important points about the study. It is noteworthy that another genetic variant was looked at, a variant of the gene responsible for serotonin production. Although maternal involvement came through again as an important factor, overall the pattern of effects was quite different and somewhat confusing. Not only did the genetic variant behave against expectations, it was the lack of intervention which engendered the reductions in drinking![8] The crudeness of the behavioural analysis also stands out compared to the technological sophistication of the genotyping; simple questionnaires relying on self-report, and all its attendant biases, gain few marks out of 10 for scientific sophistication. The study must also have been very expensive: how much better to have spent the research funding on intense, ethnographic style involvement with the families; then we might have learned something worth knowing.

A further example of the lack of critical reflexivity in genetic research, and of the perils of extrapolation into policy, comes from a recent study by Burghy et al (2012). This study provides a rare example of a longitudinal study of children and is noteworthy because it appears to provide important evidence of a link between early life stress and adult brain function: salivary cortisol levels at age 4.5 are very strongly correlated with depressed activity in the circuitry of amygdala-prefrontal cortex at age 18, as revealed by functional brain imaging. However, there are serious dangers in drawing policy conclusions from the evidence provided. First, the correlations are unfeasibly high: 0.78 is the figure quoted. That the correlation between salivary levels measured over a short interval (of weeks) is of the same order, suggests that something is awry. The correlation is also only found for girls, not boys. Do we infer from this that only girls are affected by stress, and that boys should never be removed from abusive situations? Finally, when it comes to examining actual mental health, the correlations with early life stress are either nonexistent or negligible.

Despite the difficulty in finding the elusive 'genetic modulator', there are signs that biomarkers will play an increasing role in future implementation science. A recent protocol for the evaluation of an early intervention project by the Warwick Consortium (2014) saliently states:

> In addition to a range of standardized parent-report and teacher assessment data, we have also included a number of objective assessments ... These include a number of biometric measures (e.g. hair samples to assess cortisol levels at 2 years; buccal cheek swabs to assess epigenetic changes at 3 years; accelerometers to assess activity at 7 years. (p 4)

The uncritical identification of 'biological' with 'objective' (thereby privileging such evidence) should by now be familiar, the hallmark of the neuromolecular thought style, indeed its 'psycho-marker' if you like. Leaving this aside, using genetic susceptibility to argue that only certain children should receive high-quality foster care, or any other sought-after service, because it 'won't work' for others, raises obvious major ethical issues. Indeed, we might argue, it shows the potential futility of this form of approach. Undaunted, Belsky and Van Ijzendoorn argue: '... this should not lead to ignoring replicated evidence that some individuals are more open to environmentally induced changed, for better and for worse, due to their genetic makeup' (p 1).

Conclusion

Let us end this chapter by pondering where the genetic logic might lead. It could only drive us in the direction of screening before we intervene, or screen anyway, screen for the unseen. It produces the notion of 'a new human kind: the susceptible individual' (Rose, 2010: 23), and potentially a great deal of surveillance in the name of producing better people. Surveillance has already become normalised, an inevitable part of contemporary life. In part, through medical screening programmes in the name of public health, but also in response to an international preoccupation with terrorist attacks and advances in technologies for tracking, monitoring, management and control, leading to ID cards, biometrics, social media, and border and airport controls. Like early intervention, these surveillance systems are preventive and for our own good, increasingly defining citizens through a blend of biometric information (fingerprints, retinal imagery, genetic markers and other biological data). But not all citizens are equal:

> Welfare recipients ... are more vulnerable to surveillance ... Persistent stereotypes of poor women, especially women

of color, as inherently suspicious, fraudulent, and wasteful provide ideological support for invasive welfare programs that track their financial and social behavior. [These] communities are more likely to be the site of biometric data collection ... because they have less political power to resist it. (Eubanks, 2014; cited in Giroux, 2014: 130–1)

Finally, we note the invocation by Belsky and Van Ijzendoorn of the potential of epigenetics to open up new avenues of research and policy: 'future work will hopefully extend research of this kind to determine whether ... epigenetic processes are a critical pathway by which intervention effects become instantiated' (p 4).

Biologically uniting nature and nurture, epigenetics promises a great deal, as we shall see soon. Sadly for the editors of the special issue, only one epigenetic study (on rodents) was submitted. We have already seen the spectre of genomic screening for psychological susceptibility, both to 'suboptimal' development and responsiveness to 'treatment'. Epigenetics is playing an increasing role in the discourse of policy and practice regarding what is best for families, what constitutes good parenting; it is the new kid on the block. In February 2016, the Early Intervention Foundation in England asked for evidence to be submitted on interactions between biology and the social environment, noting how 'compelling' are discoveries from biomedical science. We will now look critically at this steadily burgeoning field, and try to imagine where the emerging fascination may take us. We provided a basic overview of some of the key ideas and thought style of epigenetics in chapter two; in the following two chapters we present a detailed analysis of current research and its implications, first looking at animal studies and then research on humans.

Notes

[1] This World Bank report draws together large-scale public health interventions like provision of clean water and nutrition with parenting, developmental and educational programmes based on US prevention science.

[2] http://investinginchildren.eu/interventions/family-nurse-partnership, last accessed 19/01/2017.

[3] http://www.wsipp.wa.gov/ReportFile/1485

[4] http://www.wsipp.wa.gov/ReportFile/1387/Wsipp_Return-on-Investment-Evidence-Based-Options-to-Improve-Statewide-Outcomes-April-2012-Update_Technical-Appendix.pdf

[5] The method for measuring effect size depends on the nature of the measurement in the study, but for studies involving the calculation of means it follows a 'mean difference' method, Cohen's d or something broadly equivalent.

6   The claimed relationship relates to some eye-catching research by Ebstein in the 1990s which appeared to link the gene with the personality trait of novelty seeking (NS). Not all studies have confirmed this association. Subsequent work has linked the gene to substance misuse. Lusher et al (2001) refer to this corpus of research as something of a saga; reviewing the work they conclude that 'there may be an association with DRD4 and NS among severe drug-dependent populations', but that 'as with all sagas we shall have to wait for further developments' (p 498).

7   A term from cybernetics (Wastell, 2011). It conveys the sense that for something to control a process effectively, it must have a repertoire of responses at least as rich as the process under its jurisdiction. Here the variety of behaviours associated with the gene appears to greatly exceed the repertoire of the gene, which only directly governs the production of a single protein.

8   Another genetic polymorphism was looked at, that of the 5-HTT gene involved in the expression of serotonin. Results again indicated the importance of maternal involvement. Interestingly, no effects were found for the intervention per se; while maternal involvement did reduce self-reported drinking, this was primarily for those with the long variant of the gene and occurred in the control condition (no intervention) only. To add to the general confusion, it is the short allele which is normally associated with increased alcohol use, not the long one ... all in all, a bit of a dog's breakfast!

SEVEN

Epigenetics: rat mum to my Mum?

The last chapter reviewed the aspirations and thought styles of the various actors involved in the prevention science project. We saw that epigenetic mechanisms are starting to be invoked in the name of prevention, treatment and targeting. It is the latest technology to be brought to bear in the project of fixing people, and this chapter will dig into the epigenetic thought style in depth, by analysing some of the seminal work as well as giving a more general flavour of the mainstream research being undertaken, its methods and direction of travel. The bulk of the experimental research is on animals in laboratory settings, using behavioural paradigms which are intended to serve as meaningful surrogates for the human situation. We have witnessed this style of work before. The chapter introduces our cast of laboratory animals, examining how they are bred and handled experimentally to produce findings which seem to transfer so convincingly from the Perspex cage of the laboratory to the disadvantaged housing estate – from rat mum to your Mum.

In an informative recent review paper, Cunliffe (2015) summarises the epigenetic argument thus: 'A growing body of evidence indicates that experiences acquired during development, childhood, or adulthood induce changes in gene expression, which impart cumulative, long-lasting effects on health, well-being and vulnerability to disease' (p 59).

The statement very much captures the progressive aspirations of our times, that environmental impacts can exert profound effects on individual health and welfare, via their influence on epigenetic mechanisms, and that this understanding will provide the foundations for public health programmes of various kinds. In this chapter and the next, we aim to provide a critical examination of key developments in epigenetics, by examining relevant examples of journal science. We will consider animal evidence first, before moving to human studies in the next chapter.

Regarding animal work, the crux of the epigenetic argument is captured in the following extract, again from Cunliffe (2015):

Acutely stressful experiences can leave behind strong
memories that intensify responses when similar stimuli are
encountered again. The molecular basis of this form of
memory is poorly understood, but epigenetic mechanisms
play important roles. Classic studies in rodent animal models
and humans have demonstrated a close relationship between
elevated stress in early life and the appearance of behavioural
disorders in later life. (p 59)

The second sentence and its caveat are worth close attention; the
sentence suggests, on the one hand, that our understanding is
currently somewhat limited, yet it proceeds to declare confidently
that epigenetic processes play important roles. This certainty is further
amplified in the second sentence; the tone is now unequivocal.
But is this certainty justified? Are the 'classic studies' as decisive as
implied? We will now focus on one these studies, that of Weaver et
al, 'Epigenetic programming by maternal behavior', published in the
prestigious journal *Nature Neuroscience* in 2004. This really is a classic
paper which has been hugely influential: on typing 'epigenetic' into
Google Scholar, the paper comes up as the third most cited epigenetics
paper of all time, with 3,588 citations (as of November 2015). It is
well worth while taking a detailed look. We apologise in advance to
the reader, as our investigations eventually followed a rather longer
and more winding road than we had expected. But tracing the origins
of the 2004 classic turned out to be absolutely vital, as the reader will
see. So please bear with the twists, turns and various tangents of our
archaeological excavations.

Classic studies

One of the co-authors of the 2004 paper is Michael Meaney, whom
we encountered in chapter one. The study represents a landmark in
the development of his pioneering work on the stress response of
rodents, going back to a paper published 30 years previously (Meaney
et al, 1985). That earlier study had shown that laboratory rats which
had been handled by experimenters and separated from their mothers
for 15 minutes every day (placed in a plastic container away from the
mother's cage) showed 24% higher concentrations of the glucocorticoid
receptor (GR) in the hippocampus. The GR is an important actor in
our story, and we have already made its acquaintance in chapter two.
Such receptors within the intracellular fluid are tuned to cortisol, and
other glucocorticoids; when activated they regulate the expression of

genes concerned with the immune response and metabolism. Whereas cortisol is the predominant glucocorticoid in humans, another steroid hormone, corticosterone, is the dominant glucocorticoid in rodents.

The differential stress reactivity of the handled versus nonhandled rats was assessed using a vibratory stress test, which involved 30 minutes in a cage attached to a 'moving shakerbath'. Corticosterone levels remained significantly elevated in the nonhandled rats 90 minutes after the test, compared to the handled rats, for whom the levels had returned to baseline after 60 minutes. The study concludes: 'our findings suggest that the mechanism by which the early environment influences the stress response involves the regulation of GR concentrations in the hippocampus' (Meaney et al, 1985: 734).

Crucially, the paper does not explain why human handling and maternal separation during suckling is apparently so beneficial in developing a greater level of resistance to stress. We might plausibly expect such experiences to be rather stressful. For an explanation of this seeming paradox, we need to go back further in time, to two papers cited by Meaney et al: Levine (1962) and Ader (1970). Both papers were inspired by the idea, prevalent at that time, that 'infantile stimulation' was beneficial:

> Recent experiments have … shown that animals which have been treated in a variety of ways as infants … [such as] daily exposure to fear-producing stimuli … tend to exhibit a less pronounced physiological response to stress in adulthood … infantile stimulation of an animal produces resistance to stress. (Levine, 1962: 795)

Handling rats prior to exposure to stress was the accepted way of providing such beneficial stimulation. To examine the stress response, both the early studies involved placing rats in a 'shock chamber' where they were subjected to electric shocks. Levine found no evidence that handling helped the rats cope with this noxious experience, in fact the levels of corticosterone were higher for the handled rats. Ader's study showed a more nuanced pattern of effects: the mere fact of putting the animal in the novel environment of the shock chamber produced a larger surge in corticosterone than the subsequent electrocutions (incidentally, showing that psychological stress is more potent than physical stress); second, handling reduced the corticosterone response, particularly for female rats; third, it made no difference whether the handling occurred during weaning or after weaning, the benefits of stimulation were equivalent. The latter result is important; the authors conclude that their results:

> ... *cast serious doubt on the hypothesis that* ... *there is a critical period* during which handling will exert a maximum effect upon adrenocortical reactivity at maturity ... The reduction in adrenocortical reactivity in animals handled before or after weaning relative to non-handled controls may reflect an adaptation or *learning phenomenon.* (Ader, 1970: 839, emphasis added)

The reference to 'adrenocortical reactivity' relates to the HPA axis, introduced in chapter two, which is believed to play a central role in the regulation of the stress response. A degree of cognitive mediation is suggested by the extract; the effects do not reflect some automatic emotional response. The benefits of early stimulation would seem to reflect the experiences of a sentient creature as it learns more about the world, or so it would appear. But there is still a paradox, as it is hard to see that the experiences of the handled rats are benign: they have experienced human coercion, maternal separation, isolation in a plastic container. Such 'stimulation' would appear to be rather stressful, on the face of it. This would seem to bring us to the speculative conclusion that the handled rodents in these early studies, including Meaney et al (1985), were more resilient because they had endured a more stressful upbringing. We will return to this speculation later in the chapter, bringing forward more evidence to support its validity. Here we confine ourselves to the suggestion that it is this early stress that has better equipped the handled rats for future challenges than the rats exempted from such stress, living comfortably 'at home' with their mothers, if we may be forgiven an anthropomorphic trope.

In fact, this is not such a paradox at all, especially if we follow the anthropomorphic thread from the rat world to the human world. This gives a rather more nuanced understanding of the effects of early adversity, which in the animal studies shows a complex pattern of findings, with different studies showing contradictory effects. Reviewing the animal work and its translation to the impact of social adversity in the human situation, Rutter (1991) sagely concludes:

> Acute stresses in adults can have a 'steeling' effect and in children too there is evidence that some forms of separation may *protect* children from the stresses of hospital admission ... Presumably, it matters whether the child emerges

> successfully from the first stress with improved coping
> mechanisms or a more effective physiological response. If
> he does he may become more stress resistant [otherwise] he
> may become more vulnerable. (Rutter, 1991: 195)

Having made this important digression, we return to the 2004 classic. The focus of this study, on the face of it, is not human handling but the maternal behaviour of the rodent mothers. The paper notes that there are stable patterns of maternal behaviour (licking and grooming, LG, and arched back nursing, ABN) in rats over the first week of lactation. Evidence is cited that the offspring of high LG-ABN mothers are less fearful, and show more modest HPA responses, than their less nurtured counterparts, and that this is associated with increased hippocampal GR expression and 'more modest HPA responses to stress' (Weaver et al, 2004: 847). The authors cite a study in 1989 which shows that the beneficial effects of 'early experience' (handling) were abolished by chronic doses of corticosterone, which reduced both GR expression and the HPA response to the level of nonhandled controls. From this evidence, the authors reiterate their view that hippocampal GR expression mediates the effect of early experience on HPA reactivity.

The aim of the 'classic study' was to find the epigenetic mechanisms of this effect, focusing on the methylation pattern of a short section, or 'exon',[1] of the gene responsible for GR expression in the rat hippocampus. The section in question (exon 1_7) is around 120 nucleotide bases in length containing 17 CpG pairs, which it will be remembered from chapter two are sites of potential methylation. At one end of the exon is a 'binding site' for a transcription factor (NGFI-A); previous studies have linked expression of NGFI-A to maternal behaviour, which made this site of particular interest – it includes two CpG pairs (sites 16 and 17). But before stepping through the various experiments in the paper, we note that some key information is in the technical supplement, including the observation that the offspring of high LG-ABN mothers themselves showed more licking, grooming and arched back nursing (which is consistent with previous findings that the maternal behaviour of female offspring is highly correlated with that of the mother).[2]

The first experiment examined the effects of maternal behaviour, finding increased methylation at many of the sites in exon 1_7, and in particular at site 16 which was methylated for the offspring of all the low LG-ABN mothers, and very rarely for the offspring of high LG-ABN dams. The next experiment involved the cross-fostering of offspring. This found that the methylation status of site 16 reflected the behaviour of the adoptive, not the biological parent, suggesting it directly reflected the nurturing behaviour of the mother. This leads to the important conclusion that 'variations in maternal care directly alter methylation status of the exon 1_7 ... demonstrat[ing] that a DNA methylation pattern can be established through a behavioural mode of programming without germ line transmission' (p 849). The following experiment examined when in development this epigenetic imprint occurred, comparing the methylation of site 16 just prior to birth and at days 1, 6 21 and 91 postnatally. Before birth, site 16 was unmethylated for all offspring, and 'strikingly' one day after birth, it was equally methylated for both. Thereafter, the differences in methylation between the two groups began to emerge and were established by day 6 (P6) and sustained through to P91. The authors conclude that 'the group difference in DNA methylation occurs as a function of maternal behaviour over the first week of life' (Weaver et al, 2004: 850).

In the following experiment, attention switches to the second of our epigenetic mechanisms, histone acetylation, which we will recall from chapter two is associated with increased gene expression. The study demonstrated a significant increase in acetylation for the pups of high compared to low LG-ABN mothers; it also showed a three-fold increase in the binding of NGFI-A to exon 1_7. This is consistent with the high level of methylation at site 16 in te low LG/ABN mothers, which would be expected to inhibit binding of the transcription factor (and hence inhibit expression of the GR gene). The following experiment investigated the pharmacological reversibility of the methylation effect using a drug (trichostatin A, TSA) which inhibits enzymes involved in histone deacetylation, thereby promoting acetylation. This treatment was found to raise levels of histone acetylation and NGFI-A binding of the adult offspring of low LG-ABN mothers compared to those of high LG-ABN mothers, as well as lowering methylation levels (including site 16) to comparable levels in the two groups.[3] The following experiment focused on GR expression itself, that is, the final product synthesised by the GR gene. It demonstrated that the TSA treatment produced comparable levels of GR expression in both groups of mothers.[4] The final experiment involved subjecting the adult rats (P90) to a stress test, involving 20 minutes of restraint. Whereas corticosterone levels in the untreated adult offspring of low LG-ABN mothers were elevated as a result of stress, levels in TSA-treated pups were no different from that of the pups of high LG-ABN mothers.

In sum, a technically impressive, convergent set of experiments, producing evidence 'consistent with idea that the maternal effect on GR expression and HPA responses to stress is mediated by alterations in chromatin structure' (p 852). More specifically, the authors propose that reduced histone acetylation and increased methylation of exon 1_7 result in reducing binding of the NGFI-A to the promoter region of the GR gene, which in turns is responsible for reduced GR expression and an elevated HPA stress response. The authors conclude:

> DNA methylation represents a stable epigenetic mark; therefore, our findings provide an explanation for the enduring effect on mother–infant interactions over the first week of postnatal life on HPA responses to stress in the offspring ... We propose that effects on chromatin structure such as those described here serve as an intermediate process that imprints dynamic environmental experiences on the fixed genome, resulting in stable alterations in phenotype. (Weaver et al, 2004: 852)

Critical reflections on epigenetic programming by maternal behaviour (EPMB)

Despite the seemingly formidable body of evidence it appears to assemble, we venture to raise a number of concerns about the epigenetic programming by maternal behaviour (EPMB) classic. First, does the claim that methylation patterns once established are stable, with enduring effects, really stand up? We have noted in chapter two that the mechanisms of methylation are poorly understood and that methylated imprints are likely held in place by active regulatory processes. We have cited evidence of rapid changes in methylation in response to changing metabolic demands and psychological states. The data in the study are consistent with this lability, showing that methylation patterns develop and change rapidly in response to environmental inputs, in this case maternal care over the first week of life. But, has the study shown that such profiles once so-established are fixed for ever? This would seem odd, given their initial lability. An alternative possibility is that the environment has been stable, as we assume it will be in the laboratory as opposed to the wild. If the environment has not changed over the early life of the rat as it matures into adulthood, then why should the epigenetic marks change? It is intriguing, given the roots of the study in the literature on infant stimulation, that no behavioural manipulations were carried out post-weaning. As Ader (1970) showed, in the study cited by Weaver et al (2004), stimulation after weaning significantly modulates the stress response. It is interesting, and potentially significant, that such an intervention was not deployed and that the only remedial action taken was pharmacological.

Our second concern bears on the concluding claims which would seem to suggest that a form of epigenetic inheritance has been shown. First, we are confused. The authors talk about mothers passing on a defensive response to a threat which they have experienced; but this is not the case here, as only the pups were subjected to the stress test. Leaving aside this aporia, it is clear that epigenetic marks do not provide a mechanism for transmitting adaptive behaviours, otherwise the fostered rats would have reproduced both the epigenetic imprint and the maternal behaviours of their biological mothers. That they reproduce the maternal behaviour of their adoptive mothers indicates a behavioural mode of transmission: a cultural, not a biological, effect. What the study shows is no more than its more modest claims, that differences in maternal nurturing can induce differences in the wellbeing of offspring, in that they appear to be better able to cope with stress. When such phenotypic differences are found, correlated epigenetic modifications are observed. In the terminology of chapter two, there is no evidence that epigenetic marks are in any way causal, they are merely signs; the determining factor would appear to be the mother's behaviour. Earlier work by Meaney and his group (for example, Meaney, 2001) appears to recognise that the mode of transmission is non-genomic, but the argument in the classic paper seems somewhat confused.

Our third concern highlights the poverty of the explanation for the observed results. Although demonstrating a network of associations between DNA methylation and GR expression in the hippocampus on the one hand, and maternal behaviour and stress reactivity on the other, no explanation is offered of the mechanisms whereby this relationship operates. In particular, why is 'upregulation' of hippocampal GR expression correlated with 'downregulation' of the HPA axis? What we have is an unexplained correlation, not a functional explanation. It is necessary to turn to earlier papers to derive an understanding of how this works (Meaney, 2001). The negative feedback loop (see chapter two), whereby circulating glucocorticoids suppress hypothalamic and pituitary activation, is the claimed locus for the effect:

> Increased negative feedback sensitivity to glucocorticoids is related to increased GR expression in the hippocampus ... alterations in glucocorticoid expression are a critical feature for the effect of the early environment on negative

feedback sensitivity and HPA responses to stress. (Meaney, 2001: 1166)

There we have it, an explanation couched entirely at the level of hormonal effects; the central role of the hippocampus in learning and memory does not feature anywhere.[5] This is a tad surprising given the following extract from an extensive review of 'Brain corticosteroid receptor balance in health and disease' by de Kloet et al (1998), quoted by Meaney (2001).

It is generally accepted that hippocampal formation plays a key role in animals' reactivity to novelty and provides an essential contribution to learning and memory ... The hormone [corticosteroid] does not necessarily cause a behavioral change, but rather influences information processing and thereby affects the likelihood that a particular stimulus elicits an appropriate behavioral response. (p 283)

The rat, as a sentient, cognitive creature attempting to deal with the challenges of its somewhat meagre life in the laboratory is utterly effaced by the reduction of parenting behaviour to the methylation of one gene in one brain structure. This brings us to our next point: how do the normative concepts of good and bad mothering, so strongly implied in the study, get made?

Building the normative case: making good and bad mothers

Making normative judgements about whether features of behaviour are good or bad, adaptive or otherwise, surely means that the environment must be taken into account. But before pursuing this, let us note a seeming paradox when the classic study is lined up with the earlier work on handling. That both handling (which involves maternal separation and isolation) and high nurturance seem to confer identical benefits in terms of GR expression and stress reactivity seems, for the lay reader, rather contradictory at first sight; it did for us. Actually, there is a clear link between handling and nurturance. A paper by Meaney and colleagues in 1997 (Liu et al, 1997) reports that handling has a dramatic effect on mother–pup interactions: 'Mothers of handled pups showed increased levels of licking and grooming and arched back nursing compared with mothers of non-handled pups' (p 1660). Rates of licking and grooming roughly doubled.

The paper confirms that (human) handling is experienced as stressful by pups, noting that 'the artificial and nonspecific nature of the handling paradigm is unsettling' (p 1661) and leads to 'increased vocalisation in pups, which in turn leads to more maternal care, including licking and grooming' (p 1661). We now appreciate how handling makes rats more resilient; they have learned to cope with enforced separation through the more attentive grooming of their mothers, which was at least in part elicited by their distress.

Following the observational study of handling, the 1997 paper goes on to examine the impact of 'naturally occurring' differences in maternal care on GR expression and HPA responses in offspring. A group of mothers were examined; they were divided into two groups based on their LG-ABN scores, either above or below the mean level. Table 7.1 shows the results for both studies.

Table 7.1: Licking and grooming rates (mean number of observations out of 1,200)

Study 1: Handling study	
Handled	155
Nonhandled	78
Study 2: Maternal behaviour	
High LG-ABN	136
Low LG-ABN	72

On close inspection, the results are rather interesting from a purely behavioural of view. They suggest that a new phenotype has been appeared *ex nihilo* in study 2, the high LG-ABN 'supermum'; such a high rate of spontaneous maternal care in the second study (an average of 136 incidents of licking and grooming) is nowhere to be seen in the first experiment (the mean is 78 incidents), unless artificially produced by handling. But Liu et al neither note nor comment on this rather remarkable development; the focus is on stress responses, showing that high LG-ABN mothering was associated with both higher GR expression in the hippocampus and a reduced stress response. So, there we have it, the missing link. The reason why handling confers the same benefits as high licking and grooming is because it engenders the same style of maternal care.

But the situation is not so simple. Physiologically, the effects may be the same, but high maternal care induced by handling, as opposed to its spontaneous appearance, represent radically different situations: the former involves a degree of stress for both parties and an opportunity for the pup to learn more about its world.[6] Behaviourally and physiologically we can understand why the handled rats are more resilient: they have learned to cope with a stressful experience, and that their hippocampal GR levels are raised is entirely consistent with current understanding of the facilitative effects of moderate stress on learning, which we noted in chapter two. But no such adaptive explanation springs to mind for the apparently beneficial effects of spontaneously raised maternal care. Yet despite this, the paper would seem to strike a normative position on parenting, that more nurturing is good (supermums) and that the low LG-ABN mothers are somehow neglectful.

Let us look more closely. Three distinct phenotypes are seen over the two experiments (Liu et al, 1997 and Weaver et al, 2004): high LG-ABN in response to a distressed infant, high LG-ABN where as far as we know no particular distress is involved, and low LG-ABN in a similarly nonstressed scenario. We also note, from the first experiment, that the latter was the norm for the laboratory mother. High LG-ABN is clearly abnormal; it did not appear on the normal spectrum of maternal care in study 1, and was only produced by the intervention of the experimenters. A profound reversal has thus taken place: the normal has somehow become deficient, and the abnormal has become the new normal. This has the feel of a conjuring trick, but it is a legerdemain of the profoundest implications; normal maternal behaviour has apparently been pathologised.

We would go further and question whether the paper has really shown that low LG-ABN mothers are somehow neglectful. This means that we must attend carefully to the ecology of the laboratory; only in this context can judgements be made about whether behaviour is adaptive or otherwise.[7] In this respect, a paper by Macri and Würbel (2006) is helpful. Although in some ways, the residential circumstances of the laboratory rat can be likened to an 'ideal home' (Würbel, 2001), especially for breeding purposes (no predators, the experimenters apart; a sufficient supply of food, nesting material and so on), it possesses unique features by comparison to the wild. The concept of 'developmental plasticity' is central to Macri and Würbel's ecological analysis, referring to changes in neural circuitry as a result of environmental interactions, learning and development. The degree of such plasticity depends on environmental variation:

> If environments vary unpredictably across time, no early
> cues will be available to developing animals that predict

> the environment in which the animals will live once adult. In this case, natural selection tends to favor the evolution of limited plasticity. Thus, potential prey with limited information about the future presence of predators will develop an invariable defensive phenotype as if predators posed a continual threat (Macri and Würbel, 2006: 668)

This is surely the existential situation of the laboratory rat; there is nothing it can learn during its upbringing which will prepare it for the challenges ahead. Its life is entirely determined by the whims of the experimenter and the goals of the research programme. The all-important imperative for the rat, as for any animal, is long-term reproductive success, and there is nothing it can do to influence this. Learning has a metabolic cost: energy is inevitably expended as the animal explores its world, even the production of more GRs has a cost. Why would a cell produce more than it needs? The reduced expression for the offspring of low LG-ABN mothers may therefore be about right: as there is no useful learning to be done, why learn?! Best to do the minimum and prepare for the worst. So from the perspective of ecological behaviour, the caring style of the non-nurturing mothers is arguably the optimal one. Their offspring are right to be fearful, living in a surreal world with no means of escape; only torture and death lie ahead. They may not know this but they would be right to sense it. This leads to an interesting speculation: which of the two groups of offspring might be expected to survive best in the wild? That would be a fairer test for the low LG-ABN mothers. Long-term reproductive success is what counts, as we have said, not performance on some arbitrary test. Perhaps the less fearful, coddled offspring, their hippocampi throbbing with GR, would venture forth boldly into the world, only to be gobbled up by the first passing predator. In the laboratory, we might ask if there were a possibility of escape (say, from the stress test) which of the two types of offspring would have the better chance? Our money is on the fearful, stressed pups, not their calmer cousins.

Despite these reflections, the 2004 paper does seem to present high LG-ABN mothering as a positive ideal. It is hard to read the paper in any other way, in fact it reads as if it has been set up to demonstrate this. No attempt is made, for instance, to examine whether the maternal style of the low LG-ABN mothers is better, despite the reference to the passing on of potentially adaptive behaviours in the concluding comments. No evidence is brought forward that offspring are in any way distressed by their 'neglectful mothers'. This makes the drug treatment (TSA) all the more egregious; why not some other form of therapy, like handling, for instance? Their 'neglectful' mothering has not been shown to be negligent, so why treat it as such? Considering it to be deficient may have more to say about the ideological positions of the experimenters, than the maternal efficacy of the rat mothers. Meaney (2001) has made his normative position clear, as we saw in chapter two: 'Cold, distant parent–child relationships are associated with a significantly increased risk of depression and anxiety in later life ... warm, nurturing families tend to promote resistance to stress and to diminish vulnerability' (p 1162). Of course, like the rest of us, experimenters are perfectly entitled to hold ideological positions, but these are not morally neutral.

Finally, and most importantly, we are concerned about the sheer lack of debate and controversy regarding work that is so seminal. Within the journal science, there is some critique, though it was hard to find. Macri and Würbel (2006) challenge Meaney's linear model of stress and its mediation by maternal behaviour. They propose a rather more sophisticated model in which the impact of environmental stress on HPA reactivity takes the form of an inverted U. Stress is also recognised to impact on maternal care, such that care can mitigate the effect of stress on the HPA of offspring, but only up to a point. But critique is not the norm. The work of Meaney and his team is typically received uncritically, as we saw in chapter two, in the extract from Glover et al. Challenging findings, especially where there are significant implications, is (or should be) the normal business of science. We acknowledge that we have played devil's advocate and deliberately gone out of our way to find flaws, question interpretations and expose logical lacunae. Perhaps we have gone too far, but only in the spirit of debate. But legitimate questions there are. That no controversy seems to exist regarding such a seminal paper is a sure sign of the soaring success of a thought style.

The epigenetics of early trauma and the sins of the father

Reflecting on the findings of the EPMB classic, Cunliffe (2015) notes the possibility such work inevitably raises 'for therapeutic intervention by targeting the epigenetic machinery' (p 60). The taste for pharmacological intervention is one of the defining features emerging from much of the epigenetic literature, just as it was associated with neuroscience. To give a further sample of animal research on early stress, we now examine another study, also cited by Cunliffe (2015). The study, by Roth et al (2009), explicitly focused on dysfunctional mothering deliberately fashioned by the experimenters, unlike the naturally occurring variations studied by Meaney's group. In Roth et al, a group of rat mothers were deliberately subjected to stress immediately after giving birth: they were provided with limited nesting material in an unfamiliar environment. Their rearing behaviour was then compared to unstressed mothers afforded with abundant nesting resources in a familiar environment. The nurturing behaviour of the stressed mothers is explicitly described as 'abusive' (Roth et al, p 3): 'During the maltreatment regimen, pups were frequently stepped on, dropped during transport, dragged, actively rejected, and roughly handled. Additionally, pups were often neglected' (p 4).

The prime genetic focus of the study was the *BDNF* gene which has a recognised role in promoting synaptic plasticity. Significant suppression of *BDNF* expression was noted in the offspring of the stressed mothers in the prefrontal cortex, although not the hippocampus; this was accompanied by increased *BDNF* gene methylation in the frontal cortex which persisted into adulthood. The maternal behaviour of these 'maltreated females' themselves displayed 'significant amounts of abusive behavior towards their offspring' (p 6) and in the 'realm of normal maternal care' they frequently displayed 'low posture nursing positions', correlating with their 'aberrant *BDNF* DNA methylation'. What next? Predictably, a drug treatment was evaluated: zebularine (a methylation inhibitor) was infused into the prefrontal cortex of 'abused' pups and was found to reduce methylation levels to normal. This intervention is described as follows: 'Maltreatment-induced deficits in *BDNF* gene expression are ... *rescued* by treatment with a DNA methylation inhibitor' (p 5, emphasis added). Rescue, no less!

Cross-fostering was apparently less successful, with methylation remaining at elevated levels in the prefrontal cortex and the hippocampus: the authors lament that 'we failed to observe a complete rescue of the altered methylation patterns with cross-fostering' (p 7). While noting that the transgenerational transmission of the effects of maltreatment could include (potentially) an *in utero* hormonal component as well as the direct effect of maternal 'abuse', the authors conclude that their results demonstrate a 'surprising robustness to the perpetuation of changes in *BDNF* DNA methylation ... across the lifespan ... and from one generation to the next' (p 8). Their conclusion is noteworthy:

> As epigenetic mechanisms continue to be linked with neuronal plasticity and psychiatric illnesses, manipulating chromatin structure continues to gain support as a viable

avenue for therapeutic intervention to restore cognitive and
emotional health. This raises the intriguing speculation that
such interventions as … treatment with DNA demethylases
or histone deacetylase inhibitors, might prove useful as
therapeutic strategies for reversing persisting effects of
early-life adversity. (Roth et al, 2009: 8)

Although the authors also mention exposure to complex environments
(enrichment) and handling as potential interventions, it is remarkable
that they do not mention the single most obvious remedy which
flows directly from the design of the experiment itself: namely to
provide mothers with adequate resources to provide for their young,
and certainly to avoid taking them away lest they are thrown into a
desperate frenzy. The stress upon the mother rats was not of their own
making, but was imposed by the experimenters; had they not been
subjected to privations beyond their control, we may safely assume
that they would have brought up their pups in the normal laboratory
way. Thus, we might ask rhetorically, was it not the experimental
procedure that was truly abusive, not the rat mothers? They have
been placed in extreme adversity and are doing their best to look after
their pups, presumably becoming increasingly desperate as their pups
become more and more distressed. Are the authors self-consciously
suggesting that a relevant solution to poor housing is drug treatment
of offspring, or are they induced to do so because of the imperative
to show policy relevance and impact? For our purposes, we simply
note that this is exactly where the epigenetic thought style takes you
within the contemporary moral landscape.

Transgenerational epigenetic inheritance

We conclude this chapter on animal research with a look at
transgenerational epigenetic inheritance, as touched upon in both our
exhibits. Demonstration of this has been controversial, especially in the
female germline (that is, through inherited genetic material). Much of
the difficulty lies in the inevitable confounding of *in utero* effects with
epigenetic mechanisms: the fetus is exposed to hormonal and other
influences within the womb which could just as easily be responsible
for apparently inherited characteristics. Such effects can directly affect
not just the immediate offspring, but the next generation too. As
Martinez et al (2011) argue, and as Roth et al (2009) acknowledge,
when a mother is exposed to an environmental challenge, not only her
embryos/foetuses are exposed, but the already developing germline

for the next (F2) generation will also be potentially affected. Thus for maternal effects to be conclusively proved, phenotypic changes in the third (F3) generation must be shown.

Such third-generation effects for nutrition have been shown (Dunn and Bale, 2011): high fat diets of mothers resulted in increased body size for third-generation descendants, although only for female offspring. However, this study found that these effects were passed on via the paternal lineage, in the form of greater variability in paternal gene expression. Paternal inheritance is much more straightforward to study, and Martinez et al (2011) focused on epigenetic transmission down the male line in their work. They argue that such transmission is more conclusively shown in animal models where males are not involved in rearing their offspring. The study itself examined global gene expression of methylation signatures in the livers of male descendants of male mice whose mothers had been subjected to a restricted calorie diet (-50%) during gestation. The 'grandchildren' of the malnourished mothers showed alterations in 172 genes, a number of which are 'key players' (p 943) in lipogenesis (the process whereby energy from simple sugars is converted into fatty acids, for long-term storage in the form of fats). In a complex pattern of results, some of these changes in gene expression were related to DNA hypermethylation in the liver cells of grandchildren, and there was also evidence that the sperm of their fathers bore the same epigenetic mark. Behaviourally, the study reports higher levels of obesity and glucose intolerance in these same descendants.

Regarding maternal behaviour, evidence for transgenerational effects has been claimed. In a recent review article, Bohacek and Mansuy (2015) cite a study which they laud as 'the first in mice to demonstrate transgenerational effects of posttraumatic stress across generations' (p 11). The study is by Franklin et al (2010) and Mansuy is a co-author. We begin with the initial framing of the research question in the opening paragraph. The authors begin by averring that 'insecure attachment and unreliable, disorganized, poor maternal care' influence 'appropriate behavioral responses and cause maladaptive behaviors' (Franklin et al, 2010: 408). They continue: 'Epidemiological studies have further shown that the offspring of people with such behavioral alterations, and sometimes the generation following that offspring, are often similarly affected even if they themselves, did not experience the trauma' (p 408).

This is a strong claim, especially regarding cross-generational transmission in humans, and therefore worth interrogating. Three original research papers are invoked to support the claim. One study looked at variations in developmental pathways in children in relation to 'symptoms' of depression, anxiety, negativity in a nonclinical sample of mothers. Another looked at the transmission of maternal internalising behaviours (negative behaviours directed toward the self) across three generations in a longitudinal study of 200 young men; again the population is nonclinical. The third paper examined the effects on children of low maternal self-esteem and poor interpersonal skills in a deprived inner-city area; children of such 'vulnerable mothers' were found to have a four-fold higher risk of neglect or physical or sexual abuse. Effects were directly caused by abuse or neglect rather than other parenting features; nor was maternal adversity in the mother's childhood a factor. The study was of a single generation only. So of the three studies invoked to shore up the work, the relevance to the claim of intergenerational transmission is tangential to say the least, and even contradictory.

Regarding the study itself, of rodents it will be recalled, the stressor used was 'unpredictable maternal separation combined with unpredictable maternal stress' (Franklin et al, 2010: 409). The latter involved either 20 minutes restraint in a Plexiglass tube, or a forced swim in cold water; these stressors were applied unpredictably and randomly during separation. Arched back nursing and licking were used to assess the quality of nurturance. A 'deficit in maternal care' was apparent during the first postnatal week. But despite such deficits, F1 pups grew normally, although in the forced swim test they spent more time floating, suggesting 'depressive-like behavior' (p 409); animals also spent more time immobile in the 'tail suspension' test, another quaint 'animal model' held to assess negative mood. Female descendants of these F1 male fathers showed similar 'depressive' symptoms which could be reversed by administration of an antidepressant, again showing the predilection of animal studies for pharmacological interventions. Although male F2s did not show such symptoms, their male F3 offspring did.

Overall, these results are taken to suggest that depressive-like symptoms can be transmitted across several generations but with a complex and sex-specific mode of transmission, which is 'currently not understood but is reminiscent of that found in humans' (p 410), something of a pseudo-explanation, to say the least. DNA profiles of several genes 'implicated in the control of stress in mice' (p 413) were investigated in F1 male sperm cells. In the offspring of stressed mothers, higher levels of methylation were found in two genes, decreases in two, and no change in another; similar patterns were found in F2 males and females, although there were significant discrepancies. Undeterred by this inconsistent pattern, the authors conclude that 'early stress alters DNA methylation in the male germline and that some of the alterations can be maintained and passed to the offspring' (p 413).

A subsequent study (involving both Bohacek and Mansuy) employed the same stressor and behavioural testing regime; it found that a further epigenetic mechanism, that of microRNA (see chapter two), also played a part in transmitting phylogenetic effects across two generations of mice. The authors conclude:

> The identification of several miRNAs [micro RNAs] and putative targets as mediators of these [behavioural] effects provide molecular markers of traumatic stress for potential use for the diagnosis of stress predisposition and stress-induced disorders in humans.

Returning to the main review paper, based on over a hundred papers in which their own work is highlighted, Bohacek and Mansuy (2015) conclude as follows:

> The idea that experiences and environmental factors can lead to heritable changes in traits and behaviours has gained solid experimental support, against past controversies about the existence of such modes of inheritance. Initial evidence implicating non-genetic modifications in germ cells has accumulated, and the way in which these modifications are induced and maintained in germ cells is beginning to be delineated. (p 10)

Conclusion

Not all would agree that 'past controversies' have been resolved, and that experimental support is now solid. Indeed, the quote itself seems to concede that we only in the early stages of such work. In another recent, authoritative review ('Transgenerational epigenetic inheritance: myths and mechanisms', covering slightly more papers) Heard and Martienssen (2014) concur that for plants and very simple animals, epigenetic inheritance has been well documented. Nonetheless, considerable scepticism remains regarding the prevalence of intergenerational epigenetic transmission in mammals, and humans in particular. Although intergenerational effects (such as the maternal effects we have been describing) do appear to occur in mammals, Heard and Martienssen regard them as the exception, not the rule. In large part this scepticism arises from the epigenetic 'reprogramming' that occurs in the mammalian embryo, whereby much of the epigenetic inscription, including methylation, is removed prior to birth. This phenomenon, which we witnessed in the Meaney study, is profoundly adaptive.

> these two rounds of epigenetic erasure leave little chance for inheritance of epigenetic marks ... evolution appears to have gone to great lengths to ensure the efficient undoing of any potentially deleterious bookmarking that a parent's lifetime experience may have imposed. (Heard and Martienssen, 2014: 95)

The review acknowledges that nutrition, exposure to pollutants, alcohol and tobacco can all affect the health and welfare of offspring. However, the authors conclude that it is unlikely that such effects reflect bona fide transgenerational epigenetic inheritance over multiple generations, 'given the robust reprogramming found in the mammalian germline' (p 105). The authors observe that 'although much attention has been drawn to the potential implications of transgenerational inheritance for human health, so far there is little support' (p 106):

> On the other hand, the human transmission of culture and improved habits is clearly Lamarckian. To quote S.J. Gould ... 'What we learn in one generation, we transmit directly by teaching and writing.' In this and other respects, *perhaps it is premature to compare humans to plants.* (p 106, emphasis added)

Culture is by far the strongest song that tows us, for good or ill, in one direction or another, but as we shall see in our next chapter, where we consider human studies on epigenetic 'programming', it is the very thing that is redacted as it fails to conform with the prevailing thought style.

Notes

[1] An exon is any section of a gene that will become a part of the final RNA produced by that gene. The term refers to both the DNA sequence within a gene and the corresponding sequence in RNA transcripts.

[2] The main paper also does not describe how the two groups of rats were formed. The supplement explains that the behaviour of each dam was observed for 6 × 100-minute observation periods daily for the first 10 days postpartum and scored according to a standard protocol, counting the number of times mothers were either

licking/grooming any pup or nursing pups in an arched-back posture, as opposed to more passive postures. Based on these scores, the cohort of 32 mothers was divided into two groups: high LG-ABN mothers (scores more than one standard deviation above the mean) and low LG-ABN mothers (less than one standard deviation below the mean). Given that LG-ABN scores fall on a continuum, this implies that there were (only) five or six mothers in each group, with most mothers scoring at an intermediate level. Neither the paper nor the supplement provides detailed statistical information regarding maternal behaviour, nor that of pups.

[3] The pharmacological intervention itself provides a notable example of reductionist thinking. TSA is an inhibitor of histone deacetylation, and that provides the molecular explanation of its effects. Given that TSA was infused centrally, a generalised impact on the brain is to be expected, and an explanation in terms of psychological state would seem an alternative way of thinking about its effect on the rat. It is relevant that, at a psychological level, histone deacetylase inhibitors such as valproate have been linked to mood regulation, with antimanic effects akin to lithium. Which then is the reader's preferred explanation of the effect of TSA? That it counteracts the localised demethylation of a single gene involved in the synthesis of a protein in one brain structure? Or that it helps to stabilise the mood of a rat living in an unnatural environment faced with a life-threatening stress completely outside its normal humdrum existence, and from which it cannot escape?

[4] Although it is noted that there were significant levels of GR in the offspring of untreated low LG-ABN mothers, leading to the conclusion 'that exon 1_7 is but one of the regulatory sequences determining GR expression within the hippocampus' (Weaver et al, 2004: 852).

[5] The hippocampus is a complex structure which plays an important role, as we saw in chapter two, in many key neuropsychological processes. It connects to a number of other brain structures, including parts of the cerebral cortex, the hypothalamus and the thalamus. Like all central nervous system structures, it is composed of different types of neurons (pyramidal cells, basket cells, chandelier cells) as well as the ubiquitous glial cells. The tissue sample assayed in the EPMB study is taken from the hippocampus as a whole as if it were a homogeneous structure. Attempting to characterise the role of the hippocampus in terms of epigenetic marks on one response element of one gene in an amorphous tissue sample of indeterminate composition would seem to lack the requisite specificity (and variety) to yield meaningful insights into the function of a complex organ and its participation with other brain structures. In fairness, we do note evidence from previous studies by the group, showing handling to affect different areas (fields) of the hippocampus in the same way.

[6] Incidentally, that such radically different experiences produce the same epigenetic mark in itself shows how impoverished is the molecular level *taken alone* in explaining behaviour.

[7] Meaney (2001) does, somewhat grudgingly, acknowledge that raised stress reactivity can be beneficial, but gives an odd example, namely that nonhandled rats appear to be more resistant to allergic encephalomyelitis (p 1165). In humans, he also observes that increased reactivity, by producing a more 'timid and shy' demeanour, could help individuals avoid 'the pitfalls of criminogenic environments (p 1182).

EIGHT

Human epigenetics
prematurely born(e)?

In this chapter, we shift our focus from animals to humans and examine the extant literature on the human epigenome. We review seminal work on the impact of natural disasters on the epigenome and revisit the familiar terrain of gestation and early infancy, reconfigured as a problem to be prevented, understood and fixed at the molecular level. We interrogate the nature of the claims made within the literature and also examine the thought style and presuppositions, particularly in those studies which seek to translate findings from laboratory to clinic and public health policy. The following extract illustrates the fascination and hope inspired by epigenetic discoveries in the human realm:

> Abnormal epigenetics has been linked with diseases as diverse as cancer, diabetes, Alzheimer's and heart disease. Exposure to environmental factors such as cigarette smoke or dietary stress can affect epigenetic controls and predispose to disease. There is increasing evidence that early exposure to such factors – for instance in the womb – can increase the risk of diseases such as obesity in later life. (Houses of Parliament, 2013: 1)

Discoveries at the molecular level are thus fuelling the aspirations of the developmental origins of health and disease (DOHaD) paradigm, which we discussed at the very start of this book. It is increasingly being claimed that there is an inextricable link between maternal, perinatal and early childhood exposures and disease risk in adulthood. The 2015 International Society for DOHaD manifesto lists 'obesity, type 2 diabetes, hypertension, coronary heart disease, chronic lung and kidney disease, musculoskeletal disorders, some cancers and some mental illness' (p 1) as candidate noncommunicable diseases (NCDs) for interventions. The tone of the manifesto is markworthy. Economics and productivity feature strongly in the narrative with striking similarities to the macroeconomics of early intervention discussed in chapters four and six.

Harmful environments during early development may cause failure to achieve full physical and mental potential, and a loss of human capital. Combined with increased susceptibility to NCDs, this widens inequalities in health and has adverse economic consequences for individuals, families and communities. Moreover, an unhealthy lifestyle in prospective parents ... passes greater risk of NCDs to the next generation. This perpetuates cycles of poor health, reduced productivity and shorter life expectancy, trapping populations in a trough of low human capital from which they cannot easily escape ... Against this challenging picture, pioneering DOHaD research provides grounds for optimism. (International Society for DOHaD, 2015: 1)

Under the spotlight are individual 'choices': unhealthy eating, lack of exercise, smoking and alcohol use and wider environmental exposure to microbes or toxins. Increasingly, though, psychological 'stress' is being implicated in epigenetic changes, following an arc from laboratory rat to public health policy. The International Society for DOHaD (2015: 1) includes the following aims:

Promote and disseminate DOHaD concepts to the public and to government and non-government organizations, so as to increase awareness of the transgenerational benefits of a healthy start to life ... Support optimal timing of pregnancy, healthy weight, good macro- and micronutrient status, physical activity, sleep and other behaviours in women and their partners before, during and after pregnancy ... Promote positive maternal mental health and reduce rates of untreated depression and anxiety in pregnancy ... Support breastfeeding, healthy complementary feeding, regular physical activity, a healthy lifestyle and parenting skills, to exploit critical windows of opportunity for the optimal physical and mental development of children.

One cannot dispute the benignancy of the aspiration to purge the next generation of debilitating and often deadly disease. Yet, the goal of epigenetic optimisation carries many moral and ethical implications, not least the question of whether maximising human capital and productivity are the most important aspirations for a good society and a happy life across the developed and developing world. There is a clear focus on the reproductive years, on maternal behaviours and lifestyles from optimal timing of pregnancy to exploiting critical windows, and training adolescent girls to avoid toxicant exposure. Women's partners are mentioned only once, but they too must eat and sleep well and undertake physical activity. There is nothing modest about these policy aspirations, though we note there is no explicit reference to the alleviation of poverty and social disadvantage.

Addressing cancer at the molecular level may have an intuitive rightness about it, provided the epigenetic mechanism can be identified and properly targeted. However, even in this domain, safe, effective treatments have proved rather elusive. For example, while there have been successes with blood cancers, the troublesome habit of epigenetic drugs affecting all cells, not just cancer cells, means they can prove highly toxic. Nevertheless one can see a clear link from the molecular science to a possible pharmacological treatment for a wholly unpleasant disease. The molecular level might equally further our understandings of the impacts of toxins or infectious agents, though this has also proved controversial. An influential researcher in the field of environmental exposure and epigenetic change, Michael Skinner, has described the often thorny response his work has provoked from the toxicology establishment (Kaiser, 2014). Whether Skinner is right or wrong, the possibility of transgenerational damage through the male and female germline would be hot political stuff. It could augur litigation against governments and corporations for exposure to toxins generations previously.

We have already noted that the gendered focus of DOHaD, with women potentially treated as 'eternally pre-pregnant' (Meloni, 2016: 217; Waggoner and Uller, 2015). The concept of the 'episome' is thus born, described as: 'the totality of human environmental (i.e. non-genetic) exposures from conception onwards, complementing the genome'. It provides a framework to advance the environmental epidemiology field that has until now focused almost exclusively on single-exposure health effects (Robinson and Vrijheid, 2015: 204).

In the area of environmental toxins, new responsibilities for women seem likely to emerge: don't eat this, don't touch that, avoid this packaging, don't visit these areas, and so forth. Things become even more morally murky when policy is focused on behavioural changes, on the precautionary principle that a variety of quite ordinary 'choices' might be damaging the 'episome' for the next and even subsequent generations. The UK Houses of Parliament briefing on epigenetics and health stresses the need to equip practitioners with the competencies and skills needed to support behaviour change:

Evidence from epigenetics research is [that] epigenetic changes are potentially modifiable through lifestyle and diet. Advice to pregnant women on behaviour change to avoid exposure to potentially harmful factors during early embryonic development is likely to be particularly important. (Houses of Parliament, 2013: 4)

Public health interventions sound like a good idea, but, in these moralised contexts, there remains much to be debated. At a global level we are seeing the conflation of a range of public health 'preventions' almost by sleight of hand. A recent World Bank report draws together large-scale public health interventions, like provision of clean water and adequate nutrition, with parenting, developmental and educational programmes based on prevention science conducted largely in the relatively affluent US (Denboba et al, 2014).

Epigenomic surveillance and the privations of the mother

Let us now examine the state of knowledge in human studies and the potential social consequences of the current readings of epigenetic science. We begin with the iconic Dutch Hunger Winter, devoting ourselves to interrogating the 'facts' as they are currently assembled. The enduring effects of the winter of 1944/45 on the health of foetuses exposed to its privations (drastic food rationing imposed by the German army on the people of western Netherlands) in the final months of pregnancy is well documented. Babies were born small, metabolic effects persisted throughout their lives and they were predisposed to disease (Carey, 2012). Cunliffe summarises some key results as follows.

People who had been exposed to the food blockade as foetuses had increased likelihoods of developing diabetes, mood disorders, and obesity as adults. Moreover, fetal exposure to famine was associated with altered patterns of DNA methylation near genes likely to be involved in fetal growth and development. (Cunliffe, 2015: 62)

Here we examine some key aspects of the research, much of it initiated by Lumey (reported in a series of papers including Lumey, 1992; Lumey et al, 2011) in order to interrogate its findings more closely and reveal important details. First, we note that the head circumference of babies born to starved mothers was not affected, so we may conclude that whatever else, their brains were likely in good shape. Let us now focus on the finding of decreased birthweights. Lumey (1992) reports data from the birth logs for 1,874 deliveries before, over the period of the famine, and during its immediate aftermath. There are indeed striking reductions in birthweight, declining from 3,261 grams on average for babies conceived and born prior to the blockade, to a low point of 3,059 grams for babies experiencing the famine in the first and second trimesters of gestation. Birthweights increased for subsequent cohorts. From this pattern of results, it would seem that malnutrition during early pregnancy was the most damaging. But the situation is not that simple. Lumey also reports data for other areas of the country (rural areas and liberated areas) which were free from the blockade; a trend of declining birthweight is found for these areas too, indeed the trend is stronger, starts sooner and lasts longer, even affecting babies conceived after the end of the famine. A more detailed analysis provides confirmation of a pattern of effects which does not show a simple direct effect of famine exposure during early pregnancy on birthweight, far from it; not only are effect sizes small, but the evidence suggests that birthweight is more affected in the non-famine areas, and that in the famine areas, a reduction in weight occurs after the famine has ceased of the same magnitude as during the time of hardship.[1]

Regarding long-term health effects, we will summarise key findings from Lumey et al (2011) which reports outcomes up to the age of 60. The pattern is complex as two cohorts are reported: the Wilhelmina Gasthuis hospital in Amsterdam (WGA) and a larger cohort from Amsterdam, Rotterdam and Leiden (ARL). For fertility, no salient effects of the famine are found. For glucose metabolism, impaired glucose tolerance is reported for WGA, but not ARL, though increased incidence of type 2 diabetes was found in the latter. Blood pressure in WGA was not associated with famine, although a 'moderate increase' in systolic pressure was found for the ARL cohort. At the age of 59, cholesterol levels were increased for women but not men in the ARL cohort, but there were no effects at age 58 for the WGA cohort. No statistically significant differences were found for either coronary heart disease or indeed overall mortality, though the risk of schizophrenia was substantially increased as a result of famine exposure. Regarding the absence of an effect on long-term mortality, the authors notably comment that this 'does not exclude the possibility that there is a real effect if this effect is hidden by differences in early mortality ... weaker individuals may have experienced an excess of spontaneous abortions or early postnatal deaths' (p 12). They lament the 'paradox' that:

> for a famine to have an effect it needs to be severe, but the
> more severe the famine, the more distorted the population
> structure can become because of excess differential mortality
> and the more difficult it will be to detect a true effect among
> survivors. This dilemma is not easily resolved. (Lumey et
> al, 2011: 12)

The resonance with 'missing heritability' we met in chapter three is
striking; the effect must be there, it is just a question of looking harder!
Another recent paper co-authored by Lumey reports the (inevitable)
results of an epigenetic analysis (Heijmans et al, 2008). This examined
DNA methylation of the maternally imprinted insulin growth factor
II gene (IGF2), 'a key factor in human growth and development'
(p 17046). Methylation was compared for 60 individuals exposed to
the famine at the time of conception, with same sex non-exposed
siblings: although birthweights were normal, a small reduction of 5%
in methylation levels was noted, with a corresponding moderate effect
size. A further cohort exposed to the famine at the end of pregnancy
showed no such differences compared to controls. Birthweights were
also looked at: whereas exposure early in pregnancy showed no impact,
exposure late in gestation did, a reversal of the findings for methylation!
There also appeared to be no correlation between methylation levels
and birthweight. The authors conclude:

> The developmental origins hypothesis states that adverse
> conditions during development contribute to adult disease
> risk. Although the mechanisms behind these relationships
> are unclear, the involvement of epigenetic dysregulation has
> been proposed (22–24). Our findings are a key element in
> elaborating this hypothesis.

No explanation is offered though, of why the reductions in IGF2
methylation are to be seen as 'dysfunctional' rather than adaptive, nor
does the study link the reduction with actual health outcomes. Indeed,
for the only heath outcome reported, birthweight, not only is there
no relationship, but there is actually a double dissociation. Birthweight
may be a 'poor surrogate for nutritional status' (p 17048) but at least
we have an understanding of what it means. In contrast to the authors'
apparent faith in epigenetics, from our point of view, all it seems to
add is complexity and confusion.

We now turn to a more recent follow-up study of the hunger winter
by Scholte et al (2012). The paper begins by noting that the long-run

health outcomes are typically interpreted in terms of Barker's foetal origins/programming hypothesis (Barker, 1994) whereby metabolic adaptations *in utero* are considered to affect the risk of diseases such as cardiovascular disease, hypertension and diabetes. The focus of the study is on economic outcomes for men (employment, income) and their health up to the age of 60 (hospital admission for cardiovascular disease and cancer). Data for over 47,000 individuals, from urban districts in the west of Holland (affected by the famine) and the rest of the country (unaffected), were garnered from tax records and hospitals. The principal results of the study are summarised in table 8.1.

Table 8.1: Effects of famine exposure on employment rates and hospital admissions for cardiovascular disease.

Exposure	% In employment		% admitted to hospital for cardiovascular disease (CVD)	
	West	Rest	West	Rest
Pre-famine	75.7	76.0	11.6	13.6
Trimester 3	75.9	76.0	13.2	13.2
Trimester 2	73.8	74.7	13.5	12.9
Trimester 1	72.9	76.2	13.0	13.7
Post-famine	76.1	76.8	11.9	12.3

The columns show the percentages in work and admitted to hospital for cardiovascular disease in the year assessed by the study, 1999. Data for income is not shown (as this depends on employment) or cancer admission rates (as this showed no effects). Both effects on employment and CVD are apparent in the table. In explaining effects common to both areas, the authors mention that the winter of 1944/45 was an unusually harsh one for the whole of the country (backed up by stillbirth rates and mortality figures) and that food shortages were experienced by some cities in the east of the country as well as the famine areas. They also note that the impact of the famine would, in general, be experienced more drastically by those in lower socioeconomic groups.

Regarding employment, in-work rates are down in men with maximum exposure in the second trimester of gestation in both the famine and non-famine areas; for the famine-affected foetuses, exposure in the first semester showed the strongest effect, though no such effect appeared for the control group. Given that there were no apparent cognitive deficits at age 18 in the famine group, the authors speculate that this differential effect reflects the impact of mental disorders on productivity and career trajectories. To support this argument, Scholte et al note the finding that 'The occurrence of Ramadan during the first month of pregnancy increases the risk of mental/learning disabilities, among prime-aged men in Muslim populations in Uganda. This confirms the importance of early gestation for cognitive and mental outcomes' (Scholte et al, 2012: 17). Taken to its logical conclusion, this has interesting and potentially controversial policy implications!

Regarding cardiovascular disease, the pattern of effects is less easy to descry, not least because of the difference in pre-famine baselines. Nonetheless, using the post-famine levels as baseline, the data appear to show an increase in CVD for the famine group associated with second trimester exposure, and a comparable increase in CVD for the non-famine group in trimester 1. Regarding the increased vulnerability in trimester 2 for the famine cohort, the authors note that this goes against expectations from the epidemiological literature which 'typically finds that nutritional conditions during the third trimester are most important' (Scholte et al, 2012: 18).

In order to analyse effects in more detail, the authors proceed from the simple statistics we have looked at to examine the combined impact of famine versus non-famine areas and gestational exposure. For employment and CVD, the analysis shows two statistically significant effects: an elevated risk of unemployment associated with trimester 1 exposure to famine, and increased risk for CVD for trimester 2. But the size of these effects is small, negligible even,[2] with the authors themselves commenting as follows on their general failure to find a significant impact of famine on health and economic outcomes: 'In the light of the large sample sizes, one might have expected more coefficients to be significantly different from zero. The explanation of this apparent paradox is *that the magnitude of the estimated long-run effects is small*' (p 13, emphasis added).

In summary, in relation to other well-appreciated causes of health and economic disadvantage (for example, social class), the results of the famine study, while of considerable scientific interest, if anything indicate that hardship of this sort, when imposed out of the blue and affecting all groups of society to more or less the same extent, actually appears to have relatively little overall impact. Certainly this is so when compared to other structural sources of disadvantage, such as lack of money, lack of stable employment, or poor housing conditions, all of which have considerable bearing on health and economic outcomes. However, the contemporary gaze is turned inwards not outwards by the genetic enchantment, becoming particularly preoccupied with the inside of women's bodies during the reproductive years. Epigenetics opens new arenas for maternal responsibilisation.

Foetal programming and its thought style: the (in)hospitable womb

In the preceding section, we alluded to Barker's foetal programming hypothesis (Barker, 1994). This is an influential view, particularly associated with the DOHaD perspective introduced in chapter one. Foetal programming conveys the idea that gestational experiences critically influence susceptibility to the subsequent risk of disease throughout the lifespan. This is a field of frenetic scientific activity: an initial trawl on Google Scholar yields 30,000 hits for foetal programming. Maternal mood has generated considerable recent excitement as a potential determinant, with studies on foetal programming by adverse mood burgeoning. This work inevitably draws much inspiration from the work of Meaney and others on rats. The focus on mothers' mental state is rather odd though, given that the foetus is relatively protected from maternal stress hormones by placental enzymes.[3] Animal studies have shown that this protective mechanism can be damaged by 'inflammation' (Edwards et al, 1993) and prolonged stress, but in likelihood, given the range of environments in which human beings have thrived for millennia, we might assume that the protective mechanism normally copes! We must ask ourselves two questions: why this preoccupation with stress *in utero*, where the infant not the mother is focus of expert concern, and beyond this, where does this focus on the mother and her womb lead us as a society?

We have discussed the methodological complexities involved in manipulating the environment and behaviour of laboratory rats. As we have noted, it is hard to read such animal models as anything other than a crude, somewhat implausible, proxy for human parenting. It is unlikely that even the most enthusiastic murine zoologist would be prepared to go to such lengths to understand rat parenting and its response to stress, particularly as these are not even wild rats, which would arguably be of intrinsic interest to the naturalist. Clearly, there are insurmountable, ethical difficulties in undertaking similar work with humans. There is a paradox in the animal work. The rats are not like humans and therefore can be subject to extreme stress, which would be considered torture in human subjects, yet at the same time *are* like humans and therefore can inform understandings of our own parent–infant biosocial relations. Anthropomorphism appears to exist on one plane only to protect itself from such contradictions.

There are also considerable methodological challenges. Research papers lament the difficulties in isolating responses in particular brain regions when these are not available for postmortem examination.

Yet, despite the enormous leap, human studies of the effects of early adversity have indeed followed in droves in the wake of the rat laboratory work. As we noted in chapter four, a swathe of policy makers have made increasingly unequivocal claims about the adverse effects of pre- and postnatal exposure of the foetus/neonate to maternal stress. The serious methodological challenges have not stymied the enthusiasm for utopian fixes, though as we shall see the specific detail of what these may be is often elusive and implied.

For all the energy of its enthusiasts, what exactly is the status of the knowledge in this field? The effects of antenatal depression, anxiety and associated raised cortisol on the developing HPA axis of the foetus is the hypothesis of choice, uniting epigenetic and neuroscientific modes of inquiry (for example, Glover and O'Connor, 2002; Charil et al, 2010; Glover et al, 2010; Field, 2011). The majority of the studies draw explicitly on the work of Meaney and colleagues (but do not attend to any of the methodological and 'thought style' issues we have already outlined in the previous chapter). A thorough review paper by Tiffany Field (2010) summarises the results of a range of studies on the inhospitable uterine environment of depressed women, which purport to show associations with low birthweight and shorter gestational age. Babies are described as less responsive to stimulation, they cry more and they sleep less. The low birthweight is, in turn, associated with physical ill health in adulthood, hypertension, diabetes and coronary heart disease, as well as depression and anxiety. These effects are attributed in some studies directly to prenatal depression, rather than the mediation of birth complications, through the combined action of two of our principal actors – cortisol and the HPA axis.

> Maternal stress during pregnancy is noted to increase cortisol and corticotrophin releasing hormone levels in the mother and the fetus ... Placental corticotrophic hormone is released into fetal circulation ... In addition, elevated estrogen levels in pregnancy lead to a doubling of corticosteroid-building globulin levels resulting in a low breakdown of cortisol. (Field, 2010: 8)

A variety of other biological sequelae are noted, including effects on foetal sex hormone production which is held responsible for learning deficits in males, and anxiety, depression and an elevated HPA axis response to stress in females. All this must be rather alarming, we might speculate, to pregnant women.

Let us pause a moment though and examine some studies in more detail. Much of the epigenetic research has focused on glucocorticoid (GC) receptors in the brain, and the *NR3C1* gene which encodes the GC protein. As we saw in the previous chapter, these receptors are believed to play a key role in the regulation of the 'stress response', mediated by the HPA axis. A study by Oberlander et al (2008) found an association between maternal depression and methylation of a small number of CpG sites of the *NR3C1* gene in the neonatal cord blood in humans. There was also a short-term association with augmented salivary cortisol response in the infants at 3 months. The immediacy of this impact lays bare the confusions and predilections of the epigenetic narrative: the long-term harms that its headline stories connote are often not demonstrated by studies recruited to the cause; this study, for example, examined only short-term effects.

In another study, a large team including Meaney (McGowan et al, 2009) examined the postmortem brains of suicide victims. Three groups of 12 brains were compared: of suicide 'completers' (with or without a history of child abuse/neglect) and a control group who had died suddenly of unrelated causes. The aim of the study was to translate animal findings to humans (p 342), and it focused on the hippocampus, given its role in learning and memory. The study found both depressed expression of GC and of *NR3C1* in the suicide victims exposed to childhood abuse, compared to the other two groups, results which are marginally significant. Further investigation implicated elevated methylation at 2 out of 38 CpG sites (different from the sites in Oberlander et al) in the *NR3C1* promoter region as the putative epigenetic mechanism. The conclusion is drawn that changes in GC expression are 'closely associated with a developmental history of family adversity, in this case childhood abuse, rather than suicide completion' (McGowan et al, 2009: 345). In a subsequent paper, McGowan and Szyf (2010) reflect on the earlier study as follows:

> The data suggest that severe adversity during early childhood may have been a contributing factor to the observed epigenetic pathology ... However, it remains unclear whether the epigenetic aberrations were present in the germ line, introduced during embryogenesis or whether they were truly changes occurring during early childhood. (McGowan and Szyf, 2010: 70)

We would add a couple more caveats here including the low level of statistical significance, the presence of confounding factors (drug/

substance misuse), and the near impossibility of making unequivocal causal attributions in such complex, multifactorial comparisons. Nonetheless, the McGowan and Szyf paper ends boldly, concluding that:

> understanding the epigenetic consequences of social exposures stands not only to revolutionize medicine but also to transform the social sciences and humanities ... Epigenetic drugs are now in use in cancer and psychiatric therapy, and it is anticipated that the future will see increased use of epigenetic drugs and interventions in several other health conditions. (p 71)

Let us stand back and reflect on the epigenomic logic here. That suicide is the subject bears some irony, as the analysis of suicide and its social causation is where sociology began. How far have we come from Durkheim's assiduously researched insights and is this progress? In this context, the epigenetic revolution would seem to usher in a medicalisation of a social evil. Abuse is a moral wrong, in and of itself; it is not a wrong because it damages the genome. And if the genome had borne unscarred the brunt of this social exposure, would the abuse then be justified?

Moreover, these are studies in humans, not rats in controlled and manipulated laboratory conditions. Glover et al (2010) conclude that while animal studies 'show convincingly' a long-term effect on the HPA axis of prenatal stress 'equivalent work in humans is only just starting' (p 21). A detailed review paper by Charil et al, 2010 also cites numerous rodent studies, pointing to the relative paucity of human studies, and the inherent methodological difficulties in controlling the environment and stressors in undertaking such work. We have shown that there can never be any ethical equivalent of the animal work. Such work would involve the forced removal of infants from their mothers and then their return, just to see what happens, or taking away the basic shelter from women who have just given birth and then monitoring the result. For the laboratory rodent, such abuse can and does take place, but outside of concentration camps and war zones there is no human equivalent.

There has been some painstaking work looking at the effects of maternal stress caused by natural disaster, which is as close as we can ethically get to the laboratory rat experiences. Of particular note is a careful longitudinal study on a cohort of children born to mothers who had suffered the extreme privations of the 1988 Quebec ice storm.

Considered one of the country's worst natural disasters, the ice storm resulted in power outages, leaving residents to face severe cold and shortage of food for up to six weeks. The study is noteworthy in that it goes beyond the rodent work as researchers were able to study the effects of 'objective stress' – the number of days they were without power and damage to their homes – and disambiguate this from the subjective stress reported by the mothers. Rats are unable to speak so no such disambiguation can take place in the laboratory. Researchers found that that objective stress explained most of the variance among the children in IQ, language, BMI and obesity, insulin secretion and their immune system. Effects on autistic traits, asthma and a host of other measures are also reported in this cohort. The variance is attributed to epigenetic changes. The team note:

> These data provide first evidence in humans supporting the conclusion that PNMS (prenatal maternal stress) results in a lasting, broad, and functionally organized DNA methylation signature in several tissues in offspring. By using a natural disaster model, we can infer that the epigenetic effects found in Project Ice Storm are due to objective levels of hardship experienced by the pregnant woman rather than to her level of sustained distress. (Cao-Lei et al, 2014: 1)

The work is fascinating scientifically: for example, in children whose mothers were without electricity at any point between 14 and 22 weeks of pregnancy, the team found fingerprint asymmetries which they hypothesise might also indicate changes in the brain as fingerprints and brain tissue 'develop out of the same foetal ectoderm' during these weeks of pregnancy (Charil et al, 2010: 72). The ice storm studies, like those on the Dutch hunger winter, lack the normative tone of much of the more popularised foetal programming narratives. Mothers subject to natural disasters are not to blame, even if their subjective stress levels are high. Their privations are severe, and that they have enduring effects on the foetus is thus rather unsurprising.

Much of the work on prenatal depression and anxiety lacks this complexity and nuance. As Tiffany Field notes:

> ... none of the studies have explored the antecedent of depressive episodes as, for example, if the prenatal depression was ongoing from childhood or related to recent losses or traumas, pregnancy factors, illnesses, or family history. And,

investigators did not ask about depression before pregnancy.
(Field, 2011: 11)

The studies have a tendency to treat the womb as a sealed biological space in which the foetus is somehow metaphorically trapped against its will. The womb is some sort of 'sci-fi pod' connected to an inhospitable endocrine bath; it is not connected to the environment, or to even to the woman and her relationships, life, love or loss.

It is unsurprising that the strongest predictor of postnatal depression is prenatal depression. Thus, we may expect significant antecedents, such as social problems, and enduring psychosocial difficulties in caring and coping for their offspring in the 'depressed' group of mothers. Then there are the potential influences of antidepressant and other psychotropic medication, and we could go on. People live in complex systems. Examining the effects of prenatal stress solely at the molecular level seems curiously inhumane, and we may pertinently ask where does the vast field of research leave us in terms of clinical or social interventions? The knowledge that one's unhappiness, and being unhappy is how it would feel, is hurting one's baby is unlikely to result in a surge of 'feel good' hormones. This conundrum has not completely escaped the researchers' attention, but seems to have done nothing to disturb their thought style or research programme. In a review paper Glover et al (2010) note research by Gutteling et al (2005) which showed raised cortisol in 4-year-old children whose mothers had experienced antenatal anxiety about giving birth to a disabled child. Worrying about their unborn child, it seems, has 'hurt' their child. The circularity in the reasoning and the potential for the unintended consequence of increasing pregnancy anxiety by pointing to its 'toxic' effects is a hallmark in the literature.

Let us look at an exemplar in more detail. Buss et al (2010) examine the impact of 'pregnancy anxiety' on brain morphology in 6- to 9-year-old children. Maternal anxiety during pregnancy was measured using a pregnancy anxiety scale at 19, 25 and 31 weeks. The scale focused entirely on worries about pregnancy, health of the baby and fears about the delivery. These were simply worried women, not a clinical population with a diagnosis of mental illness. From an original sample of 557 mothers, 35 agreed to MRI scans of their children. The children were screened and none had emotional, physical or behavioural difficulties; they were 'normal' children of 'normally' worried mothers. The paper notes that pregnancy anxiety was not correlated with total grey matter volume but differences were found in a number of brain areas for women reporting higher anxiety in the first trimester.

The areas where 'deficits' were found are enumerated, but not volume increases. These must exist since total grey matter was unaffected, but presumably were felt to detract from the story being told. Despite the fact that these children are apparently normal, the authors go on to speculate that reduced volume in areas of the prefrontal cortex might lead to delayed cognitive and motor development. Further speculations follow about how 'higher concentration of stress hormones' might cause further delays, except that for these children they apparently did not. The reasoning is incorrigible. Obvious questions are not raised about the possible causes of stress in the first trimester only. Could it be that these women had hyperemesis (severe morning sickness) for example? Could this have reduced their nutritional intake? The authors finally conclude that addressing women's pregnancy-related concerns should be 'a major focus for public health initiatives' (p 149). This is, of course, a profound irony, since they have effectively fuelled maternal anxiety to some considerable degree by pointing to structural changes in the brains of (normal) children consequent upon fairly ordinary heightened anxiety in early pregnancy. It is hard to see this as progress. It also produces an ambition for the (therapeutic) state that is both extraordinarily grandiose and likely to be futile: the eradication of worrying.

Enthusiasm for screening and prevention is no guarantee of its benignancy. And where does this work lead us? In a review of the literature on stress *in utero*, Reynolds et al (2013) note:

> Lower socioeconomic position is associated with increased risk of morbidity and premature mortality from physical and mental disorders, and confers similar trans-generational consequences on the offspring. The effects on the offspring appear [to be] initiated prenatally as lower socioeconomic position also increases risk of prematurity and influences birth size. The programming insult resulting from low socio-economic status is not known and is likely to be multifactorial and operate through exposures including stress, poverty, housing, poor diet and lower education levels. (p 1845)

The authors conclude with the following 'novel pathways for early intervention either in the preconception, pregnancy or early postpartum period':

Initial findings suggest that a simple stress management instruction can improve maternal mood and reduce morning cortisol levels during pregnancy ... There is also some evidence that a motivational lifestyle intervention in obese pregnancy can moderate anxiety ... but whether this influences offspring outcomes is unknown. The observation that placental gene expression is altered in relation to maternal stress suggests that we may be able to identify those most at risk for early intervention. This may also be a target for intervention in pregnancy as a very recent study has shown that a specific dietary supplementation with the methyl donor choline in the third trimester alters the methylation profiles, and hence expression of genes in foetal derived tissues and in genes that regulate foetal glucocorticoid metabolism. (p 1847)

These are interesting suggestions for policy and practice. As is customary, targeting takes centre stage. The proposed remedies for maternal stress probably will not cause any harm, but whether they are operating at the best level conceptually or practically is highly debatable. There is no mention, for example, of identifying the source of the maternal stress, alleviating adverse social conditions or poverty, nor suggestions that it might be useful to talk with women about happiness, relationships, aspirations, fears or hopes. Instead, the stressed women can be taught to manage their stress. Like the mother rats who had their nesting material removed, it seems the human subjects can always have their methylation levels corrected pharmacologically even if they don't have a home, or enough to eat. The foetus needs a hospitable place to live and grow, but all the mother needs is a food supplement.

In a thorough sociological analysis of epigenetics and its implications, Landecker and Panofsky conclude:

With its pronounced focus on exposures during critical periods of early development, it is entangled with the culturally tender and often fraught areas of how humans care for, feed, and pollute one another and their young. The citation peaks of the scientific literature in the area of epigenetic gene regulation look like the scientific topography of modern parenting angst, featuring 'transgenerational endocrine disruptors,' 'nutritional effects,' and 'maternal anxiety behaviors' ... these narratives of maternal responsibility have profound cultural ramifications. (Landecker and Panofsky, 2013: 532)

The spectre of epi-eugenics

Epigenetic thinking is Janus faced, as Mansfield and Guthman (2014) note. It breaks out of the straitjacket of genetic determinism – we are molecularly free. We are porous, we absorb and we interact. These understandings may inform fights for social justice, add a punch to arguments for compensation following exposure to environmental chemicals, show how oppression gets under the skin. But all this plasticity has a dark side:

> This ugly side of epigenetics arises out of the heart of what makes epigenetics promising: that it focuses on plasticity, rather than determinism … makes it open to intervention and improvement, even 'optimization' … [but] The notion of optimization renders epigenetic changes as disorderly, as damage not adaptation … things once normal, in a statistical sense, can become abnormal, in the sense of not-optimal. (Mansfield and Guthman, 2014: 3, 11)

Gestation becomes the playground for epigenetic manipulations. Women are made responsible for optimising the biological environment of their bodies, making the 'right choices', consuming the remedies and therapies on offer to 'optimise' their uterine environments. Practise stress management in the mornings, consume choline supplements in the evening, and so on: the technical imperatives flow thick and fast. We thus come perilously close to losing any concept of a normal continuum: all difference is potentially suboptimal. This is, of course, a paradox because epigenetics is all about difference and adaptive variation in response to external exigencies, but by equating difference with disease, through the notion of suboptimal conditions, it creates a particularly potent form of eugenic thinking. Woman heal thyself; then, and only then, go forth and multiply. In the US this has become heavily racialised, as Mansfield and Guthman (2014) note.

This side of the Atlantic, this *modus operandi* is almost certainly going to be refracted through social class. 'Optimisation' of early life environments, and the conflation of 'suboptimal' with 'marginal maltreatment', might make the case for benignly intended public health and parenting education approaches (Barlow and Calam, 2011), but these semantic shifts also erode the 'normal' and expose particular sections of the population to increased scrutiny in the name of prevention. The State is afforded new mandates to screen and intervene, and to prevent what might have been. We can see harbingers of what might be on the way. There are epidemiological studies linking fathers' lifestyle (smoking, diet) to disease risk in the male line (Pembrey et al, 2006), and arguments from developmental biologists in favour of broad-ranging public health or environmental interventions.

> There is compelling evidence that the male germline is also vulnerable to environmental impacts which confer substantial health risks on offspring. The clear implication of these findings is that effective mitigation of environmental health risks is unlikely to be achieved by sex, or life-stage-specific behavior change, but will require action that recognizes the much greater breadth of these risks across the life course. (Cunliffe, 2015: 67)

Nevertheless, despite these arguments for a broader prospectus, the mood music in the policy world tells us that it is mothers who will bear the brunt of the current epigenetic line of reasoning.

Some hint of the policy direction flowing from epigenetics comes from a recent review, again co-authored by Meaney (Zhang et al, 2013). Drawing together animal and human studies, it reaffirms that 'epigenetic mechanisms serve to mediate the association between early childhood and gene expression', thus explaining 'in part at least, individual differences in vulnerability/resistance for specific forms of psychopathology' (p 119). More notable are the opening comments of the paper in terms of the moral direction of travel:

> Parental factors also serve to mediate the effects of adversity derived from extra-familial sources on neurodevelopment ... For example, the effects of poverty on emotional and cognitive development are mediated by parental factors to the extent that if such factors are controlled, there is no discernible effect of poverty on child development ... Treatment outcomes associated with early intervention programs are routinely correlated with changes in parental behavior. In cases where parental behavior proves resistant to change, treatment outcomes for the children are seriously limited. (Zhang et al, 2013: 111–12)

We encountered this line of reasoning in chapter six where we reviewed James Heckman's work. From the high licking and grooming supermum rats to sensitive human mothering is, for some, but a small, uncontroversial step! Glover et al (2010) note there is 'starting to be some evidence that the nature of the stress response can be modified by sensitive early mothering' (p 21). Given that the birth mother is the source of the suboptimal stress response, where else shall this sensitive mothering be found?

Biologically uniting nature and nurture, epigenetics promises a great deal and is delivering crucial new understandings of disease, but it also reconfigures relationships between parents, children and the State. The difficulties in accessing biological samples from the brains of human subjects has led to a search for reliable markers in peripheral tissues as proxies for changes in the central nervous system. A current favourite is cheek (buccal) cells. The relatively non-invasive nature of such tests opens up the population to epigenetic screening. As we noted in chapter six, in addition to parent reports and teacher assessments, a recent protocol for the evaluation of an early intervention project by the 'Warwick Consortium' (2014) includes: 'a number of biometric measures (e.g. hair samples to assess cortisol levels at 2 years; buccal cheek swabs to assess epigenetic changes at 3 years; accelerometers to assess activity at 7 years' (p 4). The utility of such proxy measures is at yet unclear, with a recent review noting:

> … despite the extreme diversity of epigenetic organization across cell-types and genomic loci within the brain, available data suggest that cerebral … epigenetic adaptations may be reflected, at least in part, in similar changes in peripheral tissues. Whether such changes may share some relationships, and through which molecular mechanisms, remains fully unknown. (Lutz and Turecki, 2014: 151–2)

Despite this, biomarkers will be deployed, one suspects more for the scientific lustre they add than any proven efficacy. The project which is the subject of evaluation by the Warwick Consortium is aimed at improving life chances of children in deprived neighbourhoods. However, the potential for the use of biomarkers, however questionable their accuracy, to make normative and consequential judgements about good and bad parenting, at the more coercive end of the State's interventions, is clear.

Policy and practice responses may potentially range from the benign promotion of simple measures, such as soothing infant massage, to intervention by the child protection system. A recent paper, entitled 'An evidence-based, pre-birth assessment pathway for vulnerable pregnant women', by Barlow et al (2015) is instructive. The opening argument refers to a prospective study of children who had been assessed or taken into care in their first year, noting that two thirds had been identified as 'at risk'. Of these, 43% were still living at the age of three with parents 'who had shown little change'. Over half the children at this age were showing serious developmental delays and behavioural difficulties; moreover, 'the long-term well-being of 60% of permanently separated children had been doubly jeopardised by late separation from an abusive family' (pp 2–3). The paper makes the case for social workers to 'work more effectively … within timescales that are consistent with the developmental and attachment process of infants' (p 3). The Children and Families Act 2014 imposes a 26-week time limit for all but the most exceptional public law proceedings in England. The paper goes on to describe the development of a new care pathway:

> … aimed at early identification, intensive support, and timely assessment and decision making for vulnerable and high-risk pregnant women. It includes a systematic method of assessing capacity to change, which involves the use of an evidence-based model of assessment and treatment that includes the repeated administration of standardised measures of family functioning and monitoring of goal attainment, consistent with recommendations of best practice. (p 3)

The pathway is based on the Parenting under Pressure (PuP) programme, 'a home-based intervention with a focus on developing a safe and nurturing relationship between carer and infant' (p 3). A pilot study of the new pathway is described in one local authority social work team; 26 cases were involved but no details of outcomes are provided apart from the illustrative case study of Jessica, 'referred to the team when she was eighteen weeks pregnant after multiple pregnancies. Her previous history included termination, miscarriages and children removed from her care who have since been adopted'. Jessica is in a new relationship 'thought to be free of abuse and was keen to receive help to enable her to keep this child' (pp 7–8).

What would have happened had Jessica not been compliant? We can only speculate, but a slide from a presentation[4] by Barlow in 2012 to a local authority in Wales proposes an indicative timescale of 8 months for any intervention to work before more radical and coercive measures are considered. The menace of such a threat is especially clear for women with few resources and social supports who are, for example, experiencing postnatal depression. Will it make things better or exacerbate their difficulties? Evidence suggests that the timescale is much too short for many women to recover from postnatal depressive episodes. A recent review concluded that in women who were receiving medical care, 50% of patients experienced depression for more than one year after childbirth, and also found that, in women who were not receiving clinical treatment, 30% were still depressed up to three years after giving birth (Vliegen et al, 2014). Of course, the many supportive qualities of the PuP programme might help women recover from depression. But in the context of an interventionist child protection system with the option of nonconsensual adoption, the implications of such a surveillance orientation, and the possible stressors this introduces for women (indeed families), are manifestly disturbing, dystopian even.

Conclusion

Put bluntly, is all this (epi)genetic thinking a good thing? Maybe, there again maybe not. The drift of our case is strongly to highlight the latter, the dark side. On the one hand epigenetics can add lustre to arguments for improvements in social welfare and public health. Herrera–Cuenca (2015), an academic from the Venezuelan Health Observatory, argues that epigenetics and public policy are very comfortable bedfellows. Adequate nutrition, safe housing, safe water and non–polluted space will diminish epigenetic risks. In turn, education will ensure that

> the population will be aware of what is important to do for themselves and their children, they will learn how to cooperate with others and understand the role of the family in the improvement of wellbeing. At the end what is interesting is that with the improvement of education, family employment and infrastructure, we are ensuring less methylation of DNA or post–translational modification of histones. (p 18)

But where does this take us? Are these not public goods with a strong moral case in their support already? Surely, epigenetics is superfluous. What if there were no effects on the epigenome of hunger, environmental toxins and other privations, would they then be acceptable? The answer surely is no. Moreover, since such provisions are so self-evidently improvements to everyday life and consequently to caring for others and coping, there should be no need for expensive (yet apparently always inconclusive) evaluations and clinical trials.

One thing is clear though; the epigenetic form of reasoning suggests greater opportunities for pharmacological remedies, and therefore lucrative profits for Big Pharma. As resources are finite, this could provide less room for social housing projects and food cooperatives, which have little currency at the molecular level and intrinsically struggle to demonstrate the 'outcomes' economists prefer to plug in to their models aimed at the optimisation of 'human capital'. It is easier in the short term to show the effects of a pill on a biomarker than the benefits of access to decent food and human company for the wellbeing of a community.

Notes

[1] A more detailed analysis using linear regression showed that babies exposed during the first and second trimesters showed the greatest reductions in birthweight, of 172 grams less than the pre-famine baseline. The corresponding weight loss for the non-famine areas was slightly greater (184 grams). Our calculations of effect size from the t values quoted showed that both these effects were small (d <0.15 in both cases). Two other results stand out. The biggest overall weight loss was 579 grams for babies in the non-famine cohort corresponding to those exposed to the famine during the middle six months of gestation: Cohen's d for this effect was in the middle range (approx. 0.3). Also of note is that babies in famine area conceived after the famine also showed a reduction in birthweight, with an effect size slightly greater than effect of exposure to famine during the first two trimesters.

[2] Using t values calculated from the estimated effects and standard errors provided in table 7 of Scholte et al's paper, we have crudely estimated Cohen's d values of around 0.02 (that is, no effect) for the impacts on employment and CVD. It is intrinsically difficult working from the processed results of analyses carried out by others to be sure that one's improvisations are correct. But we have done our best, and trust that our extemporised analysis at least provides a rough guide to the effect sizes.

[3] 11 beta hydroxysteroid dehydrogenase type 2.

[4] The full presentation is in the public domain, see: https://www.conwy.gov.uk/upload/public/attachments/512/Jane_Barlow__Wales_March_2012.pdf

NINE

Are we broken? Fixing people (or society) in the 21st century

> Must we then give up fathoming the depths of life? Must we keep to that mechanistic idea of it which the understanding will always give us – an idea necessarily artificial and symbolical, since it makes the total activity of life shrink to the form of a certain human activity which is only a partial and local manifestation of life, a result or by-product of the vital process? (Bergson, *Creative Evolution*, p xii)

We have argued throughout the book that attempts to fathom the depths of life by examining our flesh and blood create new opportunities and imperatives for the State. Through developments in biotechnology, the moral domains of deviance, normality, crime and punishment, even the making of socially useful human capital, can potentially be turned into technical matters to be sorted and shaped. Prevention and surveillance go under the skin and into the womb. We have shown how processes within scientific communities affect the ways in which findings from animal studies may be applied to human populations. Citation practices, for example, critically affect what is asked in subsequent research, and contestable findings can become rewritten as fundamental truths. Thus, research becomes 'path dependent', a furrow is ploughed, cow-paths are paved and commitment to a particular knowledge quest escalates. The research funding follows and makes the rut longer and deeper, the 'facts' get made, told and retold; the memes reproduce themselves. The structures that are created, constrain more than they enable.

In this final chapter, we raise questions about whether the neurological and molecular levels, the actions and processes within and between cells, are the most rich and appropriate domains to guide the actions of the State. The consequences of the prevailing moral and scientific settlements, we will argue, are that preferred policy responses are individualised and increasingly medicalised. A preoccupation with prevention, early intervention and particular forms of evidence are squeezing out conversations about different, and potentially more desirable and sustainable, actions to make people's lives better. Choices are being made about who to help, who needs to change and how money is spent on creating a better world. Notions of vulnerability and damage are double edged; possibly more resources flow, but these dispensations are conditional on 'compliance', 'engagement' and surveillance. Targeting, and its associated drive for evidence of outcomes, as we have seen, is expensive to deliver, soaking up resources which might be better deployed in direct support. Academic careers are made and sustained in mandating 'evidence-based interventions'. The war on poverty is no longer 'on trend'. Only a minority of the poor abuse their children or put them at serious risk of neglect, so on biological and psychological grounds, providing resources to people in poverty comes to be seen as wasteful.

On the one hand, developments in the application of biological science can be seen as a 'giant leap' in the ever ascending modernist project of human progress, of 'taking charge of the world', making nature 'susceptible to human knowledge … at the disposal of humanity' (Connolly, 1993: 2). 'God is dead', pronounced Nietzsche's madman (1974: 125) '… and we have killed him'. Portentously, he goes on to ask: 'Is not the greatness of this deed too great for us? Must we ourselves become gods simply to appear worthy of it?' Yes, it would seem so … but in a world governed by the 'drive for mastery' (Nietzsche, 1974: 2) and no longer by myth and religion, there is a darker side to the Promethean aspiration:

> The 'will to truth' will appear as the will to impose human form upon the world and then to treat that imposition as if it were a discovery. The more tenacious that will is … the more ruthless it will have to be with those people, actions and events deemed by it to be abnormal, irrational, perverse, unnatural, or anomalous. (p 10)

Our final digressions will take us from laboratory science, to social science, to policy and back. We will review our main arguments using a number of exhibits to show where the biological thought style may be taking us next in relation to policy and practice. Throughout the book, we may have made assertions which could appear definitive, but this has been done for rhetorical effect, to destabilise the dogmatism of apparently settled positions. In this last chapter, we draw on further potent exemplars from epigenetics, including a study searching for the impact of social adversity on the cells of a population in Glasgow, and on recent debates within criminology, to try to anticipate a possible future. Finally, we make our case for a more inclusive and reanimated approach to human flourishing.

Read all about it!

We begin with a report from the *Herald Scotland* in January 2012, on the study we encountered in our first chapter which claimed to have found biomarkers of disease susceptibility based on levels of social deprivation. The headline ran 'DNA could explain riddle of poor health in Glasgow' and the story, by the journalist Helen McArdle, ran as follows:

> The health of the most deprived residents of Scotland's biggest city could be impaired even before they are born, according to genetic research. … Research leader Dr Paul Shiels … said it was a 'significant' discovery which might explain why the health of people in Glasgow is much worse than in other European cities. In the study, researchers identified significant variations in a process known as methylation between DNA samples taken from people living in the most affluent and most deprived areas of Glasgow. The majority of methylation content is fixed for life from just a few weeks after conception … lower levels are known to increase a person's chances of developing diabetes and cardiovascular problems later in life.

Bold claims indeed on the origins of enduring health inequalities affecting the Scottish city. Premature death and rates of disease in Glasgow outstrip those of the cities of Manchester and Liverpool, which have similar levels of socioeconomic deprivation, making Glasgow a natural choice for researchers in the DOHaD way of thinking. This study forms the last of our major exhibits and from it we draw some conclusions about the status of the biosocial policy project, its aspirations and its potential effects. The article continues with a further quotation from the lead researcher:

> We found levels of DNA methylation were significantly lower in the samples from the most deprived areas than they were in those from the least deprived, and those samples also showed signs of an elevated risk of cardiovascular disease. Methylation levels decline throughout everyone's life as part of the natural process of ageing, and can be slightly affected in adulthood by external factors such as diet, stress and lifestyle. Those external factors have a much greater effect on babies developing in the womb, affecting

the enzymes which allow DNA methylation to occur, so it's very likely the significantly lower levels of methylation we're seeing in the most deprived areas of the city are set before birth...Further study is required... but practical outcomes from this research could include much quicker feedback on the effectiveness of public health interventions or the development of tests to identify individuals whose levels of DNA methylation suggest they are more at risk of developing health problems.

First, we should note some, now familiar, elements of methylation mythology. There are the usual causal claims made about methylation and disease, the majority of methylation is described as 'fixed for life', being only 'slightly affected' by adult lifestyle, with the pattern most likely 'set before birth'. Screening forms a central plank of the proposed public health response, both to identify those at risk and to appraise the value of interventions. Further research is, as ever, required.

Comments on the study in a covering report in the *British Medical Journal* are emblematic of the poles of the debate we have witnessed in previous chapters. Marcus Pembery, emeritus professor of paediatric genetics at the Institute of Child Health, strikes a cautionary note:

> Evidence is emerging that early experience may indeed be biologically embedded through changes in the epigenome as indicated by associations with gene promoter DNA methylation levels. It is very early days; these are only associations, and understanding the causal pathways needs both cheap, high resolution techniques for DNA methylation analysis, gene by gene, and the application of these to birth cohort followed for many decades. The measurement used in this study—global DNA methylation—only gives a partial picture, and the results should be interpreted with caution. (cited in Christie, 2012: 1)

Iona Heath, president of the Royal College of General Practitioners, in contrast, describes the findings as 'intriguing', making the case for early intervention to 'optimise' the uterine environment and the life conditions of early infancy.

> We have mounting evidence that the biographical context of individual lives affects the structure and functioning of genes and that nature and nurture are inextricably intertwined.

> The importance of optimising the life conditions of young children and pregnant women becomes ever more clear. It is a shame that political direction and fiscal policy in the UK seem to have other priorities. (Cited in Christie, 2012: 1)

Biology most certainly is political (Meloni, 2016). It is interesting that the findings are 'intriguing', not only to Iona Heath, but apparently to the scientific team too. So, let us follow our customary path and examine the journal science underpinning this media story. The primary research is reported in McGuinness et al (2012). The paper opens by reiterating the relative fixity of methylation patterns, and their susceptibility to 'lifestyle' factors, with maternal diet and mood being singled out for particular emphasis. It is further hypothesised that 'underlying chronic inflammation' (p 152) may underlie the increased disease prevalence.

Based on prior research on chronic kidney disease, a strong association is asserted by the authors between DNA methylation and inflammatory biomarkers (specifically the interleukin-6 protein, IL-6, secreted by white blood cells). This leads the team to their primary working hypothesis that 'social deprivation would be associated with ... reduced methylation content, which would in turn be associated with enhanced inflammatory status and associated disease risk' (p 152) – a veritable cornucopia of associations with what are arguably somewhat vaguely defined entities. The study examined the influence of a broad range of socioeconomic and lifestyle variables on a sample of adult individuals. The effect of the deprivation level of the participant's residential neighbourhood was assessed by comparing the bottom 5% of neighbourhoods (according to the Scottish index for multiple deprivation) with the most affluent 20%. This yielded a final sample of 239 individuals. The methylation status of DNA extracted from their peripheral white blood cells was assessed. It is noteworthy that this was a global measure; it did not specifically target the IL-6 gene responsible for IL-6 production.

Results showed that reduced methylation was correlated with deprivation and 'social class' (manual vs. nonmanual work); age showed a non-linear effect, falling for the 45–54 age group, compared to the 35–44 group, and then rising again, suggesting, it would seem, that methylation patterns are far from fixed for life, but behave in a complex fashion as a function of age. No other variables (apart from a slight trend for educational level) affected methylation status, notably including gender, income, diet, smoking, physical activity, obesity or alcohol consumption. Further analysis suggests that the biggest influence on methylation content is manual work, reducing it by 27% after correction for all other key influences. The standout result would appear to be that manual work, regardless of whether you live in a rich or poor area, or have a well-paid or a poorly paid job, reduces your methylation status.

But this is not what the authors highlight. The focus instead is on deprivation level: 'the extent of DNA methylation in the most deprived group of participants is intriguing' (p 157). This is viewed as consistent with the result for manual work (seen as 'social class'), though no statistics are reported. No attempt at all is made to address this factor (manual work) directly, despite its all-pervasive statistical influence and its obvious relationship with metabolic processes, including 'wear and tear' on the body. Briefly noting a possible link with 'environmental exposures' or 'diet during life', the authors proceed briskly to the extraordinary speculation that the methylation effects may be 'a direct consequence of developmental programming *in utero*'. Extraordinary for the simple reason that the study has not made even the remotest attempt to examine the uterine environment or early life. The authors continue:

> A link within utero programming is an *attractive explanation*, as there is some evidence supporting the effect of a poor childhood environment and an increased risk of cardiovascular disorders. Indeed, in utero epigenetic programming has been linked to the development of obesity, arteriosclerosis and diabetes and may be related to material diet. ... This is pertinent to a Glasgow-based cohort, where persistence of socio-economic deprivation can be invoked to explain specific global [sic] DNA hypomethylation, with consequent effects on health in adult life. (p 158, emphasis added)

Describing uterine programming as 'attractive' is both revealing and somewhat egregious. It is hard to see it as attractive for the people of Glasgow, and to describe it so can only be attributed to the influence of a thought style. The study concludes by examining relationships between DNA methylation and a range of biomarkers. An association of hypomethylation with IL-6 is found, as well as for fibrinogen (a protein involved in blood clotting); no relationship is found for other biomarkers, including blood pressure and cholesterol. The paper ends with some inconclusive speculations regarding potential molecular mechanisms whereby DNA methylation would work its effects on morbidity.

In summary, this is a remarkable study, but perhaps for the wrong reasons. The funders of the study, the Glasgow Centre for Population Health, fail to make any reference to the eye-catching epigenetic work in their most recent report on the origins of Glasgow's 'excess mortality' (Walsh et al, 2013). One thing would seem to be clear, DNA it seems cannot 'explain riddle of poor health in Glasgow'. Indeed, the vocabulary and thought style of the recent report differ paradigmatically from the DNA study. The hypotheses are distinctly sociological in tone, concerned with social capital, cohesion and participation. The classically Durkheimian concept of 'anomie' is also invoked, a form of boundlessness associated with a breakdown in social bonds and collective norms. The report compares Glasgow with the English cities of Manchester and Liverpool, where similar social problems exist:

> Glasgow was either favourable in comparison with, or similar to, the English cities in relation to issues such as views on the neighbourhood, civic participation (albeit very low levels were recorded across all three cities) and social networks and support, it appeared to have significantly lower levels of social participation (in terms of volunteering, and a proxy for religious attendance) and trust compared with both Liverpool and Manchester, and lower levels of reciprocity, compared with Liverpool alone. (final report, p 76)

The study concludes that participation, trust and reciprocity may influence a range of health behaviours and community social supports. These are described as plausible explanations for the 'excess' mortality in Glasgow in comparison with Liverpool and Manchester. Poverty in all three cities remains the most significant factor in explaining life expectancy. It need not be pointed out that the policy direction this suggests is rather different from the monitoring of the diet, behaviour and mood of pregnant women and parents, or indeed their biomarkers.

The neurobiological turn in criminology

In the field of criminal justice, the potential for biology to inform policy and practice has a long history, and it is worth a short digression at this point to recapitulate recent developments, as these will provide further insights into the likely direction of social policy in this area.

'Biocriminology', to coin a phrase, derives from the same 19th-century phrenological origins as biopsychiatry, being taken up by physicians of the day to explain crime in terms of sickness. In the latter half of that century, a young Italian doctor, Cesare Lombroso, opened the skull of a notorious serial rapist and murderer. Claiming to find numerous abnormalities, including an enlarged cerebellum recalling that of 'lower types of apes, rodents and birds', Lombroso formulated his (in)famous theory of 'atavistic criminality' (Pustilnik, 2009). He subsequently published his most influential work, *L'uomo delinquente*, which went through numerous Italian editions and was published in various European languages.

Over the intervening years, the same oscillations between the 'biological' and the 'social' have taken place that we witnessed for psychiatry. For much of the 20th century, it was the latter which held sway, but now the pendulum would seem to be on the move. A recent Special Issue of the journal *Criminal Justice Studies* is devoted to 'Biosocial criminology' heralding 'the emergence of a new and diverse perspective':

> Neurocriminology ties together each of the biosocial areas by explaining how environmental, biological, and genetic factors can influence behavior. Every factor that plays a causal role in the etiology of antisocial behavior must impact the functioning of the brain in some way. (Barnes and Boutwell, 2015: 2)

In a useful review article, Walsh (2011) considers the impact of neuroscience on youth justice. She begins by arguing strongly for the liberalising benefits of neuroscience, citing instances where such evidence has been used as mitigating argument. In a carefully argued critique of the neuroscience of violence in criminal law, Pustilnik also aims to co-opt neuroscience to reinforce 'progressive' movements. In similar vein, Hughes (2015) in the Special Issue mentioned above, draws attention to the high prevalence of 'neurodevelopmental disorders' in young people serving custodial sentences in the UK. The figures are striking: 12% of inmates suffer from ADHD and 15% from autism. For learning disabilities the discrepancies with the normal population are even more salient, with a prevalence of 23–32% among inmates compared to the rate of 2–4% in the general population. For communication disorders, the corresponding rates are 60–90% compared to 5–7% for the population as a whole. Based on these figures, Hughes argues the liberal case for improving our understanding of the trajectories of offending experienced by young people with specific disorders.

Walsh draws on developmental neuroscience to make the case for raising the age of criminal responsibility, citing the US case of *Roper v. Simmons*, where neuroscientific argumentation was used to 'demonstrate that adolescents are immature not only to the naked eye, but in the very fibres of their brains' (p 23). Walsh notes the work of the UK Law Commission which refers to 'poor frontal lobe development' as an example of how 'neuroscientific research is edging into such documentation' (p 27). She proceeds to speculate on the potential of brain imagery to 'definitively illustrate which parenting has good effects and which bad ones on the infant brain'. She notes, with apparent approval, the argument of the chief executive of a leading UK child welfare charity that: 'More babies should be removed from their mothers at birth before irreparable harm is inflicted. There is an argument to be made ... that even intervening at this early stage is too late' (p 32).

The seductive idea that violent crime can be attributed to a small group of incorrigibly aggressive individuals was influential in UK criminal justice policy in the first decade of this century, leading naturally to the idea that neuroimaging can yield biomarkers to identify these latent miscreants. This prefigures a future in which 'neuroscience plays a role in isolating this subgroup and identifying how to prevent their predicted criminality ... enabling social control to permeate to an even deeper level' (Walsh, 2011: 33). Whether Walsh believes this to be a good or bad thing is not entirely clear, though she does invoke the obvious civil liberties concerns and 'Clockwork Orange' scenarios, including the overenthusiastic use of ritalin to treat ADHD. She concludes:

> The incorporation of treatment into sentencing is well-established in, for instance, the area of drug policy ... There may be enormous gains to be had here, both for the individual concerned and for society, but there is also the potential to cause unimaginable harm ... Even the unborn could be screened for risk of a violent disposition. Those identified as being at risk could be helped, medically or therapeutically ... this could have political appeal to welfare minimalists wanting to make savings because resources could be targeted towards those identified as being most at risk. (pp 34–5)

But the search for biomarkers, yet in its infancy in the criminological field, has so far drawn only blanks. In a recent study, Sullivan and Newsome (2015) examined biomarkers of four variants (alleles) in several genes linked to dopamine regulation, and a serotonin transporter gene. The monoamine oxidase A enzyme was also assayed, which is responsible for the breakdown of adrenaline, serotonin and norepinephrine. Many of these biomarkers we have already encountered; they are, as it were, habitual offenders. The results of the study were interesting. The data used were derived from the National Longitudinal Study of Adolescent Health (AddHealth). Samples of saliva were obtained from 2,583 individuals for genotyping. Levels of delinquency were assessed across the various waves of the study. A psychosocial risk questionnaire was also deployed, including items concerned with family attachment and substance abuse. The results showed no association between the biomarkers and delinquency, whereas there was a notable correlation of 0.39 with the composite psychosocial risk score. Again, staying at the same level of explanation for indicator and outcome, the psychosocial, would seem best!

General concerns have been raised about the whole direction of current criminal policy. Rose (2010) identifies a strong, indeed fundamental, link between biological thinking and the management of risk. Risk thinking, he argues, dominates contemporary discourse on deviance, echoing its centrality in prevention science (chapter 6). Although noting examples where biological evidence (genetic sequences, brain images) has been used as mitigation in criminal cases, he concludes pessimistically that the more likely trajectory 'is unlikely to be in the direction of mitigation. More likely are arguments for the long-term pacification of the biologically irredeemable individual in the name of public protection' (Rose, 2010: 84–5).

For Rose, the shift from actual danger to risk is driven by the fear of 'monstrous individuals – the predators of the popular imagination – paedophiles, serial killers…' (pp 87–8). The medicalisation of 'deviant behaviour' forms an essential part of these new risk management strategies. Rose gives the example of the invention of 'dangerous and severe personality disorder' (DSPD) in 1999 as a disease category, with £100 million subsequently spent in the UK on a DSPD programme dedicated to 'ensuring the public is protected from some of the most dangerous people in society'.[1] The DSPD programme has attracted obvious criticism, with calls for its abandonment (Tyrer et al, 2010). The idea that people should be locked up for things they might do is somewhat questionable from a civil liberties perspective, to say the least, but it serves nonetheless to indicate the direction of travel.

Rose argues that a new 'style of thought' is thus taking hold, a new logic based on the identification (via neurobiological markers) of antisocial 'susceptibilities' and their pre-emptive management: 'not so much discipline-and-punish but screen-and-intervene' (Rose, 2010: 97). The logic is appealing because it is imbued with hope as well as anxiety, that brain mechanisms can be reshaped 'to nip budding psychopaths' in the bud. Given the current anxieties of policy makers, and the priority given to the precautionary principle, Rose foresees an increase in preventive but illiberal (and also ineffectual) interventions in the name of public protection:

> Historical precedents suggest such strategies are unlikely to reduce the overall frequency of the very rare incidents they seek to prevent. But they are likely to result in threshold-lowering and net-widening, and the detention of many individuals who are capable of leading lives that might sometimes be troublingly different but would pose no danger to others. (p 88)

Reclaiming Einstein: reductionism, biomarkers and the fallacy of reverse inference

> Einstein cannot simply lie back and let the cells do the job for him ... he must do the work himself, moved by his own joys and sorrows, his own memories and ambitions, his own sense of identity and free will. If these were not real, thought would stop. (Midgley, 2014: 57)

A recurring theme in this book has been the idea that there are different 'levels of explanation' or 'analysis' for describing and explaining phenomena. Often, this has been expressed dichotomously, as the simple contrast between the macro and the micro: in chapters one, two and three, for instance, the psychological level of explanation was implied to be 'macro', contrasting with the neural or genetic levels, which were seen as micro. In chapter six, we explicitly referred to the work of economists like Heckman as 'macroeconomic', implying that this was a weakness as it could not provide an explanatory account of the detailed human behaviours underlying abstract parameters in equations.

The idea of levels is a commonplace in biology, social science and other sciences, providing a handy way of reconciling different disciplinary perspectives and paradigms, although it is not without its difficulties. In everyday life, it seldom causes problems – it perfectly possible for us to cope with different levels of explanation, as Mary Midgley argues:

> When science tells us that the tables we believe to be solid are largely composed of empty space we don't have to abandon our previous views and stop putting our cups down on them. Common sense can easily accommodate two different ways of thinking about tables. (Midgley, 2014: 1)

But in science it can get us into deep difficulty. Miller (2010) points out that there is little consensus on what counts as a level. Sometimes, the difference between the micro and the macro seems merely one of statistical abstraction: for instance, whether neural activity should be analysed at the level of the individual neurone or patterns of activity in larger-scale entities. In other cases, there would appear to be more fundamental differences; the levels seem to correspond to incommensurate 'domains of discourse', such as the competing accounts of mental disorder as either a biochemical imbalance or as an existential disturbance. In the latter case, the levels of cause and effect seem naturally complementary (both psychological) and causal mechanisms can readily be constructed between the two (i.e. mental disorder and life experience); in the former, connecting across qualitatively different ontological domains (from physiology to psychology) is much more taxing, if not logically impossible, as well as having potentially undesirable consequences.

In thinking about levels and their relationships, another key concept comes into view, that of 'reductionism'. Again, this is a term with protean meanings. Often it is used opprobriously, as when researchers dismiss the work of others as 'reductionist'. Clarity in its usage has been urged, with Lilienfeld (2007) distinguishing two clearly different manifestations: eliminative and constitutive reductionism. The former posits that one level of explanation (the 'lower level', such as physiology, will eventually 'gobble up' all 'higher' levels (psychological, sociological), rendering them 'supererogatory' (p 265): 'Like the once popular computer game of Pacman, the scientific enterprise envisioned by eliminative reductionists entails a progressive cannibalization of all higher levels of explanation by a ravenously hungry lower-level monster' (p 265).

Constitutive reductionism, on the other hand, is less radical:

> It acknowledges that all mental events are ultimately rooted in the activities in the nervous system, and strives to uncover the physiological correlates of psychological events ... [It] does not assume that the physiological level of analysis is always the optimal level of analysis for understanding psychological events. (p 265)

The position we take in this book is closer to the second position regarding the relationship between psychology and biology. We follow Miller in adopting the idea of 'implementation' to characterise this relationship; this entails, 'viewing cognition and emotion as implemented in neural systems but not reducible to them' (p 724). The key challenge for eliminative reductionism is whether all the meaning of the 'higher level' construct can be captured by the 'lower level'. If so, then it can be deleted from our vocabulary. Clearly, we do not believe this is a tenable position for any of the psychological concepts we have encountered in this book. Indeed, we have contended that far from being 'supererogatory', the psychological domain is the sine qua non for the entire bio-scientific project, in either its neural or genetic version. We have alluded to the heat-map at various points to support our case for the 'logical priority' of the 'higher' (social and the psychological) versus the 'lower'. The idea of 'home' provides another example of the poverty of reductionism: from a lower-level viewpoint, a home is no more than an arrangement of bricks![2]

We now turn to a fallacy which runs through the heart of the biological project. So much of the research that we have witnessed has the character of a correlational 'fishing expedition'. A psychological condition is varied in some way, a range of 'biological markers' is examined (brain images and/or biochemistry, genetic alleles, epigenetic marks), seeking an indicator which covaries with the psychological state. This has given rise to what Poldrack (2006) has called an 'epidemic' of the reverse inference fallacy. Poldrack gives the example of Broca's area, an area of the temporal lobe which has been associated with language since the 19th century, when the French physician Pierre Paul Broca tracked down the loss of speech in two of his patients to damage in this area.

Examining the widely used 'Brainmap' database for studies reporting activity of this area (so-called Brodmann area 44), it was found to be active in 20% of 'comparisons' explicitly involving language processing, contrasting with 8% of cases where the 'language function' was not engaged. We might be tempted to conclude from this that activation of 'BA44' provides a good indicator that the language function is 'engaged'. But this would be to commit the 'reverse inference fallacy', otherwise known as 'confirming the consequent'. In mathematic terms, this entails confusing two conditional probabilities: the probability that when language is 'going on', BA44 lights up, with the converse, that when the area is activated, this means language processing is in train. Although we know the former probability (20%), we do not know the latter; and it is the latter which we need to know. A good biomarker will enable us to predict with confidence the presence of the psychosocial 'state' of interest. Here, there is ample evidence of 'false positives', with BA44 activated in 8% of comparisons without overt language engagement. Using a mathematical formalism known as Bayes theorem,[3] Poldrack estimates the strength of the 'reverse inference' of BA44 activity: while positive, it provides only a 'relatively weak increase in confidence' that language is involved. Appendix C provides further discussion of this issue and another example of the limited predictive utility of biomarkers associated with small effect sizes.

The finding of multiple brain regions being 'implicated' in any given psychological process, is – as we have seen – very much the norm, bedevilling the search for simple predictive biomarkers. Let us take the neuroscience of violence as another example, as it is particularly relevant to contemporary social policy. Two brain areas are constantly invoked: the frontal lobes and the amygdala. But as Pustilnik (2009) notes, research studies have shown the frontal lobes to be involved in every conceivable higher-level cognitive process, including general intelligence, problem solving, executive control, attention, decision making, semantic memory, perceptual analysis and self-awareness (pp 219–20). Knowing it is active is thus of little diagnostic value. Regarding the amygdala she observes that 'Numerous respected brain researchers question the localisation of fear to the amygdala and the leap from fearfulness to violence, because the amygdala can be activated by many events that have no relation to fear' (p 220). If the subject is shown a picture of scrambled eggs in an experiment to identify playing cards: 'Your amygdala will light up. This is not because the subject is afraid of or angry about scrambled eggs but because the picture is unexpected' (p 221).

But the reverse inference is rife, as shown in the following particularly spectacular example from a study by Buss et al (2010) (referred to in chapter eight) which reports grey matter reductions in the frontal cortex of children whose mothers experienced pregnancy anxiety. From this, it is confidently concluded that their higher cognitive functions must be impaired, even though there was no evidence of developmental issues emotionally or physically; moreover, the researchers did not assess cognitive performance or attempt any long-term follow-up. Too busy scanning brain images, one presumes:

> The brain regions that we have found to be affected are areas specifically associated with cognitive performance. The prefrontal cortex is sometimes described as the 'highest' structure of the brain because it is involved in executive cognitive functions such as reasoning, planning attention ... Thus elevated prenatal maternal stress/anxiety is associated with infant inability to attend and with delayed cognitive development. (Buss et al, 2010: 147)

We have characterised much of contemporary bioscience using a fishing metaphor. Technological advances have made available large databanks of brain images and genetic sequences, data which is freely shared across the research community. The size of the pool in which scientists can now fish is thus vast, and growing steadily vaster still, so we can only expect more, not less, reverse inference. The epidemic will get worse, before (hopefully) it gets better. Incidentally, the increasing role of technology and automation in the biosciences has led to important changes in the nature of research. Leonelli (2010) gives the example of genomic databases:

> The 21st century has brought immense technological advances in the production of genomic data. Sequencing is now an automated activity taking no more than a few hours; collecting data on gene expression can also be done automatically, resulting in billions of data-points per day. This level of automation means that the activity of data collecting has never been as disjointed from activities of explicit theory-building. ... The scientific focus is thus shifting from efforts to produce data, characteristic of late 20th century biology, to efforts to exploit these data as evidence towards new claims ... Accordingly, whoever is in charge of classification practices holds a considerable amount of power over the ways in which research will be conducted in the future. (Leonelli, 2010: 106)

Another manifestation of reductionist thinking inheres in the very use of animal models. For some, this appears to be a relatively trivial concern. While noting 'differences in maternal-placental-neuroendocrine processes' Glover et al (2010) nonetheless unequivocally proclaim that 'animal experiments have provided strong evidence that prenatal stress can have long-lasting and varied effects on the offspring' (p 18). One is driven to ask, do the authors really believe that complex human activities (such as parenting) and mental disorders (depression, schizophrenia) can be 'reduced' to the artificially produced behaviours (such as the forced swim test) of a rodent in a laboratory:

> How ... can anyone believe that there can be any similarity between mouse behaviour in this strange apparatus in an artificial laboratory setting and the rich meaningful, culturally embedded, historically shaped, linguistically organized, situationally framed experience of depression, anxiety and whatever else in our everyday human world? (Rose and Abi-Rached, 2013: 83)

Presumably only folks who have not read the original papers, or perhaps feel no need to as they already know the answers. Others have warned of the dangers of premature extrapolation to humans. Juengst et al (2014: 428) argue:

> Although evidence-based applications of human epigenetics may emerge in the future, premature epigenetic risk messaging is already here and its content and impact must be understood. The messages in circulation raise ethical and social concerns regardless of whether human epigenetic studies eventually confirm the murine [rodent] results.

Indeed, the degree of reduction is more extreme than it may appear at first sight to the lay reader:

> To date, the most compelling reports of methylation effects have examined rodents (a key fact conveniently omitted in many popular media reports). In rodent models, all research participants are genetically identical, and everything in their environment is held constant across treatment and control groups except the experimental manipulation. This uniformity combined with experimental control over the severity of the treatment dose makes it relatively easy to detect effects in laboratory animals, compared with humans, who are characterized by staggering levels of both genetic and environmental diversity. (Moffitt and Beckley, 2015)

Paradoxically, the imperative to optimise the sensitivity of the laboratory experiment, to eliminate all sources of unwanted variability, means that it is not clear from any study whether the results would generalise to another strain of the same species, let alone a different species altogether. Such standardisation might go some way to explain an endemic feature of the current laboratory paradigm: the difficulty of reproducing results reliably across different studies. As Rose and Abi-Rached note, the use of standardised species/strains only began at the outset of the 20th century; hitherto, it was seen as important to test hypotheses on a range of species: 'Authors aimed for generality, but they treated it as a conclusion that would or would not follow from the examination of many species'(p 91). Nowadays, such generality is treated as a given. The importance of this problem is becoming increasingly recognised: 'standardization in the characteristics of the animals used (such as age, sex, body weight and others), husbandry and test procedures—may generate spurious results, accounting for poor reproducibility' (Richter et al, 2010: 167). These authors recommend a greater degree of heterogeneity (different strains, species, more 'natural' ecology), calling for 'research into practicable and effective ways of systematic environmental heterogenization to attenuate these scientific, economic and ethical costs' (Richter et al, 2009: 257).

Summarising this section, although we have raised a number of concerns about the dangers of reductionist thinking, we reiterate that we are not dismissive of the contribution that neuroscience can make in the understanding of brains and behaviour or that epigenetics may contribute to understanding disease at the (appropriate) molecular level. Our position is much that of Lilienfeld, who argues for an 'integrative explanatory pluralism' in which 'researchers gradually assemble local linkages among neighbouring levels of analysis in a bit-by-bit fashion' (Lilienfeld, 2007: 266). Miller puts it well:

> Fundamentally psychological concepts will require fundamentally (though perhaps not exclusively) psychological explanations. Stories about biological phenomena can richly inform, but not replace, those explanations. When psychological events unfold in humans, they are implemented in biology, and those implementations are clearly important to study as well, both in their own right and to foster psychological research and clinical intervention. (Miller, 2010: 736)

It is surely time to let go of the mereological fallacy, to restore Einstein's genius to the man himself, wresting it from his mythical but not so prodigious brain.

Magic in the therapeutic State: can the thought style be budged?

> The transporting of the log is not an easy task … the natives resort to a magical rite which makes the canoe lighter. The owner or builder beats the log with a bunch of dry lalang grass and utters the following spell: 'Come down, rot! Come down fungus …' and so on, invoking a number of deteriorations to leave the log. In other words, the heaviness and slowness due to all these magical causes are thrown out of the log. (Malinowski, Argonauts of the Western Pacific, 1922: 129)

Although seeming to be opposites, technology and magic have formally much in common, as sociologists from Mauss (1902, republished 1950) to Stivers (2001) have noted. Both are instrumental, involving the deployment of a body of practical skill and knowledge to accomplish something of social value (Mauss, 1950). The primary difference lies in the apparent link between cause and effect. Whereas magic is 'pure production, *ex nihilo*' (Mauss, 1950: 175), technology accomplishes its effects through palpable labour and efficient causes. There is nothing magical about the mechanics of a steam engine, at least to us 'moderns'. But what about the new technobiologies? Perhaps there is more in common with the magic of Melanesian Waga-builder than we might care to think. Magicians in all societies are creatures of public opinion (Mauss, 1950) endowed with power by a credulous community to accomplish 'outcomes' that the society seeks, bringing rain, curing illness, and so on. Like magic, these new sciences take place in special, remote places.[4] The strict observance of procedures, like the rites of magic, is also the hallmark of laboratory science. In magic, when the spell fails, what then?

> Magic has such authority that a contrary experience does not on the whole destroy a person's belief. Even the most unfavourable facts can be turned to magic's advantage, since they can always be held to be the work of counter-magic or to result from an error in performance of the ritual …

> Fortuitous coincidences are accepted as normal facts and all contradictory evidence is denied. (Mauss, 1950: 114–15)

Belief in the efficacy of the magic is strengthened, paradoxically, by its very failure; the failed spell is blamed, not on the magic itself, but on the way the ceremony was performed, or some other procedural (methodological) flaw. Indefeasible, circular reasoning is the hallmark of magic, memorably dubbed by Mehan (1990) as 'oracular reasoning'. It would not be entirely mischievous to point out the obvious parallels with the neuromolecular thought style and its indefatigable quest for the missing genes. The same thinking shows through in the search for the biochemical imbalance or epigenetic inscriptions which will account for deviance. There is a pervasive belief system at work here which axiomatically defines the origins of all that is 'mad or bad' as biological; it is merely a question of time, effort and technological advance before the definitive biomarker is found.

Reductionism in all its forms characterises the hegemony of the biological belief system, not just of the causal origins of phenomena, but reductionism of method (animal models) and of remedy too (inevitably pharmacological). Developmentalism, as we have seen, aligns naturally with neuromolecular thinking, especially the idea that health and disease in later life are governed by early childhood experience (or earlier still, in the womb). This provides the central axiom of the DOHaD movement. That there is a normal, against which any difference is categorised as deviant, is another *idée fixe*. This leads to the progressive medicalisation of what is merely different, or which reflects an alternative moral position. The imperative to show benefits in terms of economic returns is also an important strand of the paradigm, naturally aligning with the medical model.

Magical thinking helps sustain this whole ideological nexus. Fallacious reasoning is rife: the reverse inference fallacy,[5] the mereological fallacy, circular and oracular reasoning, the streetlight effect.[6] In terms of Kahneman et al's (1982) seminal work on the fallibilities of human decision making, symptoms of the availability and anchoring heuristics[7] are endemic, with a massive dollop of confirmation bias. As we survey the literature, the whiff of technological determinism is all-pervasive; the direction of travel is ever dictated by the latest technological advance, be it brain imaging or genetic analysis: technology will always provide the needed magic. The sense of path dependency is also very strong, namely the tendency of future behaviours to be governed by what has been done before, to carry on doing more of the same. The bioscience enterprise also reminds one of the phenomenon of 'escalation of commitment in the field of project management',[8] though this is normally associated with projects of a less prodigious scale. Such amplification effects are exacerbated by what Napier et al (2006) call system justification. This is the response of an organised social system to its own failures, a form of 'doing the wrong thing righter':

> In response to such system threats, both victims and observers (e.g., the general public, commentators, policy makers) are known to engage in various forms of system justification, including direct defense of the status quo, victim blaming, stereotyping, and internalization of inequality. These processes can reduce emotional distress and restore perceived legitimacy to the system, but they may have a number of troubling consequences. (Napier et al, 2006: 57)

Stivers (2001) has dwelt at length on the relations between technology and magic in the contemporary world which he characterises as a 'technological milieu'. Technology is all-pervasive: closer than nature, keeping us safe; sustaining all needs, it has become our 'chief sacred' (p 41), offering the promise of heaven on earth. In this techno-utopia, Stivers (2001) argues that people look more and more to the State to solve all social ills. And the State is increasingly there to do just that, as seen in the zealous pursuit by politicians of a better world free from deviance, disease and social disadvantage. This has helped to assemble an actor network of formidable proportions around the bio-therapeutic project. The cast of human 'actants' includes not only politicians, researchers, professions, but funding bodies, campaigning and advocacy groups. In the academic sector, money talks; Scull refers to researchers winning big grants as 'the darlings of medical school deans, the millions upon millions of their grants and indirect cost recoveries' (p 401). This has all helped to finance the extraordinary burgeoning of 'the medical-industrial complex' in recent times. The close alliance of government and industrial interests in the psychotherapeutic State could not be better shown than by the following extract from a Houses of Parliament report:

> The global market for epigenetic therapies and technologies is predicted to reach $2.5 billion (£1.6 billion) in 2013 ... Large initiatives that are helping to establish sufficient evidence to support public health interventions include the US National Institutes of Health's $190 million Epigenomics

Roadmap project and the International Human Epigenome Consortium partly funded (€30 million) by the European Commission. (Houses of Parliament, 2013: 1)

We cannot end this section without some mention of the commercial interests which are circling. Rose and Rose (2012) present an excoriating critique of the malignant influence of 'Big Pharma', with tendrils reaching into both the professional bodies (such as the American Psychiatric Association) and the academic community, including funding bodies. The reader is referred to Rose and Rose's book for a detailed analysis and exposé of these commercial interests at work. In neuroscience, the commercial incursion is on a smaller scale. Writing with regard to neuroscience, Uttal (2016) is also scathing. Commenting on the recent proliferation of commercial organisations purveying services in areas such as lie detection, marketing and psychotherapy, he describes these businesses as 'exploiters of extravagant and scientifically unsupportable claims in nouveaux fields such as Neuropolitics and Neurolaw … [making] wildly hyperbolic effort to capitalise commercially on what is still largely unknown' (Uttal, 2016: 13).

To conclude: celebrating abundance

When contemporary proponents of long-standing arguments about the importance of the child's earliest years in determining its character and shaping is future life try to influence policy by reframing these in terms of our growing knowledge of the vulnerable developing brain … we can see signs of the potential emergence of a new regime of truth about our nature as human beings. (Rose and Abi-Rached, 2013: 227)

Questions about what is expectable of parents, what are acceptable levels of care for children, and crucially the limits of freedom and what the State can meaningfully and ethically offer, and who may profit, surely are moral ones and need informed, open debate. Humane professional practice with families demands it (Featherstone et al, 2014a). Technobiology is big business, it is also seducing, muffling and gagging. It seems, nevertheless, to be enjoying a relentless rise. Throughout this book we have attempted to trace the main contours of the contemporary utopian project aimed at fixing real people at the molecular level. This project manifests itself on a number of levels, from the individualised (medicalised) intervention to the opaque models of the macro-economists, which aim to inform social policy. It is resolutely about fixing people, not helping them to keep going, or building communities, nor indeed alleviating poverty. But we must ask, are people broken?

Normality itself is a disappearing category, with more and more of the ups and downs of life, its stresses, sorrows and disappointments, coming within the psychiatric 'gaze'. The idea that there is 'one normal', rather than many, is the fundamental problem. Inevitably, this leads to a progressive shrinkage of the membership of 'normal', as the exclusion principle operates, eventually to zero, or at least potentially to a very exclusive elite. Allen Frances (2013), formerly chairman of DSM-IV, declares it is time to save normality, to reclaim the full measure of our humanity before it is too late. But under the pervasive logic of contemporary utopianism, it is very hard to 'save normal'. New pathologies and new needs are constantly created and remedies sought.

In the policy sphere, this shapes the kinds of professional and community-based initiatives that are validated and funded. In chapter one we reported on the purported existence of the 'Welfare Trait' (Perkins, 2016) which reductively attributes the perverse incentives (to avoid work) inherent in welfare regimes, to a biologically and neurologically programmed personality type: the 'employment resistant personality'. The claims, evoking animal models, are bold: 'Selective breeding for personality causes significant genetically influenced changes in personality within as few as five generations', although Perkins concedes that 'the rate of change in human personality due to welfare-related selective breeding will be slower' (Perkins, 2016: 111). Perkins' solutions are a combination of intensive pre-school programmes and the curtailment of benefits to reduce the incentives for the poor to breed. Well, it is a position, that's for sure and one with self-evident flaws. Nevertheless, Perkins' arguments chime with those of some of our main actors: neo-eugenics may have found its time.

Where does this pessimistic form of reasoning lead us? It leads us to fixing people, not helping them, and favours some policy responses over others. The alleged relative failure of the UK's Sure Start early years programme reliably to deliver economic 'outcomes' for children (based on the ongoing longitudinal National Evaluation of Sure Start, NESS) is a case in point (Melhuish et al, 2012). The Evaluation speaks of the 'potential to generate economic benefits in the future' as all important. Its language contrasts markedly with qualitative studies which report here-and-now benefits for families in the ordinary domains of 'coping' and 'caring' (for example, Tunstill et al, 2005;

Featherstone et al, 2007; Frost and Parton, 2009), but for those doing the counting these outcomes don't count.

There are alternatives to the bio–neuro–economic models of 'success', and we would like to end this book on a more positive note, by referring to a community-based initiative in which we have recently taken part. In 2012, a scheme known as the Young Persons Development Model (YPDM) was set up by a company in the northwest of England, known as Acorn Environment Services. Acorn specialises in void clearance (restoring empty houses), cleaning and garden maintenance in the social housing sector. The aim of the scheme is to provide 14- to 16-year-olds who are struggling in the education system the opportunity to engage in a work environment and to reduce their risk of permanent exclusion from school, entering the NEET ('not in education, employment or training') category or youth offending. The work experience is a proper one, not a brief exposure; participants 'sign in' for work, normally 2 days per week, for an 18-month period. The main aim is to instil respect, confidence, teamwork, a good work ethic, positive morale and a sense of direction. Students receive constructive comments on their progress, take part in mock interviews and receive certificates of achievement, a written reference and a CV.

Over the life of the programme so far, a total of 27 students have been engaged from five schools across Salford, Lancashire and Merseyside. Comments from students include: 'it has given me the opportunity to gain life skills and is preparing me for the future', 'I wanted to go out to work, meet people and get my hands dirty', 'I am better at communicating and much more mature'. An independent evaluation conducted by one of us looked at how the model impacted on students being permanently excluded or becoming NEET. It was concluded that the risk of exclusion was reduced from 45% to 15% and the risk of NEET reduced from 65% to 23%. These are big, real effects, and the scheme is, or should be, a self-evident good. It has, however, become necessary to show benefits in economic terms, again showing the grip of the current thought style in UK public policy.

Fortunately, we have been able to show very significant savings to the public purse, given the long-term consequences of school exclusion in terms of employment. But what really matters for the instigators of the scheme, and for us, is the impact it has on the living, breathing, emoting, thinking, vital young people themselves. They are not epigenetically scarred, neurologically tainted, biologically screwed up or inherently 'employment resistant'. They are young people who have had some knocks and bruises from life, who don't fit the mould and sometimes try to break it. It matters profoundly how people are described, and it affects the way they see themselves. Those not fitting the preferred template are not a different species. The path to a good life is in knowing that the strongest inheritance we have is cultural:

> A strong song tows
> us, long earsick.
> Blind, we follow
> rain slant, spray flick
> to fields we do not know
> Basil Bunting, *Coda*

Notes

[1] Rose also notes the provisions of the Criminal Justice Act 2003 which introduced the 'indeterminate sentence for public protection', requiring inmates to show they are fit for release at the end of their stretch. Individuals considered to be a continuing threat can be detained indefinitely. In 2007, Rose notes that nearly 3,000 people were detained under these provisions with the number expected to quadruple by 2012. In fact, Ministry of Justice statistics put the figure at 6,550 as of March 2011. A government review published in October 2011 noted, however, that 'The IPP regime has not worked as intended', recommending its replacement with a 'new coherent sentencing framework'.

[2] Another simple example from the world of computers suggests itself. Consider the following string of symbols: 01000001. And another: 01011010. What do these mean? Mentioning computers is a big clue: they are both binary numbers, the first corresponding to 65 in decimal notation, the second to 90. Any the wiser? Unless you have come across the ASCII system for encoding alphanumeric characters, probably not. If you have, then you would know that 65 codes for capital A, and 90 for Z. It is clear from this that the high-level concept of the letter comes first; the binary sequence is meaningless on its own, and indeed is completely derivative. Encountering the binary sequence in a 'dump' of the computer's memory would, on its own, say nothing: 01011010 could just as well be a machine code command, an integer number or a pixel. It could also be a way of representing the state of a neural system of eight neurones (four firing and four inert) or indeed the methylation status of a CpG island.

[3] The following gives a flavour of Poldrack's analysis. Let us assume that we seek to identify, from a set of brain images, cases where the 'language function' is engaged. One way of expressing our uncertainty is to regard it as being equally likely for a given image, that is, we see the odds as 50%. How much do the odds increase if BA44 is lit up? Poldrack shows that the (conditional) probability given this 'new' evidence is 69%, and the odds have shifted from evens to 2.3. While such a shift is positive, in terms of standards within the 'Bayesian inference community', a Bayes factor between 1 and 3 represents weak evidence, between 3 and 10 moderate evidence. This means 'that the inference provides a positive but relatively weak increase in confidence' (Poldrack, 2006: 62).

4   Indeed, the remoteness grows ever greater, with so much research involving vast shared databanks of images or genetic sequences, as we noted in the previous section.

5   A related example is the conclusion that, because biochemical remedies can abate mental distress, this proves that they must have a biochemical cause. As many have pointed out, this is like concluding that headaches are caused by a deficiency of aspirin!

6   The observational bias of searching by looking where it is easiest, based on the example of the drunk searching for his keys under the streetlight, even though he lost them elsewhere. It is less charitably known as the 'drunkard's search'.

7   Respectively, the tendency to commence problem solving at a familiar position, and the difficulty of moving problem solving away from a given starting position; confirmation bias refers to the tendency to seek information which confirms an a priori hypothesis, rather than seeking evidence which disconfirms this.

8   Keil (1995: 422) defines this as 'the continued commitment of resources in the face of negative information'. Large-scale, long-term projects with high promised pay-offs are the most vulnerable. You can't get much bigger than the bioscience project!

APPENDICES

Appendix A:
Signs and codes

In this appendix, we explore the issue of the brain's coding system in more depth. As noted in the main text, Uttal (2016) makes a key distinction between signs and codes. Signs are merely neurophysiological phenomena that appear to correlate with psychological processes; a code is the actual mechanism by means by which the brain 'works'. The event-related potential (ERP), the subject of the first author's PhD research, provides a pertinent example of this distinction. The ERP is a slow perturbation in the ongoing EEG activity of the brain which is evoked by a single stimulus, such as a click or a flash. A typical ERP is shown in figure 5: it consists of a series of waves which unfold over the half second or so (500 ms) after the stimulus. By convention, negative is shown upwards, and the waves are accordingly known as P1, N1, and so on.

At that time, the dominant model of human cognition was to see the brain as an information processing system, typically represented as a block diagram involving a number of modules: for perception, attention and memory (figure 5). It was naturally tempting to think of the block diagram as a functional model of mind–brain architecture, and when juxtaposed with the ERP to speculate that perhaps the orderly progression of peaks and troughs in the waveform reflects the sequential activation of 'cognitive modules' in the brain.

The PhD examined the relationship between the amplitude of the N1–P2 complex of the ERP and the amount of information conveyed by the stimulus. In a key experiment, the research showed that when the quantity of (temporal) information in two stimuli was equated, no amplitude effects were found (Wastell, 1979a). The evidence was seemingly convincing. However, in that experiment, there was a further condition; the subjects were asked to relax and ignore the stimuli completely, rather than produce a reaction time response as in the main condition. Under these circumstances, the amplitude of N1–P2 was actually greater, even though no information was being processed at all. The seductively appealing idea that the amplitude of peaks in ERP waveform reflects the degree of information processing

Figure 5: Characteristic waveform of the human ERP (above), and model human information processing system, depicted as a block diagram (below)

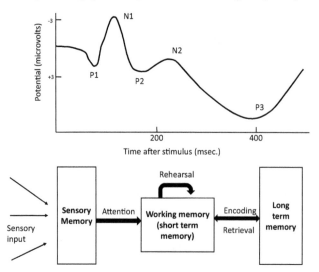

by 'brain structures' was thus contradicted by an inconvenient empirical result.[1] The ERP thus provides an instructive example of the sign/code distinction; it is manifestly a sign, deriving its allure from its formal similarity with the currently dominant model of the brain (mind) as an information-processing system.

Uttal (2011) avers that very few nervous system codes have been robustly identified. 'Beyond the transmission codes of the sensory and motor systems ... the study of higher-level cognitive processes remains virtually untouched by such progress' (p 24). Let us therefore examine such sensorimotor coding systems in more detail. When the first author did his undergraduate degree, it seemed that the coding processes of the visual system had been 'cracked', and together with an emerging understanding of the architecture of the visual pathways encompassing the eye and the visual cortex, a complete account of the processes of visual perception was within grasp.

The consensus may be summarised as follows, drawing on a 1963 article in *Scientific American*, 'The visual cortex of the brain' by the Nobel Prize-winning neurophysiologist, David Hubel, which I read avidly at the time (Hubel, 1963). In the eye, retinal ganglion cells (RGC) provide the output to the brain via the optic nerve. Each RGC received its input from a number of adjacently located receptors, and the internal wiring between RGCs (involving bipolar cells) ensures that each cell is finely tuned to stimulation at a particular location in the visual field, its receptive field. A small spot of light falling on the centre of the field would evoke a dramatic change in the firing pattern of the RGC: from a background level of intermittent firing, a flurry of spikes would be seen when the light was on.[2] In this way, the image falling on the retina appeared to produce a pattern of output that reproduced the spatial configuration of the image; this output array was relayed via the lateral geniculate body of the thalamus, and thence to the visual cortex at the back of the brain. Here a more complex pattern of neural behaviour was observed: no longer were cells simply responsive to points, they behaved as 'feature detectors' picking up lines and edges in the visual field. These simple cortical cells in turn appeared to feed into complex cells which responded to the orientation and movement of visual features.

This account is important in the present context as it highlights a number of key concepts regarding neural networks, coding processes and mind–brain relationships. First, the frequency of firing of individual neurones was thought to be central to the operation of the system, meaning that firing is more than a sign, it is the actual code used by the brain. Second, a model of visual processing is implied involving the extraction of features of progressively increasing complexity from the pattern of neural activity evoked by the visual image, and that this processing is accomplished by the rich network of interconnections between neurones. We consider each of these issues in more depth, as a somewhat more complex picture has emerged over the last half century.

First, the idea of a simple frequency code has been challenged. Let us focus on the retina, as this provides the ideal location for investigating the mechanics of neural coding: the input (visual stimulus) is under the direct control of the experimenter, the internal microanatomy is well defined and the nature of the response is also seemingly direct and interpretable. Although intuitively plausible, the candidature of frequency coding has been challenged. Writing in 2001, Van Rullen and Thorpe introduce their article as follows:

> The most commonly used code is one based on the firing rates of individual cells, but this is by no means the only option. In recent years a strong debate has opposed partisans of codes embedded in the neurons' mean firing rates and researchers in favor of temporal codes, where the precise temporal structure of the spike train is taken into account. (Van Rullen and Thorpe, 2001: 1255)

We can give only the faintest whiff of the technical issues alluded to here[3] but the limitations of firing rates as a code are easily understood. Given that the visual system can 'analyse and classify a new complex scene in less than 150 ms' (Gollisch and Meister, 2008: 1108) frequency coding is simply not fast or efficient enough to provide a feasible mechanism. This insight has prompted research to identify the 'elusive … neural code underlying this rapid visual processing' (p 1108). A limitation of early research on sensory coding was that recordings could only be made from single neurones, and hence could only suggest coding systems couched in terms of neurones acting alone. Recent technological advances now allow simultaneous recording from many neurones, which enables coding mechanisms to be explored based on the responses of multiple neurones.

Based on salamander retinal recordings, Gollisch and Meister (2008) propose a code based on the relative first spike latencies (that is, the delays between the stimulus and the first action potential generated by the cell) of pairs of ganglion cells. Evidence is presented for the effective operation of this coding mechanism, including its disruption when one member of the pair is pharmacologically disabled. Portelli et al (2014) describe another possible algorithm based on the rank ordering of first spike latencies in large populations of retinal ganglia; they demonstrate experimentally (in mice) that it provides an effective and rapid mechanism for encoding stimulus information. It should be said that while both these studies show such coding schemes to be 'candidate codes', they do not prove that these are the schemes which are actually used in the respective nervous systems of salamander and mouse.

We now consider the idea that visual perception is subserved by a hierarchy of increasingly complex feature detectors. This notion reaches its logical apogee in the idea of the 'grandmother cell', a term coined by Lettvin in 1969. In the words of Wikipedia, such a cell is 'a hypothetical neuron that represents a complex but specific concept or object which activates when a person sees, hears, or otherwise sensibly discriminates a specific entity, such as his or her grandmother'. The idea of the grandmother cell highlights an important distinction regarding two opposing general schemes regarding the representation of information in the brain. The grandmother cell represents the extreme version of so-called 'sparse coding', that objects are encoded by the activation of a relatively small set of neurones. In contrast, the idea of distributed representation holds that a specific stimulus is coded by a unique pattern of activity over a broad and distributed population of neurones. Sparse coding is open to a number of obvious problems, such as that multiple cells would be needed to code different perspectives of the same object. Remarkably, though, such cells do appear to exist. Quiroga et al (2005) describe a subset of medial temporal lobe (MTL) neurones in epilepsy patients with implanted electrodes 'that are selectively activated by strikingly different pictures of given individuals, landmarks or objects' (Quiroga et al, 2005: 1102). The example of a 'Halle Berry' neurone in one patient is cited. This unit was activated by various pictures of the actress Halle Berry (including her filmic portrayal as Catwoman) as well as by a drawing of her; it was even selectively activated by the letter string of her name. The authors conclude:

> We do not mean to imply the existence of single neurons coding uniquely for discrete percepts ... Yet, this subset of MTL cells is selectively activated by different views of individuals, landmarks, animals or objects. This is quite distinct from a completely distributed population code and suggests a sparse, explicit and invariant encoding of visual percepts in MTL. Such an abstract representation might be important in the storage of long-term memories. (p 1106)

However eye-catching the findings, the logic is not altogether convincing; far from ruling out distributed codes, it seems entirely consistent that psychological states with a common theme (for example, the idea of Halle Berry and the emotions attached to this) should evoke distributed brain states with some degree of commonality; in fact, it would be surprising if disjoint brain states were the case. Overall, the idea of such sparse coding does not represent the mainstream view, articulated in a recent review paper: 'In complex animals, information about behaviourally important variables such as sensory signals or motor actions is carried by the activity of populations of neurons' (Panzeri et al, 2015: 162).

Several key ingredients are thought to shape the capacity of such a *neural population code* to form discriminable representations of the objects of perception, including the 'diversity of neural response properties, their spatial and temporal response profiles, and the state-dependence of cortical activity' (p 162). The authors note that such networks could include sparse-coding elements to encode 'primary sensory information'. The mention of state dependence of cortical activity is also noteworthy. This alludes to generalised brain states, that is, slow-changing background levels of activity which can influence the excitability of local circuits. Mass signals such as the EEG are seen to have the potential to provide indicators of such states; the alpha rhythm, with its characteristic sine wave signature, would be a pertinent example, indicating a relaxed 'psychological state'. Broadly, the paper strikes an optimistic view of our likely ability to crack the neural code: 'Combining insights from both mass signals and multi-neurons is a key challenge for the future' (p 170). A challenge, yes; but one infers, not an insuperable one. Others, such as Uttal (2011), are less confident, as we see in the main narrative.

Notes

[1]   That 'peaks' themselves capture the attention is itself an interesting psychological phenomenon. We are naturally drawn to them as if they have some special significance, but this is pure assumption. It is noteworthy that one of the more prominent peaks of the ERP may not be a peak at all (P3), but is an artefact of the amplifiers used to record the EEG signal which filter out slow changes in electrical potential. At the time, there was a controversy regarding the authenticity of P3 as a peak, with some arguing that it reflected the resolution of a slow shift in negativity rising in anticipation of a significant event (the contingent negative variation, CNV – Wastell, 1979b).

[2]   This type of field was called an 'on' field; the opposite pattern of behaviour was also seen, with cells responding to light falling on the area immediately surrounding the centre of the field (so-called off-centred fields).

[3]   They can be intuited by considering the more familiar situation of heart rate measurement. Counting the number of beats over a period is the equivalent of the firing rate measure for neurones. There are obvious problems with this as a way of indexing heart activity, namely, that a long interval is required before the result is known, very long if an accurate result is required, and that important information is not used. In contrast, measuring the intervals between consecutive beats (that is, examining the temporal structure of the sequence of beats) allows relatively instantaneous measurement of cardiac performance and enables short-term fluctuations to be detected, such as the sinus arrhythmia associated with breathing.

Appendix B:
The amygdala: the brain's almond

Given its prominence in emotional regulation, we will attempt to summarise the status of current thinking regarding the amygdala by picking out some of the highlights from a recent review article by Hermans et al (2014). It opens as follows:

> Stressful and emotionally arousing experiences are preferentially retained in memory … It has long been known that the amygdala plays a pivotal role in this usually highly adaptive phenomenon. The notion that the amygdala is involved in affective processing dates back to the classic report by Klüver and Bucy (1937) on the effects of temporal lobectomy in rhesus monkeys.

Dramatic behavioural changes resulted from such surgical procedures, including visual agnosia, hypersexuality, and profound alterations in emotional behaviours, including tameness and loss of fear. Current thinking, based on voluminous research on rodents, has converged on the so-called 'modulation hypothesis' of amygdala function. During an emotionally arousing episode, stress hormones (epinephrine, glucocorticoids) are secreted from the adrenal glands (as well as other 'neurochemicals' such as neurotransmitters, in the brain); these are engaged by the amygdala 'to enhance the consolidation and storage of memory within other parts of the brain' (Hermans et al, 2014: 3).

The focus of much of this work is a particular region of the amygdala, the basolateral complex (BLA). Across a very broad range of training tasks, typically high arousal tasks such as fear conditioning (though low arousing tasks too, such as maze navigation), an impressive volume of evidence has accumulated which 'suggests that emotionally arousing learning experiences induce the release of norepinephrine in the amygdala' (p 4). As different training paradigms clearly imply different brain systems, it is implied that the amygdala, the BLA in particular, exerts 'influences on information processing in these different brains regions' (p 4).

Close interaction with the hippocampus in particular has been implicated: one study showed that post-training administration of glucocorticoids in the hippocampus enhanced rats' retention of inhibitory avoidance training, but that this was suppressed when noradrenergic activity in the BLA was blocked pharmacologically. Taking these findings together, the authors of the review conclude:

> there is now a wealth of evidence from experiments using primarily local drug administration supporting the hypothesis that neuromodulatory influences on the amygdala after learning promote memory processing in regions elsewhere in the brain. These regions include the hippocampus, entorhinal cortex, striatum, medial prefrontal cortex, anterior cingulate cortex, and insula, *and this list is likely to expand in the future.* (Hermans et al, 2014: 5, emphasis added)

Human studies are then reviewed, such as fMRI evidence indicating that acute stress can augment amygdala responses to emotional facial expressions, and that such reactivity can be suppressed by drugs such as propranolol which block adrenergic receptors (receptors which respond to catecholamines, especially norepinephrine and epinephrine). An fMRI study of patients with lesions in the amygdala and hippocampus showed that successful memory formation for emotional items was negatively associated with amygdala damage. The function of the hippocampus as the centre for spatial and episodic memory is noted (p 7), and the authors conclude that human studies 'are in general agreement with those of animal experiments, and confirm the critical role of arousal-associated noradrenergic activation of the amygdala in modulating memory processes that take place elsewhere in the brain' (p 7).

The authors go on to implicate the BLA in the brain's 'salience network' (SN). This network has attracted considerable recent interest:

> The human brain consists of multiple, distinct, and interacting networks ... The SN is an intrinsically connected large-scale network anchored in the anterior insula (AI) and dorsal anterior cingulate cortex. The SN also includes three key subcortical structures: the amygdala, the ventral striatum, and the substantia nigra/ventral tegmental area. (Menon, 2015: 597)

The anterior insula is its 'dynamic hub'.[1] The function of the salience network is defined by Menon as follows: the SN plays a crucial role in 'identifying the most biologically and cognitive relevant endogenous and external stimuli in order to adaptively guide behaviour' (p 609). Its functions include 'detection of salient events. ... facilitat[ion] of rapid access to the motor system ... working memory resources ... switching between [cortical] networks to keep attention focused on task-relevant goals' (p 609). Hermans et al (2014) note that 'the brain regions comprising the salience network indeed map remarkably well onto the regions modulated by the amygdala' (p 8). They go on comment that, although the attentional function (orienting to exogenous events) of the SN has been explored extensively, 'its mnemonic functions, and the role of the amygdala within these, have up to now received little attention' (p 8).

The authors then go on to consider the limitations of current technologies, the lack of temporal resolution of fMRI scans in particular:

> However, to gain a true understanding of how information is processed, stored, and passed between brain regions, it is necessary to capture and manipulate transient and oscillatory phenomena that typically take place within a time window of milliseconds. (Hermans et al, 2014: 9)

Recently they note that researchers have begun to use electrophysiological techniques to record activity directly from neuronal ensembles within the amygdala. A 'substantial hurdle' is the difficulty of 'selectively target[ing] subnuclei of the amygdala which play different roles in the neural circuitry and have distinct functional correlates' (p 9). Early results foreshadow considerable complexity ahead:

> Even within a single subregion such as the BLA, electrophysiological recordings show considerable variability in responses. Distinct populations of neurons in this region were found to respond to fear conditioning (correlating with fear expression) and fear extinction (correlating with extinction performance). (p 9)

In the penultimate section of their review, Hermans et al move on to consider the part played by the amygdala in hippocampal-neocortical exchanges involved in memory formation. A study is invoked which shows that amygdala activation facilitates the transmission of information from the entorhinal to perirhinal cortex, areas in the medial temporal lobe that are important for memory formation and which mediate communication between the hippocampus and the neocortex. They speculate that 'the amygdala may determine which information passes from the hippocampus to the neocortex' (p 10). Despite such intriguing suggestions, and the substantial body of research reviewed in the paper, they are nonetheless forced to conclude that 'our understanding of the dynamics of amygdala ensembles and their role in memory encoding and consolidation, particularly of learning experiences that are emotionally arousing and associated with noradrenergic activation, remains limited' (p 10).

But there is also a notable confidence that new technologies will 'unblock the blocks' and allow progress to be made: 'An important development that may make it possible to disentangle the internal amygdala circuitry is the new tool of optogenetics, which allows for specific manipulation of cell types, nuclei, and connections on a millisecond timescale' (p 10).

The overall conclusions of the review are particularly noteworthy. The final sentences run as follows: 'it appears essential to go beyond general processes underlying emotional memory and to understand individual differences explaining why certain individuals are more vulnerable or resilient when confronted with emotional or even traumatic experiences' (p 11).

Optimistically, it is concluded that combining insights into general processes and individual differences 'might one day provide a *mechanistic account* of mental disorders linked via mnemonic traces to stressful life events that enables *mechanistic* and individualized treatment' (p 11, emphasis added).

As a parting shot, we would note that, like many such reviews, it is an impressive piece of work, giving eloquent testimony to the industrial scale of current neuroscience. One region of the amygdala is the focus, and the amygdala is but one brain structure: there are over 300 papers covered by the review alone, and we may consider this but the iceberg's tip. Much of the work is on rodent brains. It is, to say the least, somewhat ironic to consider how much human intellectual effort and technological sophistication has been devoted to trying to understand the function of one 'subnucleus' of one brain structure of one low-level mammal, where the nucleus itself comprises around but 1 cubic millimetre of brain tissue!

Note

[1] The insula refers to a deep-seated region of the cerebral cortex in the fissure (sulcus) separating the temporal lobe from the parietal and frontal lobes. Its anterior portion has been implicated in subjective emotional experience.

Appendix C: Statistical primer

This appendix provides an introduction to the basic principles of statistical reasoning involved in the evaluation of research evidence (statistical significance, effect sizes, correlation coefficients, and so on). Such concepts are indispensable for the critical appraisal of research evidence.

Statistical significance and the genesis of scientific facts

We will begin this tutorial with an imaginary experiment, focusing on the genesis and authentication of 'factual knowledge' produced by the experiment. Although fictitious, the experiment is based on a real scientific study (Hikida et al, 2007).

We invite the reader to consider the following make-believe. You are a researcher interested in the biological basis of schizophrenia, and you believe from previous research that a certain gene is 'implicated', the Disrupted-In-Schizophrenia-1 gene (*DISC1*), which is thought to have a role in working memory. Your experiment involves a comparison of three genetically engineered mice (*tg*) with a mutant version of the gene, compared with three controls, with normal versions of the gene (wild-type: *wt*). Let us imagine that MRI scans at six weeks showed small reductions in hippocampal volume, but not other brain areas.

Behavioural analyses showed a mixed pattern: spatial memory in the Y maze paradigm showed no differences between *tg* and *wt*; time to find a hidden food pellet was found to be significantly longer for *tg* and they also remained immobile for longer (250 seconds versus 150) in the forced swim test (the mice are placed in a cylinder filled with water, from which they cannot escape). To the lay reader, this latter test may seem odd, but immobility in the forced swim test is seen by animal researchers (not uncontroversially) as a behavioural correlate of negative mood, representing a kind of hopelessness in the animal. The data for the imaginary swim test are shown in table A1.

Looking at the data, it would appear that a 'fact' has been established, the greater immobility of the *tg* mice in the swim test, from which we may seek to draw some wider conclusions. But let us pause, as alternative explanations for the pattern of results must surely be considered and ruled out before definitive conclusions may be drawn.

Table A1: Data for the imaginary swim test showing the length of periods of immobility (in seconds) for the six mice.

Genetically engineered (*tg*)	Control (*wt*)
320	190
230	190
200	70
Average = 250 seconds	Average = 150 seconds

We will take this opportunity to introduce some basic concepts of statistical reasoning. Our first statistical concept is that of the *null hypothesis*. The null hypothesis is a fundamental aspect of scientific inference in all domains. It provides a roundabout way of addressing the question: does such-and-such a pattern of results, such as table A1, reflect a genuine effect? Perhaps there are other explanations. In particular, we wish to be sure that our results are not some fluke, and that if the experiment were done again with a different sample of animals, we would find a different pattern. The established method for evaluating whether the results are genuine is to posit its opposite, that is, that the results are not real, and then to assess the likelihood of this 'null hypothesis'. If the likelihood of getting the results we have obtained is less than some threshold level of probability, then the null hypothesis can be rejected and it may be concluded that the results are 'statistically significant'.

But to evaluate the null hypothesis we have to come up with an alternative explanation for the results, on the assumption that they are not genuine. We might worry, for instance, that there are only three rats in each condition, intuitively feeling that this cannot be reliable enough evidence, that had we tested more rats, or indeed a different 'sample' of rats, we might not have found this pattern. We would certainly want to be reassured that the rats in the genetically engineered and control conditions were equivalent, apart from the genetic manipulation. As it is immature eggs which were subject to the manipulation, we would want to be sure that the mothers had not been selected in some way which predisposed those in the *tg* group to greater immobility.

Here we confront a general problem in all scientific research: we wish our 'treatment' group to be identical to our 'control' group in every respect, other than the experimental manipulation. Only then can we be sure that any effects are due to the experimental manipulation, and not to some prior disposition. But, of course, there is no way (in general) of ensuring such identity. The universally adopted solution to this problem is to allocate our experimental 'subjects' *at random* to the experimental conditions. While we cannot be sure that this makes the groups identical (except for the experimental manipulation), the principle of randomisation ensures that there is no systemic difference between them. But at the same time, it introduces an alternative explanation – perhaps randomisation itself is responsible.

What would this logic mean here? Our null hypothesis (formally denoted H_0) is that the genetic manipulation actually has no effect. In other words, the three mice in the *tg* group would have been less mobile anyway, even if their eggs had not been manipulated. It was simply the luck of the draw that these three mice ended up in the *tg* group. Let us try to quantify this. On the assumption of the null hypothesis, we simply have six mice with the observed swimming times of 320, 230, 200, 190, 190 and 70 seconds. What is the chance that the rats with the shortest times, if picked at random, of ending up in the *tg* group? Let us pick one of these six mice for the *tg* group. The probability that it will be one of the top three 'immobiles' is 3 out of 6, or 0.5. Now we have five mice, so the probability that our next pick will be of the original top three immobiles is down to 2 out of 5, or 0.4. And for the last pick, it is 1 out of 4, or 0.25. Our overall probability of picking the top three immobiles for our treatment condition is therefore 0.5 times 0.4 times 0.25, which comes out at 0.05, or 1 in 20.

In other words, if we assume the null hypothesis, then the probability of obtaining the pattern of effects we have found by chance is 1 in 20, or 5%. H_0 at this point is beginning to look rather implausible, but we need a rule to make a final decision. This threshold is referred to as the level of statistical significance. By convention, the minimum such level for rejecting the null hypothesis is, by a happy coincidence, 5%. So on this basis, we may reject H_0 and conclude that our results are statistically significant at the 5% level. In doing so, we acknowledge that setting this threshold means that we will mistakenly reject H_0 on average once in every 20 assessments, and if we wish to reduce such a 'false positive' error we should set a more demanding level of statistical significance.

But in the present case, we have set the level at 5%, so we conclude that our results are real, that a scientific fact has been established, that the *tg* mice are more docile. Whether the following embellished 'fact' has been established (that *DN-DISC1* is responsible for mental illness in humans), as is claimed in the paper on which this imaginary experiment is based, we leave to the critical judgement of the reader: 'DN-DISC1 mice displayed increased immobility in the forced swim test, which is frequently used as an indicator for depression but may parallel anhedonia found in patients with SZ [schizophrenia].'

Beyond significance: effect size matters

We now introduce a little more statistical vocabulary. In general, the process of statistical reasoning formally follows the steps that we have outlined in this *Gedankenexperiment*. A typical experiment in psychology or physiology involves some manipulation (the 'treatment' or 'independent variable') performed by the experimenter; the interest of the experimenter is in the effect this has on some measurable aspect of the experimental subject (the so-called dependent variable) with reference to a control condition (lacking the treatment). In the simplest case, there will be one treatment group and one control group, but there will often be multiple groups in the former category, and potentially more than one control. The experiment is performed and measurements are made of the dependent variable, from which a statistic is calculated to characterise the overall magnitude of the treatment effect. The null hypothesis is evaluated and statistical significance pronounced or otherwise.

Numerous descriptive statistics can be calculated for assessing the treatment effect, and tested for significance. Here, our statistic simply involved putting the swim times in rank order, noting that the top three are all associated with the *tg* condition. Other candidate statistics are available. We could, for instance, have focused on the difference in the mean swimming time (100 seconds), and carried out a widely used statistical test known as the t-test to evaluate the probability of obtaining such a difference by chance alone. Whatever statistical test is done, the underling logic is the same. The t-test, because it makes use of more information (the actual swim times and their variability, not just the rank order), potentially provides a more powerful inferential procedure than the simple test we did in the previous section (although it does make some assumptions about the nature of the underlying data, such as that it is normally distributed). The technical details of the t-test do not matter, although informally it involves taking the ratio of the difference between the two means *to the underlying variability of the data*. Intuitively, the latter makes sense, as table A2 (see below) implies. In this table, the size of the difference in averages is the same as the original data, but we note that the raw data are much less variable, clustering tightly around the means.

This reduction in scattering suggests intuitively that the difference between the means of the two groups is more robust, that is, it is less prone to be the result of chance variability simply because there is less such variability. Let us calculate t for the two cases: the values are $t = 1.86$ and $t = 6.12$, with corresponding probabilities of 7% and

Table A2: Simulated data for the genetically engineered versus control comparison. The means are the same as in table A1, but the within-group variability has been reduced.

Genetically engineered (*tg*)	Control (*wt*)
230	130
250	150
270	170
Average = 250 seconds	Average = 150 seconds

0.2%.[1] We note first that the original results are no longer statistically significant; by taking into account the manifest variability in the data and the near overlap of the two groups, the more powerful test has given what feels like a better judgement on the robustness of the treatment effect. Second, we see that for the second dataset, the t value is significant at a much more demanding level of significance, reflecting the much reduced intrinsic variation in the raw data; with such tightly clustered data, we may expect that any sample of subjects would produce a pattern of results not too distant from the 'original'.

We further note that, although t conveys a measure of the size of the treatment effect, the value of t depends on the size of the sample, which limits its ability to compare and/or combine, as we often seek to do, treatment effects across a number of similar studies perhaps involving differing sample sizes. A related statistic which does allow such combination is Cohen's d; for the present number of observations, t and d have the same value, but in general this will not be the case. Another useful statistic, commonly used to quantify the size of a treatment effect, is eta-squared. Eta-squared (η^2) has a clear intuitive meaning: it expresses the proportion of the total variability seen in a set of data that can be attributed to ('explained by') the independent variable. Here $\eta^2 = 46\%$ and $\eta^2 = 90\%$ respectively for the two datasets. Intuitively, this makes sense: there is less variation in the second case, so the proportion explained by the treatment is relatively higher.

We meet both Cohen's d and η^2 on several occasions in the main narrative of the book; they are very useful friends in assessing claims. A statistically significant result, for instance, may not necessarily represent a substantively significant effect; indeed, this is generally the case. This is simply because larger samples of observations increase the ability of an experiment to discriminate differences between groups. We would, for instance, be much more confident that an average value of 250 compared to 150 could not be attributed to chance were it based on 100 observations per group rather than 3. But that is all statistical significance means, that chance is unlikely to be the explanation, not that the effect itself is large. Cohen's d, on the other hand, does provide a measure of effect size which is independent of the number of observations. Tentatively, Cohen (1988) defined a hierarchy of 'effect size' categories: between 0.2 and 0.5 (small effect), between 0.5 and 0.8 (medium), greater than 0.8 (large). While acknowledging a degree of subjectivity and context dependency in these definitions, they do provide a useful way of characterising the relative size of treatment effects. A d of 0.2, for example, is typical of the size of effect found in studies of the effectiveness of biomarkers. Figure 6 illustrates what such an effect size means.

Figure 6: Probability density functions for two normal distributions to demonstrate the degree of overlap associated with a Cohen's d of 0.2. The total overlap is approximately 85%, and the probability of the dashed distribution yielding a higher value for the trait is half of this, i.e. approximately 7.5%.

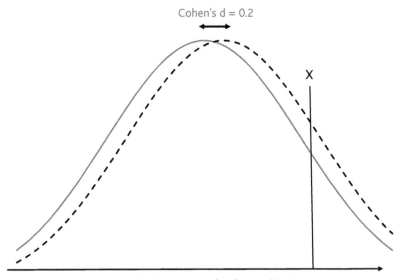

The two curves shown in figure 6 (solid black, dashed) are known as probability distributions (more correctly, probability density functions, PDF). To understand the meaning of such graphs, consider the solid black curve. The curve conveys the probability of a measurable trait of interest (such as depression, for example) falling into a range of values. The area under the whole curve for any PDF is, of course, always 1.0, that is, there is a 100% probability that some value for the trait will be obtained. Consider the peak of the distribution, which corresponds to the mean value; half of the area under the curve lies to the right, and half to the left. Probabilistically, this says that half of the population described by this PDF will be below the mean for this trait, and half above; in other words, if we picked an individual at random, there is a 0.5 probability they will be below average, and 0.5 probability they will be above. We further note that the bell-like shape of the curve means that most individuals have values for the trait which cluster around its mean value (the centre of the distribution) with more extreme values becoming progressively less common. This distribution is, of course, none other than the ubiquitous normal distribution. The spread of a distribution is given by a parameter called the standard deviation; the higher the standard deviation, the greater the spread. For a normal distribution, roughly two thirds (66%) of the distribution lies within a range of 1 standard deviation from the mean.

Consider now the vertical marker, X. The area under the solid curve to the left of X (that is, less than X) constitutes 90% of the total area, and to the right of X, 10%. Again, these areas give the probability of X falling into these two ranges: there is a 90% (0.90) chance that the trait in a given individual will be equal to or less than X, and corresponding a 10% probability (0.1) it will exceed X. Now let us consider the dashed curve. This shows the PDF for a different 'population' of individuals. The basis for this difference could be a biological feature of some sort, such as the presence of a gene variant; such a biomarker could provide an indication of susceptibility to some form of illness or deviant behaviour. We note that the curve is displaced to the right; in fact, the peak value of this PDF is exactly 0.2 standard deviations of the first distribution above its peak. Cohen's d measures effect size in precisely this way, as the separation between two probability distributions expressed in terms of the spread of underlying observations, as measured by the standard deviation estimated from both groups of data (SD). Mathematically, for two variables X and Y:

$$d = (\text{Mean}(X) - \text{Mean }(Y)) / \text{SD}$$

Expressing effect sizes relative to the underlying variability of the data is intuitively plausible, as we saw above. A difference between two means is much more impressive when the underlying variability is small than when it is large (a small rather than a big overlap). Returning to figure 6, we note the considerable overlap between the two distributions, roughly 85% in total. Cohen's d is 0.2 (both distributions have been 'standardised' to have a standard deviation of 1.0) and intuitively we can now see why a d of 0.2 is only considered to reflect a weak effect.

We can make this a little more concrete. Consider the marker X again. Let us focus on the area to the right, and further assume this extreme region represents the range of 'clinical' interest. For the solid curve, 10% of the population falls in this range. But what is the corresponding proportion for the dashed curve? The figure comes out 14%, representing a higher proportion of the population. Translating into the language of risk, we may say that the presence of the biomarker increases the risk of finding the target condition from 10% to 14%. In absolute terms, this increase (of 4%) seems quite small (consistent with a small d), that is, the biomarker has limited predictive value. But from a relative point of view, it can be portrayed as quite large: an increase of 40%. This leads naturally to a different way of conceptualising effect sizes in terms of what is known as *relative risk*, closely related to another widely used statistic, that of the odds ratio.

To make matters even more concrete, let us consider a hypothetical scenario in which we attempt to deploy a biomarker to detect some condition of concern. We assume that the prevalence of the biomarker in the population is 20%, that the target condition has a prevalence of 10% in the individuals without the biomarker, and that the effect size, as measured by Cohen's d, is 0.2. Let us imagine that the efficacy of the biomarker has been tested on a sample of 1,000 individuals, yielding table A3.

Table A3: Hypothetical scenario to evaluate the performance of an imaginary biomarker

	Target condition present	Target condition absent	Total
Biomarker present	27	173	200
Biomarker absent (normals)	80	720	800
Total	107	893	1000

We see in this table that the risk of the condition in 'normals' (no biomarker) is 0.1, as we arranged. The risk in those with the biomarker is raised to $27/200 = 0.135$, giving relative risk of 13.5%. Alternatively, we may express the raised risk in terms of the odds ratio: with the biomarker, the odds of having the condition, as opposed to not having it, are $27/173 = 15.5\%$; without the biomarker, the odds reduce to $80/720 = 11.1\%$. This gives an odds ratio of 15.5% to 11.1%, or an increase in the odds of the condition of 1.4 if the biomarker is present.

Another perspective is to consider the performance of the biomarker as a diagnostic test. Two indicators are widely used to characterise such performance: sensitivity (how well the test correctly identifies those with the target condition – the true positive rate) and specificity (how well the test correctly identifies those without the condition – the true negative rate). Here, the sensitivity is 27/107 = 25%, and the specificity is 720/893 = 81%. For practical purposes, such a low sensitivity is obviously problematic as the majority of cases are missed. A high false positive rate (173/200 = 87%) is also problematic, especially if an intervention is entailed, having both economic and moral consequences.

The reader may seem bewildered at this point. We have now encountered three commonly used measures of effect size: eta-squared, Cohen's d and the odds ratio. Mathematically, they are all related, and one can be transformed in the other, which is useful as it allows a common unit of description to be adopted which can allow the comparison and integration of findings across studies which may deploy different metrics (fBorenstein et al, 2009). It can be shown, for example, that a d of 0.2 is approximately equivalent to $\eta^2 = 1\%$ and an odds ratio 1.4 (as here). Furthermore, results expressed in terms of t values (whether for testing the significance of mean differences or other statistics such as regression coefficients) can also be transformed into Cohen's d and hence other effect estimators.

Mathematically, the three metrics may be equivalent, but psychologically they are not: an eta-squared of 1% sounds much less impressive than a 40% increase in the odds ratio. The choice of metric can thus be guided rhetorically, to accentuate or diminish a case, reminding one of the old adage about lies, damned lies and statistics! In general, choosing the right metric will depend on the judgement of the researcher according to the context and the argument being made (McGough and Faraone, 2009). For the reader, it is important to be aware of these nuances and to interrogate findings in a critical way; it has been the purpose of this statistical excursion to draw attention to this. For consistency, we have standardised on Cohen's d throughout this book: Cohen's d is very widely used for appraising effect sizes, including in meta-studies, that is, review studies which attempt to draw together findings from a range of individual investigations across a field of interest.

More on correlation coefficients

Finally, we will say a few brief words about another commonly encountered statistic, the 'correlation coefficient', mathematically abbreviated as 'r'. There are various statistics which characterise the strength of the relationship between two variables, such as height and weight. The Pearson product moment correlation coefficient is the most common. In this short discussion, when we allude to correlation, it is Pearson's r which we specifically mean.

A useful visual way of looking to see if a relationship exists between two variables is the so-called scatterplot; several examples are shown below in figure 7. One variable is plotted along the horizontal x-axis, the other along the vertical y-axis. Each point in the diagram represents a single case for which both measurements are available. Different types of mathematical relationship can, of course, exist between two variables; the simplest form is a linear relationship, whereby when one variable increases, we expect to see a proportionate increase in the other. Height and weight again serve as a good example. Pearson's r simply measures the strength of such a linear relationship; it varies between 0 and 1, with a value of zero indicating no relationship, and a value of 1 indicating a perfect linear relationship. Incidentally, the relationship could be an inverse one, with one variable decreasing as the other increases (weight and time to run a marathon would, in general, be expected to show such a relationship). Negative correlations indicate such inverse relationships, with a value of -1 indicating a perfect negative relationship.

Figure 7 provides a number of illustrative examples. In each case, a line has been drawn which, in an intuitive sense, provides the closest fit to the points, in that the overall distance of the points from the line has been minimised. The statistical method of 'linear regression' provides a mathematical procedure for determining the position of such a line of 'best fit'. Let us consider the first scatter-plot. 'Eye-balling' the graph, the situation does not seem hopeful: the points seem to swarm around in an amorphous crowd, and it is not obvious where the line of best fit should go. The graph suggests there is no relationship between the variables, and indeed r equals 0, reflecting this. In the next graph, there does seem to be a trend, suggesting an optimum position for the line of best fit; but the relationship is not a strong one, reflected in r = 0.3. The third graph suggests a much stronger relationship; there is little 'scatter' around the line and r = 0.7. Not shown is the scenario where r = 1; here the points would sit exactly along the line; there would be no scattering at all.

Figure 7: Four scatter-plots to illustrate how the strength of a relationship between two variables is reflected in the correlation coefficient, according to the variability of the data and the nature of putative trend

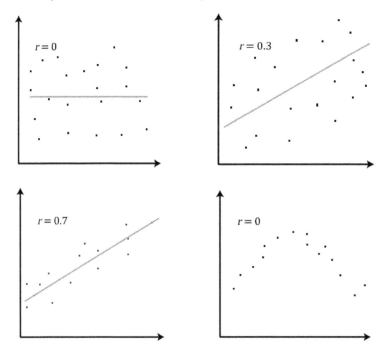

Real-world experiments seldom yield values of r = 1.0 or even close to it; there is always a degree of scatter ('noise', if you like). As an example of a strong correlation, we would expect a person's height as a child to be strongly predictive of their height as an adult. Empirical data confirm this; the correlation is of the order of 0.8. But what exactly does this mean; how should such-and-such a value of r be interpreted? Fortunately, a straightforward way of interpreting r exists which is consistent with our earlier discussion of effect sizes. The square of r (denoted R^2) corresponds to eta-squared (η^2), that is, it expresses how much of the variability of one variable can be explained (predicted) from knowledge of the other. As the square of 0.8 is 0.64, this means that 64% of the variability in adult height can be predicted from knowledge of heights in childhood.

As with most statistics, the issue of statistical significance arises. Consider for example, a study by Beach et al (2010) which showed that there is a correlation of 0.21 between early abuse and antisocial behaviour in men. To appraise statistical significance, we must first posit the null hypothesis, that the true value of r is zero, and that the result we have observed has come about merely by chance. The logic is always the same; here we need to appraise the likelihood of obtaining a value of r = 0.21 purely by chance. In this case, the probability is less than the standard criterion of 5%, so H_0 may be rejected and statistical significance claimed. Again, note that this does not mean the effect is a strong one, just that it is not a 'statistical artefact' (a fluke). To assess its strength, we square the correlation which gives an R^2 of less than 4%, so we might conclude that, although significant, early abuse is only one small causal influence in the aetiology of antisocial behaviour, with 96% of its variation arising from other causes.

Several final points regarding correlation will now be made. First, we proffer the usual health warning that 'correlation does not imply causality'. The correlation coefficient just measures the strength of association between two sets of numbers; finding, for instance, a correlation between the size of a family's house and the educational attainment of the children does not mean the house size is directly responsible for the latter. A corollary of this is that the direction of any claimed causality is arbitrary; finding an association between X and Y does not mean X causes Y, any more than Y causes X. Judgement and argument must be used to establish causal priority. For example, we might just as well claim that the child's attainment determines the size of the house, purely on the basis of a significant correlation coefficient. Such an argument would be tenable if we had measured parental educational attainment; then a plausible case for causality could, of course, be made.

More subtly, and importantly, the reader must always keep in mind that correlation coefficients only test for the presence of linear relationships. Relationships need not be linear and many important ones are not. Consider the final graph in figure 7. There is clearly a very strong relationship between the horizontal variable and the vertical one, but rather than a straight line it looks like an inverted U (mathematically, this would be described as a quadratic relationship). Such relationships are highly relevant in this book, where psychological stress is an important theme. The relationship between stress and performance (or wellbeing) is characteristically quadratic; too little or too much stress are deleterious – moderate amounts produce the highest level of performance. The reader will note that, although the scattergram clearly reveals the quadratic trend, the correlation coefficient is zero. The lesson of this simple example is that one should always 'eye-ball' one's data first, before proceeding to formal statistical analysis. Indeed, eye-balling is probably the most important statistical procedure of all. But in the rush to test 'pet models' and evaluate statistical significance 'it is a custom more honour'd in the breach than the observance', with the consequence that important relationships may be missed and erroneous conclusions drawn.

Note

[1] Strictly speaking, these are the probabilities of obtaining a value of t this extreme, *or more extreme*, on the assumption of the null hypothesis. The need to couch the logic in terms of ranges rather than individual values is because the probability of getting any particular value for a continuous variable (like t) is strictly speaking 0.0, as there is an infinity of possible values depending only on the resolution of the measurement.

Appendix D:
The definition of autism spectrum disorder (ASD)

The definition is extracted from the Centers for Disease Control and Prevention website (http://www.cdc.gov/ncbddd/autism/hcp-dsm.html).

Table A4: The diagnostic criteria for 299.00 Autism Spectrum Disorder

A. Persistent deficits in social communication and social interaction across multiple contexts, as manifested by the following, currently or by history (examples are illustrative, not exhaustive):   Deficits in social-emotional reciprocity, ranging, for example, from abnormal social approach and failure of normal back-and-forth conversation; to reduced sharing of interests, emotions, or affect; to failure to initiate or respond to social interactions.   Deficits in nonverbal communicative behaviors used for social interaction, ranging, for example, from poorly integrated verbal and nonverbal communication; to abnormalities in eye contact and body language or deficits in understanding and use of gestures; to a total lack of facial expressions and nonverbal communication.   Deficits in developing, maintaining, and understand relationships, ranging, for example, from difficulties adjusting behavior to suit various social contexts; to difficulties in sharing imaginative play or in making friends; to absence of interest in peers.
B. Restricted, repetitive patterns of behavior, interests, or activities, as manifested by at least two of the following, currently or by history (examples are illustrative, not exhaustive):   Stereotyped or repetitive motor movements, use of objects, or speech (e.g., simple motor stereotypes, lining up toys or flipping objects...).   Insistence on sameness, inflexible adherence to routines, or ritualised patterns of verbal or nonverbal behavior (e.g., extreme distress at small changes, difficulties with transitions, rigid thinking patterns ... need to take same route or eat same food every day).   Highly restricted, fixated interests that are abnormal in intensity or focus (e.g., strong attachment to or preoccupation with unusual objects, excessively circumscribed or perseverative interests).   Hyper- or hypo-reactivity to sensory input or unusual interest in sensory aspects of the environment (e.g., apparent indifference to pain/temperature, adverse response to specific sounds or textures, excessive smelling or touching of objects, visual fascination with lights or movement).
C. Symptoms must be present in the early developmental period (but may not become fully manifest until social demands exceed limited capacities, or may be masked by learned strategies in later life).
D. Symptoms cause clinically significant impairment in social, occupational, or other important areas of current functioning.
E. These disturbances are not better explained by intellectual disability ... or global developmental delay. Intellectual disability and autism spectrum disorder frequently co-occur; to make comorbid diagnoses of autism spectrum disorder and intellectual disability, social communication should be below that expected for general developmental level.

Appendix E:
Critique of Cunha et al, 2010

In this appendix, we present our summary and critique of Cunha et al (2010) in some depth, to the extent that we are able as it is a formidable technical edifice. The published paper (Cunha et al 2010) is 50 pages long and is dense with mathematical equations and esoteric economic terminology; the supplement with additional important detail is a further 50 pages, and is equally arcane. Condensing this without distortion has been a challenge, but we have endeavoured to pick out key features, limitations, assumptions and implications. Representing a collaboration of three authors, Cunha, Heckman and Schennach, we will henceforth refer to the model presented in their paper as the CHS model.

Befitting economists, Cunha et al refer to their Model of Skill Formation as a 'production function', jargon for a mathematical function which describes the relationship between the input (factors of production, such as labour and capital) and the outputs of a 'production' system. Treating skill formation in these terms sees the level of skill, at any period in the development of an individual, as the output of inputs from the previous period. The overall time course of skill formation is divided into a number of stages, with each stage made up of several consecutive periods. In the empirically tested model, as we shall see, two such developmental stages are distinguished: 0 to 6 years, and 7 to 14 years, each comprising four two-year periods (the first period is age 0). The model implies that the shape of the production function is specific to each stage, and makes an important distinction between cognitive (intellectual) and noncognitive (socio-emotional) skills.

Key components of the model are described as follows, simplifying slightly from p 886:

> Each agent is born with initial conditions θ_1. Family environments and genetic factors may influence these initial conditions. We denote by θ_P parental cognitive and noncognitive skills. θ_t denotes the vector of skill stocks in period t. Let η_t denote shocks and/or unobserved inputs that affect the accumulation of cognitive and noncognitive skills. The technology of production of skill k in period t and developmental stage s depends on the stock of skills in

period t, investment at t, $I_{k,t}$, parental skills, θ_p, shocks in period t, $\eta_{k,t}$ and the production function at stage s,

$$\theta_{k,t+1} = f_{k,s}(\theta_t, I_{k,t}, \theta_p, \eta_{k,t})$$

Note that investment here refers to 'parental investment', to be explicated below. To this basic model, Cunha et al add an important additional parameter, which they designate 'elasticity of substitution'. This is a uniquely economic concept. In a production situation, it measures the substitutability between inputs (or goods), that is, how easy it is to substitute one input for another. For example, in the manufacture of four-legged stools, there are two inputs (factors of production), seats and legs. If these factors cannot be substituted for one another, then production is ultimately limited by whichever input is in shortest supply. With 120 legs but only 10 seats, for instance, only 10 stools can be made, and a glut of legs remains. What does this mean in terms of CHS? We admit that we have struggled with this concept, which is somewhat obscure for non-economists. In Cunha et al's own words,[1] elasticity of substitution affords a 'a measure of how easy it is to compensate for low levels of cognitive and non-cognitive stocks inherited from the previous period with current levels of parental investment' (p 887).

Cunha et al describe the mathematical nature of the production function as 'monotone ... twice continuously differentiable, and concave in I [parental investment]' (p 886). The terminology is important; translated into nontechnical language, the first two of these characteristics simply mean that skill formation proceeds smoothly upwards at either an accelerating or decelerating pace. The third epithet is more salient. Figure 8 provides an example of a concave curve; mathematically it is defined as a curve which is above any line connecting two points on the curve. Necessarily, a concave curve tends to accelerate more sharply at the outset before tapering off towards the end point of its trajectory. This choice is important in the present context, as it implies that parental investments made earlier in any stage will have a greater effect on skill formation. Other growth curves are, of course, possible. The figure also shows a sigmoid curve: such a curve could, for instance, describe the growth of a human population: first the growth is slow, then it accelerates as the population reproduces and the economy expands, only to decline as the availability of resources comes under increasing pressure. It could also, of course, describe the developmental trajectory of a child who learns slowly at the outset, perhaps due to adverse extrinsic circumstances, before later catching up.

Figure 8: This illustrates two possible growth functions as described in the text: a simple concave function and a more complex S-shaped curve

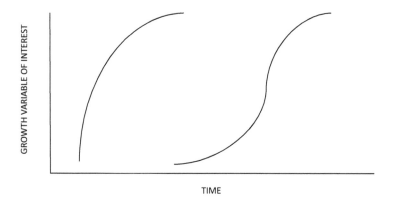

In order to evaluate the model, a substantial empirical study is carried out using data from the Center for Human Resource Research at Ohio State University. The data derive from the National Longitudinal Survey of Youth initiated by the Center in 1979. Regular interviews with the survey participants have been carried out since that time, including regarding their children. In 2004, 7,538 participants were interviewed, and from this dataset, Cunha et al analysed data for 2,207 *first-born white children* of these interviewees. The survey includes a broad range of seemingly well-established instruments for measuring the cognitive ability, temperament, motor and social development and so on of children, as well as their home environment.

In terms of the CHS model, key variables were measured as follows: *cognitive skills* up to the age of 4 years were assessed by several standard educational instruments (Parts of the Body Score, Memory for Location Score and the Peabody Picture Vocabulary Test); after the age of 5 years the Peabody Individual Achievement Test (PIAT) for mathematics and reading recognition was used throughout. Up to age 4, the Temperament Scale was used to assess *noncognitive skills*; over age 4, the Behavior Problem Index was used. The assessment of *parental skills* is limited to the mother: her cognitive skills are measured with a battery of tests (Arithmetic Reasoning, Word Knowledge, Mathematical Knowledge and so on), and her noncognitive skills through a set of self-assessed questions appraising self-esteem and related issues ('I am a person of worth', 'I am a failure', 'I have no control' and so on). Of particular interest is the method used to measure *parental investment*. This involved a subset of items from the Home Observation

Measurement of the Environment questionnaire developed by Bradley and Caldwell (1984). A selection of the HOME items used by Cunha et al is shown in table A5.

Table A5: Selected list of HOME items

the number of books the child has	whether the child has a musical instrument
how often the mother reads to the child	whether the family receives a daily
the number of soft toys or push/pull play	newspaper
toys the child has	whether the child receives special lessons/
how often child eats with mom/dad	activities
how often mom talks to child from work	whether the child is taken to musical
whether the child has tape recorder/CD	performances
player	how often the child sees family friends
how often child is taken to museum	

Cunha et al go on to report the results of various analyses, all aimed at estimating key parameters of the CHS model for the development of both cognitive and noncognitive skills. We have not included the latter here partly to simplify what is already a complex presentation, and partly because it is scholastic performance which is of the greatest interest. The various analyses of cognitive skill differ in relatively minor technical respects (such as the handling of measurement error); we present here the fourth of these analyses, although the broad qualitative pattern of effects does not differ substantially. Table A6 shows the estimates reported in table IV[2] of the original paper, on which Cunha et al base their own discussion (section 4.3, 'Interpreting the estimates').

Estimates of parameters are shown in columns 2 and 4 of the main section of table A6, taken directly from table IV in Cunha et al, which also shows the error terms for the estimates. Presented in this bald way, it is hard to make sense of these statistics. Neither levels of statistical significance nor effect sizes are shown. A large value, for instance, does not mean the parameter is an important predictor (unless the measures have been standardised); how well it predicts is reflected in the 'standard error' associated with the estimate, that is, the degree to which the estimate would be expected to vary for different samples of observations, based on the variation within the present sample. Such error terms can be used to appraise statistical significance, but significance only provides a limited way of evaluating the parameters. The majority will be statistically significant, given the large sample size. As we emphasised in appendix C, what matters is not statistical significance but the magnitude of the effect exerted by the various factors; this is especially so in the practical world of evidence-based

Table A6: Parameter estimates and effect sizes for the various factors modelled to influence cognitive skill in consecutive periods.

	Next period cognitive skill			
Current period	First stage (0–6 years) Parameter	Cohen's d	Second stage (7–14 years) Parameter	Cohen's d
Current period cognitive skill (self-productivity)	0.479	0.79	0.831	3.22
Current period noncognitive skill (cross-productivity)	0.070	0.12	0.001	0.01
Current period parental investment	0.161	0.46	0.044	0.31
Parental cognitive skill	0.031	0.10	0.073	0.39
Parental noncognitive skill	0.258	0.38	0.051	0.16
Elasticity of substitution[3]	1.457	0.10	0.446	0.42

policy, where concern should focus on their likely impact when translated into real-world interventions. Using the standard errors provided in the Cunha paper, we have attempted[4] to compute rough effect sizes for each factor, using Cohen's d (appendix C). Although we cannot be certain of the validity of this improvisation, it nonetheless incorporates information about the inherent variability for each parameter, and we trust that it therefore provides a comparable basis for appraising their relative impact. If our analysis is way off the mark, our riposte is that we have merely done our best and invite Cunha et al to provide their definitive counter-analysis, respectfully questioning why this essential work was not presented in the first place in a systematic and transparent way. To reiterate, size matters!

Looking at these effect sizes, much of the table makes intuitive sense, using the crude categorisations of effect size based on those of Cohen (appendix C): d < 0.2, negligible effect; between 0.2 and 0.5, small effect; between 0.5 and 0.8, medium; d > 0.8, large). By far the most important factor influencing cognitive performance in any period is cognitive performance in the prior period (this is designated self-productivity by Cunha et al). Effect size is large in terms of Cohen's categories in both stages. Indeed, once the child has gone to school, our estimated effect size could only be described as prodigious, stonking even! This is exactly what might be expected, with children's past performance increasingly constraining future performance, leading them to be set into streams in terms of their level of ability. The underlying psychometric assessments are likely to be more stable at this stage too. The table suggests that crossover from noncognitive to cognitive skills seems unimportant at either stage (small or no effect). Parental investment in stage 1, with the child primarily at home, is more effective than in stage 2; again, according with common sense. Once the child is in full-time schooling, the parent's cognitive skill seems to matter more (small/medium effect), whereas their noncognitive skills are less influential. Again, this seems intuitive as they are now in a better position to help with schoolwork. Elasticity of substitution plays a very limited role in stage 1, but the results suggest that it does exert more of an effect in stage 2, with it becoming harder for parents to compensate once students are established in school, another quite plausible effect.

Let us now examine Cunha et al's interpretation of these figures; it is somewhat different from our own. Paraphrasing slightly, they claim that the parameter estimates show:

(a) Self-productivity becomes stronger as children become older for both cognitive and noncognitive skill formation.
(b) The elasticity of substitution for cognition is smaller in second stage production. It is more difficult to compensate for the effects of adverse environments on cognitive endowments at later ages than it is at earlier ages. This ... helps to explain the evidence on ineffective cognitive remediation strategies for disadvantaged adolescents ...
(p 921)

It is difficult not to see these implications as selective and somewhat tendentious when read against our own rather more comprehensive interpretation. Assuming our analysis to be broadly valid, the results of the study do not seem to show elasticity of substitution as being an important factor in stage 1, let alone as supporting the case for early 'remediation'. If anything, this factor only begins to exert influence once the child has gone to school. As we have said, our analysis appears to bring out a coherent pattern of findings which provides a comprehensive and intuitively meaningful overview of all the factors of interest, rather than highlighting a limited subset of factors and neglecting others.

To explore the policy implications of their findings, Cunha et al present a policy planning simulation. They pose the following scenario: there is a cohort of H children and the task of the 'social planner' is to 'determine [the] optimal allocations of investments from a fixed budget ... to maximize the average education of the cohort' (p 921).

The budget comprises 2H 'investment units' and this is held constant. Crucially, the simulation

> *assumes that the state has full control over family investment decisions.* We do not model parental investment responses to the policy. These simulations produce a measure of the investment that is needed from whatever source to achieve the specified target. (p 921, emphasis added)

Various 3D diagrams are presented to show the effectiveness of investments as a function of the child's initial level of cognitive and noncognitive skill, and the mother's cognitive and noncognitive skills. A pair of graphs in their supplement demonstrates a key finding to best effect. The figures plot the percentage increase in investment over that required for a child with average parental and personal endowments to attain high school graduation. For developmental stage 1, the results show that 'Eighty percent more investment is required for children with the most disadvantaged personal endowments ... The corresponding figure for children with the most disadvantaged parental endowments is 95%' (Supplement, p 43). Given that the 'investment profiles are much flatter' for stage 2, the important conclusion is drawn that 'the optimal policy is to invest relatively more in the disadvantaged compared to the advantaged in the early years' (p 43). Significantly, a simpler version of their production function, that ignores noncognitive skills and multiple stages, generates the opposite result, namely, that 'the optimal policy is to invest relatively more in the early years of the *initially advantaged* ... it is optimal to *perpetuate initial inequality* and not to invest relatively more in disadvantaged young children' (main paper, p 927, emphasis added).

We will conclude with some critical reflections on Cunha et al. We would make several points. First, that the model omits any consideration of socioeconomic status, reflecting a sceptical position articulated explicitly by Heckman elsewhere:

> The widely discussed correlation between parental income in the child's college-going years and child college participation arises only because it is lifetime resources that affect college readiness and college-going ... Job training programs targeted at the disadvantaged do not produce high rates of return and fail to lift participants out of poverty ... these programs are largely ineffective and cannot remedy the skill deficits accumulated over a lifetime of neglect. (Heckman and Masterov, 2007: 475)

In this vein, it is important to remember that when Cunha et al talk of 'disadvantage', this does not designate poverty, just a decrement in either cognitive or noncognitive skill. Equally, investment does not mean State investment, it means parental investment, as measured by the HOME inventory (time spent with children, the provision of toys and music lessons). Regarding such investments, it must be recalled that the overall budget in the simulation is fixed; it assumes a zero sum gain. The policy simulation appears to assume that such investments can be redistributed, somehow taken away from families with bright children and given to families with underachieving children. No wonder parental decisions are not considered and the policy maker has full control!

And it is not just the losing mothers who would resist. The operationalisation of parental investment in terms of the HOME inventory embodies a normative, somewhat bourgeois, model of how parenting should be done, of people who want to do the best for their kids to propel them into a similarly middle-class career. But not every mother or family necessarily wants this, which of course is the real crux of the whole argument:

> Sizeable differences in achievement by parental income are already evident by very young ages ... This raises the possibility that a generation's fate may be sealed by the time it enters school. Economic and social policy requires convincing answers to the vexing question: Why do poor children perform so poorly? Given the importance of family investments for early child development, we concentrate on understanding why low-income families invest so much less in their young children. (Caucutt et al, 2015: 1–2)

A better understanding of parental decision making is clearly part of this. A recent study by Attanasio, which draws on Cunha et al's model, shows a rather more sophisticated understanding of some of the complexities which are involved:

> What determines parental choices? What are the constraints that parents face? How do parents react to a specific policy? These are all questions that are key to the successful design of early years interventions. And yet, much still needs to be learned. Parental decisions are complex and several factors ... interact to determine them. Parents will invest in children by dedicating time to them and buying toys

and books depending on the costs of these investments, how effective they think these activities are ... They will also consider the trade-offs between spending time with children, work and leisure ... Finally, parents often have to make decisions to allocate scarce resources among several children, who differ in their age, gender, perceived ability and so on. (Attanasio, 2015: 18)

As a final epistemological point, we will focus again on the concept of elasticity of substitution, given its prominence. Consider again the stool-making factory. Imagine our surprise if we discovered that rather than 10 stools and 80 spare legs, the factory had produced 20 stools and no spare legs. How could this be? It would appear that seats and legs were substitutable after all. And from a macroeconomic modeller's point of view, that explanation would seem to be enough; the elasticity of substitution is perfect, no more to be said. But there is much more that could be said, surely much more to know before the matter is settled. The inquisitive mind will want to know how and why legs and seats are apparently interchangeable, as they seem such different things. One thing is for sure, that no equation can provide the answer – we will have to go and look for ourselves. The reader might like to speculate on what has transpired, but we will give a couple of clues: the seats of the stool are square, as are the legs. So that's how it's done! you exclaim on entering the factory and talking to the staff. They have improvised, gluing four legs together to make a seat. By this means, 8 legs are required to make a stool, and hence the excess of 80 legs have been turned into 10 stools. All is now clear!

But what of the elasticity of substitutability in Cunha et al? The concept is a tad obscure; it is invoked with all the seductive prestige of a complex, quasi-mathematical concept, but it is very hard to understand exactly what it means. Just like the stool-making factory, access to the real world is needed to demystify the macro-economic abstraction. But no such access is available; we cannot go and look. Nor, in truth, are the more apparently intelligible elements of the model particularly clear. How do parental investments help, and so on? Fundamentally, the issue is epistemological. Again, we encounter the poverty of reductionist accounts based on a single level of explanation. An adequate explication of the relationships between socio-emotional circumstances, cognitive development and parental investments, and how these play out throughout the course of schooling, cannot be answered by a mathematical equation; ascent to the particulars of the real world is needed!

Complex maths and esoteric terminology complicate the policy translation process, just as we saw for brain images. There is an obvious concern that policy makers (and practitioners) are seduced by the vocabulary and the equations and do not raise key questions, that their critical faculty is daunted by the economic wizardry. But the relationships in which Cunha et al are interested can be explored using much simpler and accessible techniques, in bespoke, carefully designed and therefore better investigations. In such experiments, the investigators would have direct control over the choice of measures, drawing on a broad range of quantitative and qualitative data garnered to provide adequate explanations of the phenomenon of interest. A study by Bradley and Caldwell (1984), who originally developed the HOME instrument used by Cunha et al, provides a good example. In a simple study of the benefits of emotional support and cognitive stimulation in the home environment, they show, for instance, that there are correlations between various aspects of the early home environment (at age 12 months and 24 months) and subsequent academic performance at first grade, 6 years later. The correlations are strongest for the provision of toys (averaging around 0.5), which the authors speculate directly stimulate intellectual development, and weakest for maternal responsivity and involvement. Not flashy, but much better science in our view, more intelligible and more useful.

Notes

[1] We have replaced mathematical symbols in the original with corresponding words for ease of reading and comprehension.

[2] Variance of shocks also plays a big part in both phases. This is potentially interesting, suggesting a big role for external events, although Cunha et al seem not to show any interest in this factor in either the main paper or the supplement. No examples of what they meant by shocks is provided. Accordingly we have excluded shocks from our narrative.

[3] Standard errors are not provided for elasticity of substitution in Cunha et al; they are given for complementarity from which it is derived. We have derived our effect size (Cohen's d) for elasticity of substitution from the effect size for complementarity.

[4] By calculating intermediate t values.

References

Ader, R. (1970) The effects of early experience on the adrenocortical response to different magnitudes of stimulation, *Physiology and Behavior*, 5: 837–839.

Ainsworth, M. and Wittig, B. (1969) Attachment and exploratory behavior of one-year-olds in a strange situation, in B. Foss (ed) *Determinants of infant behavior* (Vol. IV), London: Methuen, pp 113–136.

Alberts, B., Bray, D., Hopkin, K. et al (2014) *Essential cell biology*, New York: Garland Science.

All Party Parliamentary Group for Conception to Age 2: the First 1001 Days (2015) *Building Great Britons*, http://www.1001criticaldays. co.uk/buildinggreatbritonsreport.pdf

Allen, G. (2011a) *Early intervention: Next steps,* Cabinet Office: London.

Allen, G. (2011b) *Early intervention: Smart investment, massive savings,* Cabinet Office: London.

Allen, G. and Duncan Smith, I. (2009) *Early intervention: Good parents, great kids, better citizens,* Centre for Social Justice and the Smith Institute.

Antaki, C. (1994) Common sense reasoning: arriving at conclusions or travelling towards them?, in J. Siegfried (ed) *The status of common sense in psychology*, Norwood, NJ: Ablex.

Armstrong, D. (1995) The rise of surveillance medicine, *Sociology of Health and Illness*, 17(3): 393–404.

Attanasio, O. P. (2015) The determinants of human capital formation during the early years of life: theory, measurement and policies, *Journal of the European Economic Association*, 13(6): 949–997.

Baddeley, A. (2000) The episodic buffer: a new component of working memory?, *Trends in Cognitive Sciences,* 4(11): 417–423.

Baddeley, A. D. and Hitch, G. J. (1974) Working memory, in Bower, G.A. (ed) *The psychology of learning and motivation*, pp 47-89, Academic Press.

Bales, S. N. (2004) *Making the public case for child abuse and neglect prevention,* Washington, DC: FrameWorks Institute.

Barker, D. J. P. (1994) *Mothers, babies, and disease in later life*, London: British Medical Journal Publishing Group.

Barkley, R. (2010) *ADHD in adults: What the science says,* New York: Guilford Press.

Barlow, J. and Axford, N. (2014) Giving children a better start in life: from science to policy and practice, *Journal of Children's Services*, 9(2).

Barlow, J., Bennett, C., Midgley, N., Larkin, S., and Wei, Y. (2015) Parent–infant psychotherapy for improving parental and infant mental health: a systematic review, *Campbell Systematic Reviews*, 11(6).

Barlow, J. and Calam, R. (2011) A public health approach to safeguarding in the 21st century, *Child Abuse Review*, 20(4): 238–255.

Barnes, J. C. and Boutwell, B. B. (2015) Biosocial criminology: the emergence of a new and diverse perspective, *Criminal Justice Studies*, 28(1): 1–5.

Barre, R., Yan, J., Egan, B., Treebak, JT., Rasmussen, M., Fritz, T., Caidahl, K., Krook, A., Donal, J., O'Gorman, DJ. Zierath, JR. (2012) Acute exercise remodels promoter methylation in human skeletal muscle, *Cell Metabolism*, 15: 405–411.

Barthes, R. (1973) *Mythologies*, St Albans, UK: Paladin.

Beach, S.R.H., Brody, G.H., Gunter, T.D., Packer, H., Wernett, P. and Philibert, R.A. (2010) Child maltreatment moderates the association of MAOA with symptoms of depression and antisocial personality disorder, *Journal of Family Psychology*, 24: 12–20.

Beach, S.R.H. and Sales, J.M. (eds) (2016) Special issue: Refining prevention: genetic and epigenetic contributions, *Frontiers in Psychology*. Lausanne: Frontiers Media.

Beauregard, M., Courtemanche, J., Paquette, V. and Landry St-Pierre, E. (2009) The neural basis of unconditional love, *Psychiatry Research: Neuroimaging*, 172(2): 93–98.

Beers, C. W. (1921) *The mental hygiene movement,* New York: Longmans, Green & Co.

Bell, C. (2013) *The Daily Telegraph*, 16 October 2013, http://www.telegraph.co.uk/news/science/10369861/Epigenetics-How-to-alter-your-genes.html#disqus_thread

Belsky, J. and de Haan, M. (2011) Parenting and children's brain development: the end of the beginning, *Journal of Child Psychology and Psychiatry*, 52(4): 409–428.

Belsky, J. and van Ijzendoorn, M. H. (2015) What works for whom? Genetic moderation of intervention efficacy, *Development and Psychopathology*, 27: 1–6.

Bennett, M. R. and Hacker, P. M. S. (2003) *Philosophical foundations of neuroscience*, Oxford: Blackwell Publishing.

Bentovim, A. (1995) *Trauma-organized systems: Physical and sexual abuse in families*, Karnac Books.

Bergson, H. (2011) *Creative evolution*, Digireads.com

Bernier, A., and Meins, E. (2008) A threshold approach to understanding the origins of attachment disorganization, *Developmental Psychology*, 44(4): 969.

Bion, W. R. (1962) *Learning from experience*, London: Heinemann; New York: Basic Books.

Bohacek, J. and Mansuy, I.M. (2015) Molecular insights into transgenerational non-genetic inheritance of acquired behaviours, *Nature Reviews Genetics*, advance online publication, Doi: 10.1038/nrg3964. pp 1–12.

Bonazza, S., Scaglione, C., Poppi, M. and Rizzo, G. (2011) Did Goethe describe attention deficit hyperactivity disorder?, *European Neurology*, 65(2): 70–71.

Borenstein, M., Hedges, L.V., Higgins, J.T.P. and Rothstein, H.R. (2009) *Introduction to meta-analysis*, Chichester, UK: John Wiley.

Boyce, W.T., Sokolowski, M.B. and Robinson, G.E. (2012) Toward a new biology of social adversity, *Proceedings of the National Academy of Sciences*, 109(Supplement 2): 17143–17148.

Bridges, J.W. (1928) The mental hygiene movement, *Public Health Journal*, 19: 1–8.

Bradley, R.H. and Caldwell, B.M. (1984) The relation of infants' home environments to achievement test performance in first grade: a follow-up study, *Child Development*, 55: 803–809.

Broadhurst, K., Alrouch, B., Yeend, E. et al (2015a) Connecting events in time to identify a hidden population: birth mothers and their children in recurrent care proceedings in England, *British Journal of Social Work*, 45(8): 2241–2260.

Broadhurst, K., Shaw, M., Kershaw, S. et al (2015b) Vulnerable birth mothers and repeat losses of infants to public care: Is targeted reproductive health care ethically defensible?, *Journal of Social Welfare and Family Law*, 37(1): 84–98.

Broer, T. and Pickersgill, M. (2015) (Low) Expectations, legitimization, and the contingent uses of scientific knowledge: engagements with neuroscience in Scottish social policy and services, *Engaging Science, Technology, and Society*, 1: 47–66.

Brown, R. and Ward, H. (2013) *Decision-making within the child's timeframe*, Childhood Wellbeing Research Centre, Loughborough University, Working Paper 16.

Bruer, J.T. (1999) *The myth of the first three years*, New York: Free Press.

Bufkin, J.L. and and Luttrell, V.R. (2015) Neuroimaging studies of aggressive and violent behaviours, *Trauma, Violence and Abuse*, 6: 176–191.

Burghy, C.A., Stodola, D.B., Ruttle, P.L. et al (2012) Developmental pathways to amygdala-prefrontal function and internalizing symptoms in adolescence, *Nature Neuroscience*, 15(12): 1736–1741.

Burman, E. (1994) *Deconstructing developmental psychology*, London: Routledge.

Burt, C.H. and Simons, R.L. (2014) Pulling back the curtain on heritability studies: biosocial criminology in the postgenomic era, *Criminology*, 52: 223–262.

Buss, C., Davis, E.P., Muftuler, L.T., Head, K. and Sandman, C.A. (2010) High pregnancy anxiety during mid-gestation is associated with decreased gray matter density in 6–9-year-old children, *Psychoneuroendocrinology*, 35(1): 141–153.

Butler, P. (2014) Policymakers seduced by neuroscience to justify early intervention agenda, *The Guardian*, 6 May 2014. http://www.theguardian.com/society/2014/may/06/policymakers-neuroscience-justify-early-intervention-agenda-bruce-perry

Bywaters, P. (2015) Cumulative jeopardy? A response to Brown and Ward, *Children and Youth Services Review*, 52: 68–73.

Cafcass (2015) *Care applications in October 2015*, https://www.cafcass.gov.uk/media/266884/october_2015_care_demand.pdf

Callon, M. (1986a) Some elements of a sociology of translation: domestication of the scallops and the fishermen of St Brieuc Bay, In J. Law (ed) *Power, action and belief: a new sociology of knowledge?*, London: Routledge, pp 196–223.

Callon, M (1986b) The sociology of an actor-network: the case of the electric vehicle, in M. Callon, J. Law and A. Rip (eds), *Mapping the dynamics of science and technology: sociology of science in the real world*, Basingstoke, UK: Macmillan, pp 29–30.

Carey, J. (ed) (1999) *The Faber book of utopias*, London: Faber & Faber.

Carey, N. (2012) *The epigenetics revolution*, London: Icon Books.

Cartwright, N. and Munro, E. (2010) The limitations of randomized controlled trials in predicting effectiveness, *Journal of Evaluation in Clinical Practice*, 16(2): 260–266.

Cao-Lei, L., Massart, R., Suderman, M.J. et al (2014) DNA methylation signatures triggered by prenatal maternal stress exposure to a natural disaster: Project Ice Storm, *PLoS ONE*, 9(9): e107653.

Caucutt, E.M., Lochner, L. and Park, Y. (2015) *Correlation, confusion or constraints: why do poor children perform so poorly?*, Human Capital and Economic Opportunity Global Working Group. Working Paper 2015-55.

Chafe, W. (1986) Evidentiality in English conversation and academic writing, in W. Chafe and J. Nichols (eds) *Evidentiality: the linguistic coding of epistemology*, Norwood, NJ: Ablex.

Charil, A., Laplante, D. P., Vaillancourt, C. and King, S. (2010) Prenatal stress and brain development, *Brain Research Reviews*, 65(1): 56–79.

Charlton, B. G. (1990) A critique of biological psychiatry, *Psychological Medicine*, 20: 3–6.

Cheng, W., Rolls, E.T., Gu, H., Zhang, J. and Feng, J. (2015) Autism: reduced connectivity between cortical areas involved in face expression, theory of mind and the sense of self, *Brain*, doi: http://dx.doi.org/10.1093/brain/awv051

Christie, B. (2012) DNA methylation may be associated with health inequalities, *BMJ*, 344: e722.

Cicchetti, D. (2015) Neural plasticity, sensitive periods, and psychopathology, *Development and Psychopathology*, 27: 319–320.

Cleveland, H.H., Schlomer, G.L., Vandenbergh, D.J. et al (2015) The conditioning of intervention effects on early adolescent alcohol use by maternal involvement and dopamine receptor D4 (*DRD4*) and serotonin transporter linked polymorphic region (*5-HTTLPR*) genetic variants, *Development and Psychopharmacology*, 27: 51–67.

Cohen, J. (1988) *Statistical power analysis for the behavioral sciences*, Hillsdale, NJ: Lawrence Erlbaum Associates.

Coie, J.D., Watt, N.F., West, S.G. et al (1993) The science of prevention: a conceptual framework and some directions for a national research program, *American Psychologist*, 48(10): 1013–1022.

Connolly, M., Morris, K., Pennell, J. and Burford, G. (2009) *FGC research annotated bibliography*. Denver, CO: American Humane Association.

Connolly, W.E. (1993) *Political theory and modernity*, Ithaca, NY: Cornell University Press.

Conrad, P. (2007) *The medicalization of society*, Baltimore, MD: John Hopkins University Press.

Cooper, R. (2014) *Diagnosing the diagnostic and statistical manual of mental disorders*, London: Karnac.

Coppen, A. (1967) The biochemistry of affective disorders, *British Journal of Psychiatry*, 113: 1237–1264.

Cunha, F., Heckman, J.J., Lochner, L. and Masterov, D.V. (2006) Interpreting evidence on life cycle skill formation, in E. Hanushek and F. Welch (eds) *Handbook of the economics of education*, Amsterdam: North Holland, pp 697–812.

Cunha, F., Heckman, J.J., and Schennach, S.M. (2010) Estimating the technology of cognitive and noncognitive skill formation, *Econometrica*, 78(3): 883–931.

Cunliffe, V. (2015) Experience-sensitive epigenetic mechanisms, developmental plasticity, and the biological embedding of chronic disease risk, *Systems Biology and Medicine*, 7: 53–71.

Damasio, A.R. and Maurer, R.G. (1978) A neurological model for childhood autism, *Archives of Neurology*, 35: 777–786.

Dartington Social Research Unit, University of Warwick and Coventry University (2015) *The best start at home*, Early Intervention Foundation, http://www.eif.org.uk/publication/the-best-start-at-home/

Davies, J. (2013) *Cracked: Why psychiatry is doing more harm than good*, London: Icon Books.

Dawson, G., Hessl, D. and Frey, K. (1994) Social influences on early developing biological and behavioural systems related to risk for affective disorder, *Development and Psychopathology*, 6: 759–779.

De Brito, S.A., Viding, E., Sebastian, C.L. et al (2013) Reduced orbitofrontal and temporal grey matter in a community sample of maltreated children, *Journal of Child Psychology and Psychiatry*, 54(1): 105–112.

De Kloet, E.R., Vregdenhil, E., Oitzl, M.S. and Joels, M. (1998) Brain corticosteroid receptor balance in health and disease, *Endocrine Reviews*, 19: 269–301.

Delamont, S. and Atkinson, P. (2001) Doctoring uncertainty: mastering craft knowledge, *Social Studies of Science*, 31(1): 87–107.

Denboba, A.D., Sayre, R.K., Wodon, Q.T. et al (2014) *Stepping up early childhood development: investing in young children for high returns*, Washington, DC: World Bank Group, http://documents.worldbank.org/curated/en/2014/10/20479606/stepping-up-early-childhood-development-investing-young-children-high-returns

Dillon, A. and Craven, R.G. (2014) Examining the genetic contribution to ADHD, *Ethical Human Psychology and Psychiatry*, 16(1): 20–28.

Donzelot, J. (1979) *Policing the family*, New York: Pantheon.

Dugdale, R. (1877) *"The Jukes": A study in crime, pauperism, disease and heredity*, New York, London: G.P. Putnam's Sons.

Dunn, G.A. and Bale, T.L. (2011) Maternal high-fat diet effects on third-generation female body size via the paternal lineage, *Endocrinology*, 152(6): 2228–2236.

Duschinsky, R., Greco, M. and Solomon, J. (2015) Wait up! Attachment and sovereign power, *International Journal of Politics, Culture, and Society*, 28: 223–242.

Edwards, C.E., Benediktsson, R., Lindsay, R.S. and Seckl, J.R. (1993) Dysfunction of the placental glucocorticoid barrier: a link between the foetal environment and adult hypertension?, *Lancet*, 341: 355–357.

Edwards, R., Gillies, V. and Horsley, N. (2015) Brain science and early years policy: hopeful ethos or 'cruel optimism'?, *Critical Social Policy*, 35(2): 167–187.

Eklund, A., Nichols, T.E. and Knutsson, H. (2016) Cluster failure: why fMRI inferences for spatial extent have inflated false-positive rates, *Proceedings of the National Academy of Sciences*, 113(28): 7900–7905.

Ellul, J. (1965) *Propaganda: The formation of men's attitudes,* New York: Vintage Books.

Farah, M.J. and Hook, C.J. (2013) The seductive allure of 'seductive allure', *Perspectives in Psychological Science,* 8(1): 88–90.

Faraone, S. V., Perlis, R. H., Doyle, A. E. et al (2005) Molecular genetics of attention-deficit/hyperactivity disorder, *Biological Psychiatry*, 57: 1313–1132.

Farmer, R.L. (2009) *Neuroscience and social work practice: the missing link.* Thousand Oaks, CA: Sage Publications.

Featherstone, B., Manby, M. and Nicholls, N. (2007) What difference does outreach make to family support?, in J. Schneider, M. Avis and P. Leighton (eds) *Supporting children and families: lessons from Sure Start for evidence-based practice in health, social care and education,* London: Jessica Kingsley Publishers.

Featherstone, B., White, S. and Morris, K. (2014a) *Re-imagining child protection: towards humane social work with families,* Bristol: Policy Press.

Featherstone, B., Morris, K. and White, S. (2014b) A marriage made in hell: Early intervention meets child protection, *British Journal of Social Work*, 44 (7):1735–49.

Fenton Glynn, C. (2015) *Adoption without consent*, Brussels: The European Union.

Field, F. (2010) *The Foundation Years: Preventing poor children becoming poor adults: The report of the Independent Review on Poverty and Life Chances,* HM Government, http://webarchive.nationalarchives.gov.uk/20110120090128/http://povertyreview.independent.gov.uk/media/20254/poverty-report.pdf

Field, T. (2011) Prenatal depression effects on early development: a review, *Infant Behavior and Development*, 34(1): 1–14.

Finsterwald, C. and Alberini, C.M. (2014) Stress and glucocorticoid receptor-dependent mechanism in long-term memory: from adaptive responses to psychopathologies, *Neurobiology of Learning and Memory*, 112: 17–29.

Fisher, M. and Marsh, P. (2015) The research–practice relationship and the work of Edward Mullen, in H. Soydan and W. Lorenz (eds) *Social work practice to the benefit of our clients: scholarly legacy of Edward J. Mullen,* Bolzano, Italy: Bozen-Bolzano University Press, pp 47–63.

Fitzpatrick, P. (1992) *The mythology of modern law*, London: Routledge.

Fleck, L. (1979) *Genesis and development of a scientific fact,* Chicago: University of Chicago Press.

Forrester, D. (2012) Evaluation research, in M. Gray, J. Midgley and S. Webb (eds) *The Sage handbook of social work,* London: Sage Publications, pp 440–453.

FrameWorks Institute (2010) *More to genes than that: Designing metaphors to explain epigenetics,* Washington, DC: FrameWorks Institute.

Frances, A. (2013) *Saving normal,* London: Harper Collins.

Frankl, V. (1962) Existential dynamics and neurotic escapism, in *Psychotherapy and existentialism,* New York: Penguin.

Franklin, T.B., Russig, H., Weiss, I.C. et al (2010) Epigenetic transmission of the impact of early stress across generations, *Biological Psychiatry*, 68: 408–415.

Frost, N. and Parton, N. (2009) *Understanding children's social care: Politics, policy and practice,* London: Sage Publications.

George, M.S., Padberg, F., Schlaepfer, T.E. et al (2009) Controversy: Repetitive transcranial magnetic stimulation or transcranial direct current stimulation shows efficacy in treating psychiatric diseases (depression, mania, schizophrenia, obsessive–compulsive disorder, panic, posttraumatic stress disorder), *Brain Stimulation*, 2: 14–21.

Ghezzi, P.M., Doney, J.K. and Bonow, J.A. (2014) Psychological theories of childhood autism, in J. Tarbox et al (eds) *Handbook of early intervention for autism spectrum disorders,* New York: Springer, pp 105–116.

Giddens, A. (1984) *The constitution of society,* Cambridge: Polity Press.

Giroux, H.A. (2014) Totalitarian paranoia in the post-Orwellian, surveillance state, *Cultural Studies*, 29(2): 108–140.

Glover, V. and O'Connor, T.G. (2002) Effects of antenatal stress and anxiety: implications for development and psychiatry, *British Journal of Psychiatry*, 180(5): 389–391.

Glover, V., O'Connor, T.G. and O'Donnell, K. (2010) Prenatal stress and the programming of the HPA axis, *Neuroscience & Biobehavioral Reviews*, 35(1): 17–22.

Goddard, H. (2012) *The Kallikak family: A study in the heredity of feeble-mindedness,* Macmillan, New York.

Gollisch, T. and Meister, M. (2008) Rapid neural coding in the retina with relative spike latencies, *Science*, 319: 1108–1111.

Greenberg, G. (2010) *Manufacturing depression: The secret history of a modern disease,* New York: Simon & Schuster.

Greenhalgh, T. and Russell, J. (2006) Reframing evidence synthesis as rhetorical action in the policy making drama, *Healthcare Policy*, 1(2): 34–42.

Grill-Spector, K., Sayres, R. and Ress, D. (2006) High-resolution imaging reveals highly selective nonface clusters in the fusiform face area, *Nature Neuroscience*, 9(9): 1177–1185.

Gutteling, B. M., De Weerth, C. and Builelaar, J.K. (2005) Prenatal stress and children's cortisol reaction to the first day of school, *Psychoneuroendocrinology*, 30: 541–549.

Guze, S. B. (1989) Biological psychiatry: Is there any other kind? *Psychological Medicine*, 19: 315–323.

Hacking, I. (1990) *The taming of chance*, Cambridge: Cambridge University Press.

Heard, E. and Martienssen, R. A. (2014) Transgenerational epigenetic inheritance: myths and mechanisms, *Cell*, 157: 95–109.

Heckman, J.J. (2013) *Giving kids a fair chance (a strategy that works)*, Boston, MA: MIT Press.

Heckman, J.J. and Masterov, D.V. (2007) The productivity argument for investing in young children, *Review of Agricultural Economics*, 29(3): 446–493.

Heijmans, B.T., Tobi, E.W., Stein, A.D. et al (2008) Persistent epigenetic differences associated with prenatal exposure to famine in humans, *Proceedings of the National Academy of Sciences*, 105: 17046–17049.

Hermans, E.J., Battaglia, F.P., Atsak, P. et al (2014) How the amygdala affects emotional memory by altering brain network properties, *Neurobiology of Learning and Memory*, 1112: 2–16.

Herrera-Cuenca, M. (2015) From epigenetics to public policy: a new perspective for early action, *Advances in Food Technology and Nutritional Sciences*, 1(5): 16–18.

Hikida, T., Jaaro-Peled, H., Seshadri, S. et al (2007) Dominant-negative DISC1 transgenic mice display schizophrenia-associated phenotypes detected by measures translatable to humans, *Proceedings of the National Academy of Sciences*, 104(36): 14501–14506.

Houses of Parliament, Parliamentary Offices of Science and Technology (2013) *Epigenetics and health*, http://researchbriefings.parliament.uk/ResearchBriefing/Summary/POST-PN-451#fullreport

Howard-Jones, P.A., Washbrook, E.V. and Meadows, S. (2012) The timing of educational investment: A neuroscientific perspective, *Developmental Cognitive Neuroscience*, 25: S18–S29.

Hubel, D. (1963) The visual cortex of the brain, *Scientific American*, Nov, 2–10.

Hughes, N. (2015) Understanding the influence of neurodevelopmental disorders on offending: utilizing developmental psychopathology in biosocial criminology, *Criminal Justice Studies*, 28(1): 39–60.

Huntsinger, E.T. and Luecken, L.J. (2004) Attachment relationships and health behavior: The mediational role of self-esteem, *Psychology & Health*, 19(4): 515–526.

Huttenlocher, P.R. (1979) Synaptic density in human frontal cortex: Developmental changes and effects of aging, *Brain Research*, 163(2): 195–205.

International Society for DOHaD (2015) The Cape Town Manifesto, https://dohadsoc.org/wp-content/uploads/2015/11/DOHaD-Society-Manifesto-Nov-17-2015.pdf

Ioannidis, J. (2005) Why most published research findings are false, *PLoS Medicine,* 2: 696–701.

John, I. D. (1990) Discursive style and psychological practice, *Australian Psychologist*, 25(2): 115–132.

Joseph, J. (2012) The 'missing heritability' of psychiatric disorders: elusive genes or non-existent genes?, *Applied Developmental Science*, 16(2): 65–83.

Juengst, E.T., Fishman, J.R., McGowan, M.L. and Settersten, R.A. (2014) Serving epigenetics before its time, *Trends in Genetics*, 30(10): 427–429.

Kagan, J. (1998) *Three seductive ideas*, Harvard, MA: Harvard University Press.

Kahneman, D., Slovic, P. and Tversky, A. (1982) *Judgment under uncertainty: heuristics and biases*, Cambridge: Cambridge University Press.

Kaiser, J. (2014) The epigenetics heretic, *Science*, 343(6169): 361–363.

Kaliman, P., Alvarez-Lopez, MJ., Cosın-Tomas, M., Rosenkranz, M.A., Lutz, A. and Davidson, R.J. (2014) Rapid changes in histone deacetylases and inflammatory gene expression in expert meditators, *Psychoneuroendocrinology*, 40: 96–107.

Keil, M. (1995) Pulling the plug: Management and the problem of project escalation, *MIS Quarterly*, 19(4): 421–427.

Kiesler, D. J. (1966) Some myths of psychotherapy research and the search for a paradigm, *Psychological Bulletin*, 65: 110–136.

Kendall-Taylor, N., Lindland, E., O'Neil, M. and Stanley, K. (2014) Beyond prevalence: An explanatory approach to reframing child maltreatment in the United Kingdom: the most prevalent form of maltreatment, child neglect, gets the least attention from the public and policymakers, *Child Abuse & Neglect*, 38(5): 810–821.

Khan, F. (2010) Preserving human potential as freedom: a framework for regulating epigenetic harms, *Health Matrix*, 20: 259–323.

Klein, M. (1952) Some theoretical conclusions regarding the emotional life of the infant, in *Envy and gratitude and other works 1946–1963*, London: Hogarth Press and the Institute of Psycho-Analysis, (published 1975).

Kuhn, T. (1962) *The structure of scientific revolutions,* Chicago, London: University of Chicago Press.

Landecker, H. and Panofsky, A. (2013) From social structure to gene regulation, and back: a critical introduction to environmental epigenetics for sociology, *Annual Review of Sociology*, 39: 333–357.

Latham, J. and Wilson, A. (2010) The great DNA data deficit: Are genes for disease a mirage? The Bioscience Research Project, http://independentsciencenews.org/health/the-great-dna-data-deficit/

Latour, B. (1987) *Science in action*, Harvard, MA: Harvard University Press.

Latour, B. (1993) *The pasteurization of France*, Cambridge, MA: Harvard University Press.

Latour, B. (1999) *Pandora's hope: Essays on the reality of science studies*, Cambridge, MA: Harvard University Press.

Law, J. (1994) *Organizing modernity*, Oxford: Blackwell.

Lee, S., Aos, S., Drake, E., Pennucci, A., Miller, M. and Anderson, L. (2012*) Return on investment: evidence-based options to improve statewide outcomes*, Document No. 12-04-1201. Olympia: Washington State Institute for Public Policy.

Legrenzi, P. and Umilta, C. (2011) *Neuromania: On the limits of brain science*, Oxford: Oxford University Press.

Leonelli, S. (2010) Documenting the emergence of bio-ontologies: or, why researching bioinformatics requires HPSSB, *History and Philosophy of the Life Sciences*, 32(1): 105–125.

Lester, D. (1989) The heritability of alcoholism: science and social policy, in E.S. Lisansky (ed) *Current issues in alcohol/drug studies*, New York: Haworth Press, pp 29–69.

Levendosky, A.A., Bogat, G.A., Huth-Bocks, A.C., Rosenblum, K. and von Eye, A. (2011) The effects of domestic violence on the stability of attachment from infancy to preschool, *Journal of Clinical Child and Adolescent Psychology*, 40(3): 398–410.

Levine, S. (1962) Plasma-free corticosteroid response to electric shock in rats stimulated in infancy, *Science*, 135: 795–796.

Lewontin, R., Rose, S. and Kamin, L. (1984) *Not in our genes: Biology, ideology and human nature*, New York: Pantheon

Lilienfeld, S.O. (2007) Cognitive neuroscience and depression: legitimate versus illegitimate reductionism and five challenges, *Cognitive Therapy and Research*, 31: 263–272.

Liu, D., Diorio, J., Tannenbaum, B. et al (1997) Maternal care, hippocampal glucocorticoid receptors, and hypothalamic–pituitary–adrenal response to stress, *Science*, 277: 1659–1662.

Lloyd Jones, E. (2013) Decision making within a child's timescale: Who decides? *Family Law*, 43(8): 1053–1055.

Loi, M., Del Savio, L. and Stupka, E. (2013) Social epigenetics and equality of opportunity, *Public Health Ethics*, 6(2): 142–153.

Lowe, P., Lee, E. and Macvarish, J. (2015) Growing better brains? Pregnancy and neuroscience discourses in English social and welfare policies, *Health, Risk & Society*, 17(1): 15–29.

Lumey, L.H. (1992) Decreased birthweights in infants after maternal *in utero* exposure to the Dutch famine winter of 1944–45, *Paediatric and Perinatal Epidemiology*, 6: 240–253.

Lumey, L.H., Stein, A.D. and Susser, E. (2011) Prenatal famine and adult health, *Annual Review of Public Health*, 32, doi:10.1146/annurev-publhealth-031210-101230.

Lusher, J. M., Chandler, C. and Ball, D. (2001) Dopamine D4 receptor gene (DRD4) is associated with novelty seeking (NS) and substance abuse: the saga continues…, *Molecular Psychiatry*, 6: 3497–3499.

Lutz, P.E. and Turecki, G. (2014) DNA methylation and childhood maltreatment: from animal models to human studies, *Neuroscience*, 264: 142–156.

McArdle, H. (2012), http://www.heraldscotland.com/news/13045497.DNA_could_explain_riddle_of_poor_health_in_Glasgow/

McCabe, D.P. and Castel, A.D. (2007) Seeing is believing: the effect of brain images on judgements of scientific reasoning, *Cognition*, 107(1): 343–352.

McCrory, E., De Brito, S. and Viding, E. (2012) The link between child abuse and psychopathology: a review of neurobiological and genetic research, *Journal of the Royal Society of Medicine*, 105: 151–156.

McGough, J.J. and Faraone, S.V. (2009) Estimating the size of treatment effects: moving beyond P values, *Psychiatry*, 6: 21–29.

McGowan, P.O. and Szyf, M. (2010) The epigenetics of social adversity in early life: implications for mental health outcomes, *Neurobiology of Disease*, 39: 66–72.

McGowan, P.O., Sasaki, A., D'Alessio, A.C. et al (2009) Epigenetic regulation of the glucocorticoid receptor in human brain associates with childhood abuse, *Nature Neuroscience*, 12(3): 342–348.

McGue, M. (1992) When assessing twin concordance, use the probandwise not the pairwise rate, *Schizophrenia Bulletin*, 18(2): 171–176.

McGugin, R.W., Van Gulick, A.E. and Gauthier, I. (2016) Cortical thickness in fusiform face area predicts face and object recognition performance, *Journal of Cognitive Neuroscience,* 28(2): 282–294.

McGuinness, D., McGlynn, L.M., Johnson, P.C.D. et al (2012) Socio-economic status is associated with epigenetic differences in the pSoBid cohort, *International Journal of Epidemiology,* 41: 151–160.

McWilliams, L.A. and Bailey, S. . (2010) Associations between adult attachment ratings and health conditions: evidence from the National Comorbidity Survey Replication, *Health Psychology,* 29(4): 446–453.

Marchal, C. amd Miotto, B. (2015) Emerging concept in DNA methylation: Role of transcription factors in shaping DNA methylation patterns, *Journal of Cellular Physiology,* 230: 743–51.

Macri, S. and Würbel, H. (2006) Developmental plasticity of HPA and fear responses in rats: a critical review of the maternal mediation hypothesis, *Hormones and Behavior,* 50: 667–680.

Malinowski, B. (1922) *Argonauts of the western Pacific,* London: G. Routledge & Sons.

Manolio, T.A., Collins, F.S., Cox, N.J. et al (2009) Finding the missing heritability of complex diseases, *Nature,* 461: 747–753.

Mansfield, B. and Guthman, J. (2014) Epigenetic life: biological plasticity, abnormality, and new configurations of race and reproduction, *Cultural Geographies,* 1474474014555659.

Martinez, D., Pentinat, T., Ribo, S. et al (2011) *In utero* undernutrition in male mice programs liver lipid metabolism in the second generation offspring involving altered *Lxra* methylation, *Cell Metabolism,* 19: 941–951.

Mauss, M. (1950) *A general theory of magic,* London: Routledge.

Maximo, J.O., Cadena, E.J. and Kana, R.K. (2014) The implications of brain connectivity in the neuropsychology of autism, *Neuropsychological Review,* 24(1): 16–31.

Meaney, M. (2001) Maternal care, gene expression, and the transmission of individual differences in stress reactivity across generations, *Annual Review of Neuroscience,* 242: 1161–1192.

Meaney, M., Aitken, D.H., Bodnoff, S.R., Iny, L.J. and Sapolsky, R.M. (1985) The effects of postnatal handling on the development of the glucocorticoid receptor systems and stress recovery in the rat, *Progress in Neuro-psychopharmacology and Biological Psychiatry,* 9: 731–734.

Mehan, H. (1990) Oracular reasoning in a psychiatric examination, in Grimshaw, A.D. (ed) *Conflict talk,* New York: Cambridge University Press, pp 160–177.

Melhuish, E.C., Belsky, J. and Leyland, A.H. (2012) *The impact of Sure Start local programmes on seven-year-olds and their families,* Project Report, Department for Education, London, UK.

Mellon, M. (2015) The 'Named Person' debate: the case against, *Scottish Journal of Residential Child Care*,14(3).

Meloni, M. (2016) *Political biology: Science and social values in human heredity from eugenics to epigenetics*, New York and Basingstoke, UK: Palgrave Macmillan.

Meloni, M. and Testa, G. (2014) Scrutinizing the epigenetics revolution, *BioSocieties*, 9(4): 431–456.

Menon, V. (2015) *Brain mapping: An encyclopedic reference*, vol. 2, pp 597–611.

Midgley, M. (2014) *Are you an illusion?*, London: Routledge.

Miller, G.A. (2010) Mistreating psychology in the decades of the brain, *Perspectives on Psychological Science*, 5(6): 716–743.

Moffitt, T.E. and Beckley, A. (2015) Abandon twin research? Embrace epigenetic research? Premature advice for criminologists, *Criminology*, 53(1): 121–126.

Montagu, A. (1972) Sociogenic brain damage, *American Anthropologist*, 74(5): 1045–1061.

Napier, J.L., Mandisodza, A.N., Andersen, S.M. and Jost, J.T. (2006) System justification in responding to the poor and displaced in the aftermath of Hurricane Katrina, *Analyses of Social Issues and Public Policy*, 6(1): 57–73.

Nietzsche, F.W. (1974) *The gay science*, New York: Vintage Books.

Oberlander, T.F., Weinberg, J., Papsdorf, M., Grunau, R., Misri, S. and Devlin, A.M. (2008) Prenatal exposure to maternal depression, neonatal methylation of human glucocorticoid receptor gene (NR3C1) and infant cortisol stress responses, *Epigenetics*, 3(2): 97–106.

Olds, D.L., Arcoleo, K.J., Henderson, C.R. et al (2010) Enduring effects of prenatal and infancy home visiting by nurses on maternal life course and government spending, *Archives of Paediatric Medicine*, 164(5): 419–424.

Owen, I.R. (1999) The future of psychotherapy in the UK: discussing clinical governance, *British Journal of Psychotherapy*, 16(2): 197–207.

Paes de Barros, R., Ferreira, F., Molinas Vega, J. and Saavedra Chanduvi, J. (2009) *Measuring inequality of opportunities in Latin America and the Caribbean,* Washington, DC: World Bank.

Pam, A. (1995) Biological psychiatry: science or pseudoscience?, in Ross, C.A. and Pam, A. (eds) *Pseudoscience in biological psychiatry: Blaming the body*, New York: John Wiley & Sons, pp 7–84.

Panzeri, S., Macke, J H., Gross, J. and Kayser, C. (2015) Neural population coding: combining insights from microscopic and mass signals, *Trends in Cognitive Sciences*, 19(3): 162–172.

Papez, J.W. (1937) A proposed mechanism of emotion, *Archives of Neurology and Psychiatry*, 38(4): 725–743.

Pearce, W., Raman, S. and Turner, A. (2015) Randomised trials in context: practical problems and social aspects of evidence-based medicine and policy, *Trials*, 16(1): 394.

Pembrey, M.E., Bygren, L.O., Kaati, G. et al (2006) Sex-specific, male-line transgenerational responses in humans, *European Journal of Human Genetics*, 14: 159–164.

Perkins, A. (2016) *The welfare trait: How state benefits affect personality*, New York: Palgrave Macmillan.

Perroud, N., Paoloni-Giacobino, A., Prada, P. et al (2011) Increased methylation of glucocorticoid receptor gene (*NR3C1*) in adults with a history of childhood maltreatment: a link with the severity and type of trauma, *Translational Psychiatry*, 1, e59, doi:10.1038/tp.2011.60, pp 1–9.

Perry, B.D. (1997) Incubated in terror: neurodevelopmental factors in the 'cycle of violence', in J. Osofsky (ed) *Children, youth and violence: the search for solutions*, New York: Guilford Press, pp 124–148.

Perry, B.D. (2002) Childhood experience and the expression of genetic potential: what childhood neglect tells us about nature and nurture, *Brain and Mind*, 3: 79–100.

Perry, M.W. (ed) (2000) *Eugenics and other evils, An argument against the scientifically organized society, G.K. Chesterton*, Seattle, WA: Inkling Books.

Petticrew, M. and Roberts, H. (2003) Evidence, hierarchies, and typologies: horses for courses, *Journal of Epidemiology and Community Health*, 57: 527–529.

Pickersgill, M. (2010) From psych to soma? Changing accounts of antisocial personality disorders in the *American Journal of Psychiatry*, *History of Psychiatry*, 21(3): 294–311.

Pickersgill, M. (2016) Epistemic modesty, ostentatiousness and the uncertainties of epigenetics: on the knowledge machinery of (social) science, *Sociological Review Monographs*, 64(1): 186–202.

Poerksen, U. (1995) *Plastic words: The tyranny of modular language*, University Park, PA: Pennsylvania State University Press.

Poldrack, R.A. (2006) Can cognitive processes be inferred from neuroimaging data?, *Trends in Cognitive Sciences*, 10(2): 59–63.

Portelli, G., Barrett, J., Sernagor, E., Masquelier, T. and Kornprobst, P. (2014) *The wave of first spikes provides robust spatial cues for retinal information processing,* Research Report 8559, INRIA.

Posner, M. I., Sheese, B. E., Odludas, Y. and Tang, Y. Y. (2006) Analyzing and shaping human attentional networks, *Neural Networks,* 19: 1422–1429.

Posner, M. I., Rothbard, M. K., Sheese, B. and Voelker, P. (2014) Developing attention: behavioral and brain mechanisms, *Advances in Neuroscience,* 1–9.

Pribram, K. (1991) *Brain and perception: holonomy and structure in figural processing,* Hillsdale, NJ: Lawrence Erlbaum Associates.

Ptashne, M. (2013) Epigenetics: core misconcept, *Proceedings of the National Academy of Sciences of the USA,* 110(18): 7101–7103.

Pustilnik, A.C. (2009) Violence on the brain: a critique of neuroscience in criminal law, *Wake Forest Law Review,* 44: 183–237.

Quiroga, R. Q., Reddy, L., Kreiman, G., Koch, C. and Fried, I. (2005) Invariant visual representation by single neurons in the human brain, *Nature,* doi:10.1038/nature03687

Qiu, A., Rifkin-Graboi, A., Chen, H. et al (2013) Maternal anxiety and infants' hippocampal development: timing matters, *Translational Psychiatry,* 3(9): e306.

Raabe, P. (2013) *Philosophy's role in counseling and psychotherapy,* Lanham, MD: Rowman & Littlefield.

Rafter, N. H. (1997) *Creating born criminals,* Chicago: University of Illinois Press.

Rafter, N. H. (1988) *White trash: The eugenic family studies, 1877–1919,* Boston, MD: Northeastern University Press.

Ramani, D. (2009) The brain seduction: the public perception of neuroscience, *Journal of Science Communication,* 8(4): 1–8.

Read, J. (2010) Can poverty drive you mad? 'Schizophrenia', socioeconomic status and the case for primary prevention, *New Zealand Journal of Psychology,* 39(2): 7–19.

Reese, H.W. (1996) How is physiology relevant to behavior analysis? *The Behavior Analyst,* 19: 61–70.

Reid, W. J. and Shyne, A.W. (1969) *Brief and extended casework,* New York: Columbia University Press.

Ren, H., Collins, V., Clarke, S.J. et al (2012) Epigenetic changes in response to tai chi practice: a pilot investigation of DNA methylation marks. *Evidence-Based Complementary and Alternative Medicine,* doi:10.1155/2012/841810

Reynolds, R.M., Labad, J., Buss, C., Ghaemmaghami, P. and Räikkönen, K. (2013) Transmitting biological effects of stress in utero: implications for mother and offspring, *Psychoneuroendocrinology*, 38(9): 1843–1849.

Richter, S.H., Garner, J.P. and Würbel, H. (2009) Environmental standardisation: cure or cause of poor reproducibility I animal experiments?, *Nature Methods*, 6(4): 257–261.

Richter, H., Garner, J., Auer, C., Joachim Kunert, J. and Würbel, H. (2010) Systematic variation improves reproducibility of animal experiments, *Nature methods*, 7: 167–8.

Rietveld, M.J., Hudziak, J J., Bartels, M., van Beijsterveldt, C.E. and Boomsma, D.I. (2003) Heritability of attention problems in children: I. Cross-sectional results from a study of twins, age 3–12 years, *American Journal of Medical Genetics B Neuropsychiatric Geneticst*, 117: 102–113.

Rimke, H. and Hunt, A. (2002) From sinners to degenerates: the medicalization of morality in the 19th century, *History of the Human Sciences,* 15(1): 59–88.

Robinson, O. and Vrijheid, M. (2015) The pregnancy exposome, *Current Environmental Health Reports*, 2(2): 204–213.

Rose, N. (1989) *Governing the soul: tThe shaping of the private self*, London: Routledge.

Rose, N. (2010) 'Screen and intervene': governing risky brains, *History of the Human Sciences,* 23(1): 79–105.

Rose, N.S. and Abi-Rached, J.M. (2013) *Neuro: the new brain sciences and the management of the mind*, Princeton, NJ: Princeton University Press.

Rose, H. and Rose, S. (2012) *Genes, cells and brains: The Promethean promises of the new biology*, London: Verso.

Ross, C.A. and Pam, A. (eds) (1995) *Pseudoscience in biological psychiatry: Blaming the body*, New York: John Wiley & Sons.

Rothstein, M.A., Cai, Y. and Marchant, G.E. (2009) The ghost in our genes: legal and ethical implications of epigenetics, *Health Matrix Cleveland*, 19(1): 1–62.

Roy John, E. (1972) Switchboard versus statistical theories of learning and memory, *Science*, 177: 850–864.

Roth, T.L., Lubin, F. D., Funk, A.J. and Sweatt, J.D. (2009) Lasting epigenetic influence of early life adversity on the *BDNF* gene, *Biological Psychiatry*, 65(9): 760–769.

Ruhe, H.G., Mason, N.S. and Schene, A.H. (2007) Mood is indirectly related to serotonin, norepinephrine and dopamine levels in humans: a meta-analysis of monoamine depletion studies, *Molecular Psychiatry*, 12: 331–359.

Rutter, M. (1991) *Maternal deprivation reassessed*, London: Penguin.

Saarni, S.I. and Gylling, H.A. (2004) Evidence-based medicine guidelines: a solution to rationing or politics disguised as science? *Journal of Medical Ethics*, 30(2): 171–175.

Schildkraut, J.J. (1965) The catecholamine hypothesis of affective disorders: a review of supporting evidence, *American Journal of Psychiatry*, 122: 509–522.

Scholte, R., van den Berg, G. and Lindeboom, M. (2012) Long-run effects of gestation during the Dutch Hunger Winter famine on labor market and hospitalization outcomes, *Netspar Discussion Paper*, DP 01/2012-031.

Schrödinger, E. (1967) *What is life?* with *Mind and matter* and *Autobiographical sketches*, Cambridge: Cambridge University Press.

Scottish Government (2015) Consultation on the draft Statutory Guidance for Parts 4, 5 and 18 (Section 96) and related draft orders of the Children and Young People (Scotland) Act 2014, http://www.gov.scot/Publications/2015/02/185p1/14

Scull, A. (2015) *Madness in civilisation,* London: Thames & Hudson.

Shaw, P. (2012) Insights into childhood psychiatric disorders from developmental neuro-imaging, in Garralda, M.E. and Raynaud, J.-P. (eds) *Brain, mind and developmental psychopathology in childhood*, Plymouth: Jason Aronson Inc, pp 53–72.

Shemmings, D. and Shemmings, Y. (2014) *Assessing disorganized attachment behaviour in children: an evidence-based model for understanding and supporting families*, London: Jessica Kingsley.

Shonkoff, J.P. and Phillips, D. (eds) (2000) *From neurons to neighborhoods: the science of early childhood development,* Washington, DC: National Academies Press.

Shonkoff, J.P and Bales, S. (2011) Science does not speak for itself: translating child development research for the public and its policymakers, *Child Development,* 82(1): 17–32.

Skinner, B.F. (1950) Are theories of learning necessary?, *Psychological Review*, 57: 193–216.

Slater, E. (1968) A review of earlier evidence on genetic factors in schizophrenia, in Rosenthal, D. and Kety, S. (eds) *The transmission of schizophrenia*, Oxford: Pergamon Press, pp 15–26.

Sloboda, Z. and Petras, H. (2014) *Defining prevention science*, New York: Springer.

Solomon, J. and George, C. (2008) The measurement of attachment security and related constructs in infancy and early childhood, in J. Cassidy and P.R. Shaver (eds) *Handbook of attachment: Theory, research, and clinical applications*, 2nd edn, New York: Guilford Press, pp 383–416.

Stainton Rogers, R. and Stainton Rogers, W. (1992) *Stories of childhood: shifting agendas of child concern*, Hemel Hempstead: Harvester Wheatsheaf.

Stevens, A. (2011) Telling policy stories: an ethnographic study of the use of evidence in policy-making in the UK, *Journal of Social Policy*, 40(02): 237–255.

Stiles, W.B. and Shapiro, D.A. (1989) Abuse of the drug metaphor in psychotherapy process-outcome research, *Clinical Psychology Review*, 9: 521-543

Stiles, W.B., Shapiro, D.A. and Elliott, R. (1986) Are all psychotherapies equivalent?, *American Psychologist*, 41: 165–80.

Stivers, R. (2001) *Technology as magic: the triumph of the irrational,* New York: Continuum.

Struhl, K. (2014) Is DNA methylation of tumour suppressor genes epigenetic?, *eLife*, 3:e02475, 1-3

Sullivan, C. J. and Newsome, J. (2015) Psychosocial and genetic risk markers for longitudinal trends in delinquency: an empirical assessment and practical discussion, *Criminal Justice Studies*, 28(1): 61–83.

Szasz, T. (1974) *The myth of mental illness:Foundations of theory of personal conduct*, New York: Harper Collins.

Szasz, T. (2008) *Psychiatry: The science of lies,* New York: Syracuse University Press.

Tallis, R. (2011) *Aping mankind: Neuromania, Darwinitis and the misrepresentation of humanity*, Durham: Acumen.

Thome, J. and Jacobs, K.A. (2004) Attention deficit hyperactivity disorder (ADHD) in a 19th century children's book, *European Psychiatry*, 19(5): 303–306.

Thompson, R.A. (2000) The legacy of early attachments, *Child Development*, 71(1): 145–152.

Tunstill, J. and Blewett, J. (2015) Mapping the journey: outcome-focused practice and the role of interim outcomes in family support services, *Child & Family Social Work,* 20(2): 234–243.

Tunstill, J., Meadows, M., Akhurst, S. et al (2005) *Implementing Sure Start Local Programmes: an in-depth study*, London: Department of Children, Schools and Families.

Turda, M (2010) *Modernism and eugenics,* Basingstoke, UK: Palgrave Macmillan.

Turkheimer, E. (2011) Commentary: variation and causation in the environment and genome, *International Journal of Epidemiology,* 40: 598–601.

Tyrer, P., Duggan, C., Cooper, S. et al (2010) The successes and failures of the DSPD experiment, *Medicine, Science and the Law,* 50: 95–99.

US Department of Health and Human Services (2010) *Head Start Impact Study: Fnal report,* Washington, DC.

Uttal, W.R. (2011) *Mind and brain: a critical appraisal of cognitive neuroscience,* Cambridge, MA: MIT Press.

Uttal, W.R. (2016) *Macroneural theories in cognitive neuroscience,* New York: Psychology Press.

Valentine, C.A., Valentine, B., Aptheker, H. et al (1975) Brain damage and the intellectual defense of inequality [and Comments and Reply], *Current Anthropology,* 16(1): 117–150.

Van Ijzendoorn, M.H., Schuengel, C. and Bakermans-Kranenburg, M.J. (1999) Disorganized attachment in early childhood: meta-analysis of precursors, concomitants, and sequelae, *Development and Psychopathology,* 11, 225–249.

Van Rullen, R. and Thorpe, S.J. (2001) Rate coding versus temporal order coding: what the retinal ganglion cells tell the visual cortex, *Neural Computation,* 13: 1255–1283.

Verhoeff, B. (2014) Stabilizing autism: a Fleckian account of the rise of a neurodevelopmental spectrum disorder, *Studies in History and Philosophy of Biological and Biomedical Sciences,* 46: 65–78.

Vliegen, N., Casalin, S. and Luyten, P. (2014) The course of postpartum depression: a review of longitudinal studies, *Harvard Review of Psychiatry,* 22(1): 1–22.

Vul, E., Harris, C., Winkelman, P. and Pashler, H. (2009) Puzzlingly high correlations in fMRI studies of emotion, personality and social cognition, *Perspectives on Psychological Science,* 4(3): 274–290.

Waggoner, M.R. and Uller, T. (2015) Epigenetic determinism in science and society, *New Genetics and Society,* 34(2): 177–195.

Walsh, C. (2011). Youth justice and neuroscience, *British Journal of Criminology,* 51(1): 21–39.

Walsh, D., McCartney, G., McCullough, S., van der Pol, M., Buchanan, D. and Jones, R (2013) *Exploring potential reasons for Glasgow's 'excess' mortality: Results of a three-city survey of Glasgow, Liverpool and Manchester,* Report published by the Glasgow Centre for Population Health, Glasgow, UK.

Ward, H. and Brown, R. (2013) Decision-making within a child's timeframe: a response, *Family Law*, 43: 1181–1186.

Warwick Consortium (2014), http://betterstart.dartington.org.uk/wp-content/uploads/2013/10/Warwick-Consortium-Evaluation-Executive-Summary.pdf

Wastell, D.G. (1979a) Temporal uncertainty and the recovery function of the auditory EP, in C. Barber (ed) *Proceedings of the International Evoked Potentials Symposium*, Lancaster, UK: MTP Press, pp 835–839.

Wastell, D.G. (1979b) On the independence of P300 and the CNV: a critique of the principal components analysis of Donchin et al (1975), *Biological Psychology*, 9: 171–76.

Wastell, D. (2007) The myth of alignment, in T. McMaster et al (eds) *Organizational dynamics of technology-based innovation: Diversifying the research agenda,* Dordrecht and New York: Springer, pp 513–518.

Wastell, D.G. (2011) *Managers as designers in the public services: Beyond technomagic,* Axminster, UK: Triarchy Press.

Wastell, D.G., Brown, I. D. and Copeman, A. K. (1982) Differential effects of workload on system performance in cord and cordless public telephone switchrooms, *Ergonomics*, 25, 1041–1952.

Wastell, D. and White, S. (2012) Blinded by neuroscience: social policy and the myth of the infant brain, *Families, Relationships and Societies*, 1(3): 397–414.

Weaver, I.C.G., Cervoni, N., Champagne, F. A. et al (2004) Epigenetic programming by maternal behaviour, *Nature Neuroscience*, 7(8): 847–854.

White, S. and Wastell, D.G. (2013) Response to Brown and Ward, 'Decision-Making within the Child's Timeframe', available at SSRN: http://dx.doi.org/10.2139/ssrn.2325357

White, S., Wastell, D., Smith, S. et al (2015) *Improving practice in safeguarding at the interface between hospital services and children's social care: a mixed-methods case study,* Southampton (UK): NIHR Journals Library; 2015 Feb. (Health Services and Delivery Research, No. 3.4.)

Wiener, H. (1995) The genetics of preposterous conditions, in Ross, C.A. and Pam, A. (eds) *Pseudoscience in biological psychiatry: Blaming the body*, New York: John Wiley & Sons, pp 193–210.

Williams, N.M., Franke, B., Mick, E. et al (2012) Genome-wide analysis of copy number variants in Attention Deficit Hyperactivity Disorder: the role of rare variants and duplications at 15q13.3, *American Journal of Psychiatry*, 169: 195–204.

Williams, Z. (26 April 2014) Misused neuroscience defining child protection policy, *The Guardian,* http://www.theguardian.com/education/2014/apr/26/misused-neuroscience-defining-child-protection-policy. Response: *The Guardian* (29 April 2014) (Letters) Early years interventions and social justice, http://www.theguardian.com/society/2014/apr/29/early-years-interventions-social-justice

Winnicott, D.W. (1973) *The child, the family, and the outside world,* Harmondsworth, UK: Penguin.

Würbel, H. (2001) Ideal homes: housing effects on rodent brain and behaviour, *Trends in Neurosciences,* 224(4): 207–211.

Yehuda, R., Daskalakis, N.P., Bierer, L.M., Bader, H.N., Klengel, T., Holsboer, F. and Binder, E.B. (2016) Holocaust exposure induced intergenerational effects on FKBP5 methylation, *Biological Psychiatry,* 80: 372–80.

Yurgelun-Todd, D.A., Renshaw, P.F., and Femia, L.A. (2006) Applications of fMRI to psychiatry, in Faro, S.H. and Mohamed, F.B. (eds) *Functional MRI: Basic principles and applications,* New York: Springer, pp 183–220.

Zhang, T,Y., Labonte, B., Wen, X.L., Turecki, G. and Meaney, M.J. (2013) Epigenetic mechanisms for the early environmental regulation of hippocampal glucocorticoid receptor gene expression in rodents and humans, *Neuropsychopharmacology,* 38: 111–123.

Zhou, X., Panizzutti, R., de Villers-Sidani, E., Madeira, C. and Merzenich, M.M. (2011) Natural restoration of critical period plasticity in the juvenile and adult primary auditory cortex, *Journal of Neuroscience,* 31(15): 5625–5634.

Index

Beers, C.W., mental hygiene 10
behavioural approach, autism 80
behavioural explanations 152–3
  DNA methylation, rat mothers
    161–2
Belsky, J. 115, 149, 151, 154, 155
Bentovim, Arnon, attachment 13–14
Bernier, A., disorganised attachment
    16, 17, 18
Best start at home, The (Early
    Intervention Foundation) 125–6
bias 65–6, 146, 217, 223
Big Pharma 198, 219
biocriminology 206
biological psychiatry 62–7, 78–82
'biologisation' (of mental disorder) 70,
    81
biomarkers 3, 5–6
  attention training 47
  cortisol test 124
  for criminality 208
  DNA methylation 204
  limited predictive utility 212
  performance of hypothetical 242–3
  and State intervention 153–4, 195
biometric data and surveillance 154–5
biosocial criminology 206
birthweight
  and famine exposure 181, 198
  no correlation with methylation levels
    182
  and prenatal depression 186
'blackboxing' 28–9, 30–1
Blaming the body (Ross and Pam) 65
Blewett, J., 'outcomes theology' 146
Bohacek, J., transgenerational effects of
    PTSD 172, 174
Bradley, R. H., early home
    environment and subsequent
    achievement 134, 136, 258
brain-based treatments, rTMS 72
brain damage, sociogenic theory 22,
    89, 93, 106–7
brain development 89–90, 93, 94,
    97–8, 101, 115
brain images 38–42
  ADHD 73–4
  aggression studies 43
  Allen Report 95, 106–7, 121–2
  autism 70–1
  reverse inference fallacy 211–13, 222
  simplistic ideas about 34–5
brain plasticity *see* plasticity of the brain
brain power 8
  and synaptic profusion 97–8, 99
brain science, implicating in policy
    92–4, 97

Brodmann areas
  BA44, language function 211–12,
    222
  in dorsal ACC, attention 45–6
Broer, T., Scottish social policy 91
Brown, Rebecca 17, 31, 113–18
Bruer, J.T. 48, 107, 139
  myth of first three years 96–102
Building Great Britons (parliamentory
    report) 92
Burghy, C.A., effects of early life stress
    on adults 153
Bush, President George, 'decade of the
    brain' 93
Buss, C., pregnancy anxiety 190,
    212–13
Butler, Patrick 122–3

C

Caldwell, B.M., early home
    environment and subsequent
    achievement 134, 136, 258
Cameron, David 111
cancer treatments 179, 188
cardiovascular disease (CVD) 183, 184,
    201, 204
Carey, N., DNA methylation 51, 52
Castel, A.D., brain images and scientific
    reasoning 40
catecholamines 59
  depression hypothesis 64, 81
categories of mental disorders 68–9,
    81–2
causality 17, 36, 38, 202, 210, 246
cell memory/specialisation 51
cells 49–50
certainty 100, 104, 158
Charil, A., rodent vs human studies
    188
cheek (buccal) cells, epigenetic
    screening 195
chemical imbalance theory 64, 81
Cheng, W., functional connectivity in
    ASD 84
child abuse
  and antisocial behaviour in men
    245–6
  brain image, Allen report 107–8,
    121–2
  children raised in orphanages 115
  and methylation 52–3, 187
  neuromania 32–3
child protection issues 18, 31, 111,
    114, 121
  Parenting under Pressure programme
    196–7
Child Trauma Academy 105

Rose, S., critique of Kallmann's work 65
Ross, C.A., pseudoscience 65
Roth, T.L., dysfunctional mothering of stressed rat mothers 169–70
Rothstein, M.A., ethical and legal implications of epigenetics 6
Ruhe, H.G., monoamines and mood 81
Russell, J., evidence for policy making 90
Rutter, M., early adversity, humans 160–1

S

salience network (SN) 44, 232–3
Schildkraut, Joseph, chemical imbalance theory 64
schizophrenia
  chromosomal anomalies 75
  failure to identify genes 78
  gene implicated in 62, 237
  Kallmann's research 65
  and poverty 67
  prevalence and heredity 65–6
  psychological/behavioural features defining 79–80
Scholte, R., long-run effects of hunger during gestation 182–4
school exclusions 221
Schrödinger, Erwin 20–1, 22
scientific change 25–6
scientific research, citation practices 24, 199
Scotland
  social deprivation study 201–5
  social policy 131
screening 154, 155, 191, 195, 202, 207
script codon 49
Scull, Andrew, madness in civilisation 48, 81–2
secure attachment 14, 101, 103, 104
Selye, Hans, flight/fight response 55
sensitive periods 95–6, 100, 107, 115–16
  for attachment 13–14
sensory deprivation
  in animals 101–2
  in children 105–6
serotonin 64, 81, 153, 156, 208
Shapiro, D.A., drug metaphor 144
Shonkoff, Jack 97, 111–12, 118, 119
sigmoid curve 250–1
sign-code distinction 36–7, 225–30
significance level 150, 237
simplification of science 27, 91–2
skill formation model, Cunha 133–6, 249–58

Skinner, B.F. 80
Skinner, Michael 179
social adversity, attempts to reverse effects of 5–6
social engineering 9, 20–2, 23, 129
social work, use of RCT in 145–6
sociogenic brain damage theory 22–3, 89–90, 93
sparse coding 228–9
specialised cells 49–50
Spurzheim, Johann Gaspar, phrenology 64
Stainton Rogers, R. 13
Stainton Rogers, W. 13
State intervention 5–6, 89–90, 111–13, 114, 124
statistical significance 62, 235–7, 245–6
statistics 62, 235–47
steroid hormones 50–1
Stevens, A., use of evidence in UK policy-making 90–1
Stiles, W.B., drug metaphor 144
Stivers, R., magic and technology 216, 218
Strange Situation Test 14–15
stress/stress response
  during pregnancy 191–2
  effect on developing foetus 29, 185–6
  effect of prolonged exposure to 125
  in infancy. effects of 31
  maternal, effect on offspring 169–71
  maternal, natural disasters 188–9
  and performance 56, 246
  protective effects 160–1
  role of HPA axis 30, 55–7, 187
  studies on rodents 158–63
    critique of 163–9
  transgenerational effects 172–4
Struhl, Kevin, epigenetic inheritance 54
suboptimal concept 5–6, 119–21, 193–4
suicide 129, 187–8
Sullivan, C.J., biomarkers of delinquency 208
Sure Start, UK 97, 220–1
surveillance 12–13, 154–5
swim test, rodents 62, 173, 235, 237
synapses 95, 98–9
  effect of early experiences on 101–2
  effect of stress on 56, 57, 107–8
system justification 218
Szasz, T., *The myth of mental illness* 83
Szyf, M., social adversity in early life 187–8

T

Tallis, Raymond, brain imaging 39, 40

'targeted early intervention' 89–90, 95–6
  economic models 132–9
targeted parenting programmes 132, 137–8, 139–42
'targeting', prevention science 126, 130, 132
  genetic targeting 147–54
technology 28, 35, 36, 45, 47, 49
  brain imaging 38–48
  and magic 216–18
  medical–industrial complex 218–19
  surveillance 154–5
temporal lobe
  Broca's area 211–12
  fusiform face area 42–3
Thorpe, S. J., frequency coding 227–8
'thought collective' 26–7, 61
'thought styles' 26, 32
  epigenetic 25, 48–52
  foetal programming 185–93
  medical 68–9
  neuroscientific 32–8, 57
  prevailing policy 111–12
toxic stress 31, 111, 118–19
toxin exposure 4–5, 178–9
training
  in executive control 46–7
  family justice professionals 113
  tasks, animal experiments 44, 231–2
transcription regulators 50, 51, 54, 60
transgenerational epigenetic inheritance 171–5
'translational imperative' 27–8
trauma 106, 107–8, 169–74
  PTSD treatment 57
TSA (trichostatin A) drug treatment to reverse methylation effect 162, 168–9, 176
Tunstill, J., 'outcomes theology' 146
Turkheimer, E., gene-environment interaction 66
twin studies 66–7, 74–5, 83–4

U

uncertainty 100, 104
unconditional love, brain regions for 39–40
unintelligent man, Schrödinger 20–1
utopias/utopian thinking 7, 8–9, 98
Uttal, W.R.
  aggression, brain structures 43
  appeal of brain images 40
  signs and codes 36–7, 225–7

V

Valentine, C.A., cultural anthropology 22, 23

van Ijzendoorn, M.H. 16, 149, 151, 154, 155
van Rullen, R., frequency coding 227–8
Verhoeff, B., autism 68–70, 78, 79
violence 34, 43, 94, 101, 206, 207, 212
visual cortex 37, 43, 98, 102
  critical period study 99–100
visual system coding processes 226–8
voxels (activation sites), brain imaging 59, 84

W

Waddington, Conrad 49
Walsh, C., youth justice 206, 207
Ward, Harriet 17, 31, 113–18
Warwick Consortium 154, 195
Weaver, I.C.G., programming by maternal behaviour 158–63
Webb, Sidney 9
Welfare Trait, The: How State Benefits Affect Personality (Perkins) 31, 220
Wiesel, Torsten 'critical periods' 99–100
Williams, N.M., ADHD paper 74–5
Williams, Zoe 119–21
Wilson, A., DNA data deficit 79
wisdom, neurobiology of 39
World Bank 9, 132, 155, 180
Würbel, H, developmental plasticity of HPA 167–8, 169

Y

Yerkes-Dobson law 56
Young Persons Development Model (YPDM) 221–2
youth justice 206–7
Yurgelun-Todd, D.A., brain imaging 71

Z

Zhou, X., plasticity of auditory cortex 100